the JESUS LEGEND

G. A. Wells

Foreword by R. Joseph Hoffman

OPEN COURT Chicago and La Salle, Illinois

Books by G.A. Wells

Herder and After (1959)

The Plays of Grillparzer (1969)

The Jesus of the Early Christians (1971)

Did Jesus Exist? (1975; second edition, 1986)

Goethe and the Development of Science (1978)

The Historical Evidence for Jesus (1982)

The Origin of Language: Aspects of the Discussion from Condillac to Wundt (1987)

Religious Postures: Essays on Modern Christian Apologists and Religious Problems (1988)

Who Was Jesus? A Critique of the New Testament Record (1989)

Belief and Make-Believe: Critical Reflections on the Sources of Credulity (1991)

What's in a Name? Reflections on Language, Magic, and Religion (1993)

The Jesus Legend (1996)

Edited Works

Language: Its Origin and Relation to Thought (co-edited with D.R. Oppenheimer), by F.R.H. Englefield (1977)

The Mind at Work and Play (co-edited with D.R. Oppenheimer), by F.R.H. Englefield (1985)

J.M. Robertson: Liberal, Rationalist, and Scholar (1987)

Critique of Pure Verbiage: Essays on Abuses of Language in Literary, Religious, and Philosophical Writings (co-edited with D.R. Oppenheimer), by F.R.H. Englefield (1990)

the JESUS LEGEND

Open Court Publishing Company is a division of Carus Publishing
Company.

Copyright © by Carus Publishing Company

First printing 1996

Printed and bound in the United States of America

Library of Congress Cataloging-in-Publication Data

Wells, George Albert, 1926–
    The Jesus legend / G.A. Wells.
    p.   cm.
    Includes bibliographical references and indexes.
ISBN 0-8126-9334-5 (pbk. : alk. paper)
    1. Jesus Christ—Historicity.   2. Jesus Christ—History of doctrines—
Early church, ca. 30-600.   3. Bible. N.T.—Criticism, interpretation, etc.
I. Title.
BT303.2.W427   1996
232.9'08—dc20   96-42944
                                                                      CIP

Contents

Foreword

It is no longer possible to dismiss the thesis that Jesus of Nazareth never existed as the "marginal indiscretion of lay amateurs" (to paraphrase a sentence once imposed on Matthew Arnold's biblical criticism by his theological critics). The direction of biblical criticism since Albert Schweitzer's day has circled back with dizzying regularity to the implied question of Jesus's existence but has sought without success to answer it. Perhaps this is so because Schweitzer himself had pronounced his own investigations a failure:

> There is nothing more negative than the result of the critical study of the life of Jesus. The Jesus of Nazareth who came forward publicly as the Messiah, who preached the Kingdom of God, who founded the Kingdom of Heaven upon earth, and died to give his work its final consecration, never had any existence. He is a figure designed by rationalism, endowed with life by liberalism, and clothed by modern theology in an historical garb. (*The Quest of the Historical Jesus* [New York: Macmillan, 1968], 19)

Schweitzer's familiar verdict needs to be seen in its proper light. He was not saying that Jesus of Nazareth never existed, but rather that the Jesus of late nineteenth-century liberal Protestantism, the moral rhapsodist praised for his "sweet

reasonableness" (Arnold) and the superiority of his ethical teaching by a protestant establishment weary of debating the miraculous and supernatural aspects of the New Testament record, had
been discredited by historical-critical study of the gospels.
Indeed, Schweitzer was content to say that the figure portrayed in
rudimentary hellenistic Greek in the gospels and known to Paul
as "Christ, the Lord" was a man of his time and culture, and thus
bound to be a "stranger and an enigma" to our own time.

Notoriously, theologians (perhaps New Testament scholars
especially) are unhappy with enigmas. The negative results of
the 'old' quest have given rise to a variety of newer quests, each
of them stemming from dubious starting points. In the past
generation, the 'real' Jesus has been variously a magician (Smith),
a Galilean rabbi (Chilton), a marginal Jew (Meyer), a bastard
(Schaberg), a cipher (Thiering), a Qumran dissident (Allegro et
al.), a gnosticising Jew (Koester), a dissident Jew (Vermes), a hap-
pily married man and father of sons (Spong), a bandit (Horsley),
an enthusiastic (possibly Zealot?) opponent of the Temple cult
(Sanders). Perhaps most remarkable of all is the 'real' Jesus of the
Westar Project/Jesus Seminar whose existence has been pinned
on just over thirty 'authentic' sayings, derived from an eclectic
application of biblical-critical axioms and confirmed by vote of
the seminar members.

It is a shame that with reference to the above the absurd must
be grouped with the sane—Thiering with Sanders—but the field
has now gotten so muddy and strewn with theories (some already
dead, some dying) that it is only possible to talk about good and
bad examples of a theological genre: the modern Jesus biography.

It is clear to most readers of modern Jesus biographies—at
least those who have read any two of the above—that Jesus cannot have been all of the things he is said to have been in the same
(reportedly) short lifetime. Nor, it is safe to say, would a sober
reading of the Gospel of Mark, still usually reckoned to be the
earliest, offer the reader a Jesus who is, self-evidently, any of
these things. In the most extreme examples, scholarship has re-
invented an apocryphal Jesus no less un-real than the morally
sublime figure of post-Kantian Christian theology, but marked
with the cynicism and cultural desperation of the late twentieth

century. We will not wait much longer for a Jesus who left Nazareth, age eighteen, the victim of child abuse in a dysfunctional one-parent family, to find his real identity among other Jewish boys forced to live a lie in the homophobic backwater of Empire, and died the patsy of his cousin-lover Judas who himself had felt threatened by Jesus's growing affection for the Roman procurator—one who perhaps reminded him of his gentile father, Panthera. This is less a frivolous comment on the direction of current scholarship than a scenario waiting to be played. It is also evidence that the claim to be doing 'serious' biblical scholarship is no protection against the profiteering that seems to characterise the worst examples of the genre.

A cautious approach to the array of new-quest Jesuses offers a different question: What is it about the character of the New Testament literature that makes so many contradictory theories available? Schweitzer had pointed to the "disintegration" of a theological Jesus "by the concrete historical problems which came to light one after another." Yet within a year of the publication of Schweitzer's *Von Reimarus zu Wrede*, translated into English as *The Quest of the Historical Jesus* (1910), it was asserted by some scholars—Arthur Drews (1865–1935) and J. M. Robertson (1856–1933), to cite only the best known—that the prior question of Jesus's actual historical existence could be raised equally in connection with misgivings about legendary and doctrinal overlay: after all, it was not only the Christian church of the nineteenth century that had contributed to the mythicizing of its 'founder'. The New Testament literature itself begins with the story of the saviour-revealer-god (Christ the Lord) in Paul's letters and moves only later, and painfully, to the elaboration of the saviour's life in the form of gospels. Nor was this elaboration without difficulty: it was widely accepted in German biblical scholarship by 1900 that the liturgical drama of the passion (the soi-disant 'passion narrative' both of canonical gospels and of early apocryphal accounts such as the *Gospel of Peter*) arose before other elements of the story, driven perhaps by the antecedent tradition of the saviour's last meal with his disciples. Thus even in the gospels, whose distinction from Paul's letters and priority in the canon was traceable to the Church's early insistence on their historical character, liturgical rather than 'historical' elements were primary—that is to say, earlier than either teaching elements (the beatitudes, for example) or the records of Jesus's supernatural displays of healing and wonders. The successful discovery of analogues in Jewish and late hellenistic literature for virtually all of the forms and elements of the gospels left the historical Jesus, by Bultmann's day, without a clear location in his own. He was, as Bultmann is reported to have said of Schweitzer's famous verdict, less an enigma than an improbability (*Unwahrscheinlichkeit*).

The myth theorists, often naive or sloppy in handling historical elements, were anthropologically naive as well: looking to Fraser's *Golden Bough* or to Hesiod for correlates, they too often overlooked the fact that myth arises colloquially from local traditions and ignored the mythology of local Jewish tradition—the Wisdom tradition, for example—in favour of ambitious panhellenistic mythologies not known to have been current in Jewish theology. Jesus was seen as Apollo, as Pan, as Hermes, Ahura Mazda, Dionysus, Herakles, or an uneven mix of savior gods. In short, the old Christ myth school fell victim to its own rather amateurish approach to the anthropology of religion, its fascination with the ways of the *Religionsgeschichtliche-Schüle*, especially its obsession with the etiology of myth and language, and its own determination to debunk the originality of the Christian story of salvation by a god incarnate.

What Schweitzer and the old style myth theorists failed equally to see was that tendencies observable in German theology were equally observable in the primary literature, and that the eschatological prophet was as much a stock figure of hellenistic Jewish folklore as the liberal democrat was in Victorian England. Drews had asked the question flatfootedly in 1912:

> What evidence do the words of Jesus afford of his historical reality [especially as] we are not at all sure that the traditional 'words of the Lord' are the words of a single historical individual—namely the historical Jesus? Theologians assume [that they are] but they are merely begging the question: Words of the Lord are . . . merely words which the Lord (Yahweh) gives to his followers through the spirit, [so] that even in granting the existence of an historical Jesus it would be impossible to discriminate what is due to the 'spirit' in the

collection and what to Jesus. (*Witnesses to the Historicity of Jesus* [Gordon: 1912], 118)

In making the ancient Church (fashionably called by turn-of-the-century theologians the 'primitive community') rather than Jesus the fundamental historical point of reference, the focus might reasonably have shifted to the link between the things Jesus is reported to have said and whether an historical individual said them. Unfortunately for the proponents of non-historicity, the question was soon muddied by a disarray of myth theories (there was never only one) which delighted in finding analogues for every detail of the life of Jesus, both word and deed, in ancient Near-Eastern and Mediterranean lore, sufficiently disparate in their conclusions to make Jesus's historical existence seem a temperate position. Intemperance had predictable results. So determined was the onslaught against the 'myth theories' in the period between the two world wars that a whole subspecies of theological literature, the Historicity Genre, was born. Two typical examples are Shirley Jackson Case's *The Historicity of Jesus* (1920) and Arthur Weigall's *The Paganism of our Christianity* (1928): their common theme was that while the "constricted Jesus of theology is dated" (Weigall), having lived "at a time when men believed in Olympus and drenched altars with the blood of sacrificial victims," the essential (possibly unrecoverable) historical core of Christianity is traceable to an historical founder whose message was, basically, ethical. This de-eschatologized Jesus was reckoned to have spoken very little about the next world; to have laid down principles of conduct by which men might live (Case); and always transcended the superstitions of church and culture. The Historicity Genre strongly implied that the elimination of the historical figure would spell the end of Christian ethics. Hence, to deny him was to deny the noblest and best of ethical systems. Its main thrust however was to affirm the existence of sources outside the gospels which shaped 'primitive Christianity' (Bultmann's *Urchristenheit*) including mythological sources, vocabulary, cultic borrowings—in short, the cultural apparatus which formed the outer wrapping of the story of Jesus—while maintaining that the core, albeit elusive, was nonetheless historical. Even Bultmann's radical

reworking of the gospel message in existential terms, which presupposed acknowledgement of the essentially mythical character
of the story and its protagonist, clung resolutely to the postulate
of an historical core.

The 'historicity genre' today is a much-changed approach to
the life and times of Jesus of Nazareth, emphasizing that the way
to recovery of the historical individual is through the social
context which explains him—or rather, the community's apprehension of him. It uses the social sciences, especially cultural
anthropology, archaeology, linguistic analysis, papyrology, and
various species of literary criticism, to answer questions which
an older generation of scholars would have looked only to theology and philology to settle. Its methodological sophistication
and the self-assurance which seems to characterize its approach
to the ancient texts seems at odds with the depressing lack of
clarity which has emerged from over a generation of contextual
studies.

The quest goes on with something close to the fervour of
scientific discovery. At the risk of provoking controversy, it goes
on mainly in Christian circles and among Christian theologians.
The Jesus of 'history' has always been obscure to Jewish scholars
whose enforced involvement in the discussion of Jesus's stature is
largely the result of the triumph of imperial Christianity in the
fourth century, by which time no clear record of Jesus existed
except that foisted on Jewish scholars by Christian teachers.
Perhaps the historical vagueness of the figure to all but a few Jewish scholars is a further hindrance to locating Jesus, as liberal
theologians wish to do, within the context of emergent and belea-
guered first-century rabbinism.

George Wells is known to swim against the stream in the contemporary debate. The most articulate contemporary defender of
the non-historicity thesis, Wells's questions are the ones that need
to be answered at this juncture in Jesus research. What is the link
between the Pauline and gospel traditions? Why is Paul utterly
silent about the historical Jesus? (his apostolic inferiority com-
plex is now widely rejected as a plausible explanation); if the
Johannine tradition is a 'spiritualization' of historical tradition,

what tradition is it spiritualizing? Why is the core historical episode of the gospel tradition, the story of Jesus's death on the cross, completely lacking in convincing historical detail, being rather a liturgical drama built up from the Psalms and prophetic texts? What role can the recovery and analysis of 'Q' (the hypothetical 'sayings source') play in deciding the matter of historicity?

Wells argues a "persistent," even a nagging, thesis, marked by unusual clarity and consistency. The arguments against it have ranged from ad hominem attacks on his qualifications (despite his professorial appointment in German at Birkbeck College, London having made him a closer student of German theology than many of his Anglo-American contemporaries) to the familiar and often unargued proposition that the non-historicity of Jesus makes the rise of Christianity and the writing of the gospels all but impossible to explain. If Wells has been charitable towards his theological opponents, he has been tireless in searching out inconsistencies and 'changes of mind' in their own work— changes that bring the via media of opinion closer to his own reading of the gospels and his own opinion closer to being the via media. It is not too much to hope that this most recent examination of the Jesus question will help believers and unbelievers to a fuller understanding of how god became man.

R. Joseph Hoffmann
Westminster College Oxford
Feast of St Mary Magdalen

About the Notes and Abbreviations

If notes include anything more than references to sources, readers feel that they are being asked to read two books at the same time. I have nevertheless sometimes used notes to elaborate or justify statements in the text, thinking that these notes can be ignored by readers not interested in the elaboration or justification.

Abbreviations

I. TERMINOLOGY

OT and NT designate the Old and the New Testaments.

I use the terms Matthew, Mark, Luke, and John sometimes to designate the author of the relevant gospel and sometimes to designate that gospel itself. Which meaning is intended will be clear from the context. These traditional names remain convenient, although the real authors of all the gospels are in fact unknown.

In references to a chapter or to a chapter and a verse of a gospel, Matthew, Mark, Luke, and John are abbreviated to Mt., Mk., Lk., and Jn. The book 'Acts of the Apostles' is designated 'Acts'.

I follow the usual terminology in calling the first three of the four canonical gospels 'the synoptics'. The term 'synoptic' means 'what can be seen at a glance' and owes its origin to the fact that, if the complete texts of all three are put side by side in parallel columns, one can see immediately what material has been added to, omitted from, or adapted in each.

II. QUOTATIONS FROM SCRIPTURE

Scripture quotations are (except when otherwise indicated) from the Revised Version (which I call RV), published 1881–85, of the Authorized Version or King James Bible of 1611 (which I call AV). Very occasionally I refer also to the following other English versions:

NEB *The New English Bible*, copyright of Oxford and Cambridge University Presses.

RSV *The Revised Standard Version*, copyright of the Division of Christian Education, National Council of the Churches of Christ in the United States.

In some cases brief scriptural phrases have been rendered literally or adapted to the syntax of my sentences.

III. OTHER QUOTATIONS

In each of my chapters, once details of works have been given, further references to them are normally given simply as page references in my text or notes.

My four earlier books on Christian origins or on Jesus are designated as follows:

JEC *The Jesus of the Early Christians*, London: Pemberton, 1971.

DJE *Did Jesus Exist?*, 2nd edition, London: Pemberton, 1986.

HEJ *The Historical Evidence for Jesus*, Buffalo: Prometheus, 1982, reissued in 1988.

WWJ *Who Was Jesus? A Critique of the New Testament Record*, La Salle, Illinois: Open Court, 1989.

I also make occasional reference to the following three books of mine, all published by Open Court:

Religious Postures. Essays on Modern Christian Apologists and Religious Problems, 1988.

Belief and Make-Believe. Critical Reflections on the Sources of Credulity, 1991.

What's in a Name? Reflections on Language, Magic and Religion, 1993.

Certain books, articles, symposia or journals—mostly those mentioned in more than one of my chapters—are denoted by the following abbreviations:

Anti-Judaism I	*Anti-Judaism in Early Christianity*, volume 1, *Paul and the Gospels*, edited by P. Richardson, Waterloo (Ontario): Laurier, 1986.
Anti-Judaism II	*Anti-Judaism in Early Christianity*, volume 2, *Separation and Polemic*, edited by S.G. Wilson, Waterloo (Ontario): Laurier, 1986.
Barr, *Biblical*	J. Barr, *Biblical Faith and Natural Theology*, Oxford: Clarendon, 1993.
Barrett, *John*	C.K. Barrett, *The Gospel According to St. John: An Introduction with Commentary and Notes on the Greek Text*, 2nd edition, London: SPCK, 1978.
Beare, *Matthew*	F.W. Beare, *The Gospel According to Matthew*, Oxford: Blackwell, 1981.
Bowden, 'Nerve'	J. Bowden, 'A Loss of Nerve', in *Thirty Years of Honesty. 'Honest to God' Then and Now*, edited by himself, London: SCM, 1993, pp. 74–83.
Brown, *Death*	R.E. Brown, *The Death of the Messiah*, New York: Doubleday (The Anchor Bible Reference Library), 2 volumes with continuous pagination, 1994.
Bruce, *Documents*	F.F. Bruce, *The New Testament Documents. Are they Reliable?* 5th edition, Leicester: Inter-Varsity Press, 1960.
Ehrman, *Corruption*	B.D. Ehrman, *The Orthodox Corruption of Scripture. The Effect of Early Christological Controversies on the Text of the New Testament*, New York: Oxford University Press, 1993.

Feldman, *Josephus*	L.H. Feldman, *Josephus and Modern Scholarship*, Berlin: De Gruyter, 1984.
Furnish, *Jesus*	V.P. Furnish, *Jesus According to Paul* (in the series 'Understanding Jesus Today'), Cambridge: Cambridge University Press, 1993.
Goulder, *Midrash*	M. Goulder, *Midrash and Lection in Matthew*, London: SPCK, 1974.
Haenchen, *JE*	E. Haenchen, *Das Johannesevangelium*, Tübingen: Mohr, 1980.
Harvey, *Commands*	A.E. Harvey, *Strenuous Commands: The Ethic of Jesus*, London: SCM, and Philadelphia: Trinity, 1990.
JBL	Journal of Biblical Literature
JTS	Journal of Theological Studies
Käsemann, *Essays*	E. Käsemann, *Essays on New Testament Themes*, English translation London: SCM, 1964.
Kümmel, *Introduction*	W.G. Kümmel, *Introduction to the New Testament*, English translation of the revised 17th German edition, London: SCM, 1975.
Lindars, *John*, 1972	B. Lindars, *The Gospel of John* (New Century Bible), London: Oliphants, 1972.
Lindars, *John*, 1990	B. Lindars, *John* (in the series 'NT Guides') edited by A.T. Lincoln, Sheffield: Academic Press, 1990.
Mack, *Myth*	B.L. Mack, *A Myth of Innocence: Mark and Christian Origins*, Philadelphia: Fortress, 1988.
Mack, *Lost Gospel*	B.L. Mack, *The Lost Gospel: The Book of Q and Christian Origins*, Shaftesbury (Dorset): Element, 1993.
Mason, *Josephus*	Steve Mason, *Josephus and the New Testament*, Peabody (Massachusetts): Hendrickson, 1992.

Meier, *Marginal*   J.P. Meier, *A Marginal Jew: Rethinking the Historical Jesus*, volume 1, New York, London: Doubleday (The Anchor Bible Reference Library), 1991.

Montgomery, *Crisis*   J.W. Montgomery, *Crisis in Lutheran Theology*, 2nd edition, Minneapolis: Bethany, 1973.

Montgomery,   J.W. Montgomery, *The Law Above the Law:*
The Law   *Why the Law Needs Biblical Foundations. How Legal Thought Supports Christian Truth*, Minneapolis: Bethany, 1975.

Nineham, *Mark*   D.E. Nineham, *The Gospel of St. Mark*, Harmondsworth: Penguin (Pelican NT Commentaries) 1969 or 1992 reprint.

Nineham,   D.E. Nineham, *Explorations in Theology I*,
Explorations   London: SCM, 1977.

Nov Test   *Novum Testamentum.*

NTS   *New Testament Studies*

Räisänen, *Secret*   H. Räisänen, *The 'Messianic Secret' in Mark*, English translation Edinburgh: Clark, 1990.

E.P. Sanders,   E.P. Sanders, *The Historical Figure of Jesus*,
Historical Jesus   London: Lane, 1993.

J.T. Sanders, *Jews*   J.T. Sanders, *The Jews in Luke-Acts*, London: SCM, 1987.

J.T. Sanders,   J.T. Sanders, *Schismatics, Sectarians, Dissi-*
Schismatics   *dents, Deviants: The First One Hundred Years of Jewish-Christian Relations*, London: SCM, 1993.

Sandmel, *We Jews*   S. Sandmel, *We Jews and Jesus*, London: Gollancz, 1965.

Shanks, *Scrolls*   H. Shanks (ed.), *Understanding the Dead Sea Scrolls*, London: SPCK, 1992.

D.B. Taylor, *Mark*   D.B. Taylor, *Mark's Gospel as Literature and History*, London: SCM, 1992.

V. Taylor, *Mark*

V. Taylor, *The Gospel According to St. Mark: The Greek Text with Introduction, Notes and Indexes*, 2nd edition, London: Macmillan, 1966.

TLS

Times Literary Supplement

Vermes, *Jesus*

G. Vermes, *Jesus and the World of Judaism*, London: SCM: 1983.

Vermes, *Religion*

G. Vermes, *The Religion of Jesus the Jew*, London: SCM, 1993.

Wenham, *Redating*

J. Wenham, *Redating Matthew, Mark, and Luke: A Fresh Assault on the Synoptic Problem*, London: Hodder and Stoughton, 1991.

Wrede, *Secret*

William Wrede, *The Messianic Secret*, English translation Cambridge and London: Clarke, 1971.

Acknowledgements

I am grateful to the Lawyers' Christian Fellowship, particularly to its officers, for inviting me to address them (see chapter 4 below) and for welcoming me on another occasion when their beliefs were being discussed. I also thank Mr. R.N. Tyler for friendly discussions in which he has criticized me from his Catholic standpoint. One can feel a certain solidarity with committed proponents of views to which one is hostile, without pretending that there is no conflict. I hope I have kept to the principle formulated by the Basel theologian and colleague of Nietzsche, Franz Overbeck, namely in argument to bring out differences in belief with maximum sharpness and clarity, while keeping a friendly peace in personal contact with the opponent.

Dr. D.V. Banthorpe and Mr. D. O'Hara have—as on previous occasions—helped me with comments on my manuscript, and Dr. David Ramsay Steele of Open Court has made helpful suggestions. My wife, Elisabeth, has been, as always, very supportive, and my former secretary Mrs. Evelyn Stone has once again done the typing. I wish to thank them all.

Actual Historical Order of Writing of
New Testament Books

Dates   *Books*

Not later   ⎫   Pauline letters: 1 Thessalonians, Romans,
than 60   ⎬   1 and 2 Corinthians, Galatians, Philippians,
             ⎭   Philemon
                                                              ⎫ Early
                                                              ⎬ epistles
Possibly   ⎫   Epistle to the Hebrews
earlier than ⎬
70   ⎭   Early post Paulines ⎫ 2 Thessalonians,
                  ascribed to Paul   ⎭ Colossians, Ephesians
                  James
                  1 Peter

                  1, 2 and 3 John

                  Revelation (the New Testament apocalypse)
After 70,   ⎫
probably as ⎬   Mark
late as 90   ⎭   ⎫ Gospels
                                                              ⎬ and
                  Matthew, Luke, John   ⎭ Acts
                  Acts

110   Pastoral epistles: 1 and 2 Timothy, Titus ⎫
                                                              ⎬ Later
                  Jude   ⎬
                                                              ⎭ epistles
120   2 Peter

Introduction: The Making of a Legend

The question 'Did Jesus exist?' has often been asked, and is normally answered with an unqualified 'yes' and a sense of outrage that the matter should even have been raised. But things are not as simple as this would suggest, for Jesus is not depicted uniformly throughout the twenty-seven books of the New Testament (NT), and the portraits of him in the four canonical gospels are certainly open to question. These gospels make him a teacher and miracle-worker in Palestine when Pontius Pilate was governor of Judea, that is, some time between A.D. 26 and 36, but were written fifty or more years later. They are generally admitted *not* to be the earliest extant Christian documents. The earliest are those among the letters ascribed to Paul which are genuinely his (and not the ones written later in his name). They include the four major epistles (Romans, 1 and 2 Corinthians, and Galatians) and several others, all written by A.D. 60—at any rate before Jerusalem began to suffer during the war with Rome which began in A.D. 66 and culminated in Jerusalem's capture and destruction in A.D. 70; for Paul mentions current dealings he is having with a Christian community there, which was obviously still untroubled by any such upheavals. The gospels, on the other hand, were written later, but before the end of the first century, and in some of them there are clear indications that the war with Rome was already a thing of the past at their time of writing. Paul never suggests that Jesus had been a teacher or miracle-worker, nor active in Galilee, but portrays him as a supernatural personage who had come briefly to earth as a Jew descended from David, had lived obscurely and been crucified in circumstances which Paul never specifies, but which he does not seem to regard as recent. There is no suggestion that he was a near-contemporary who died at Jerusalem under Pilate. It is not only Paul who depicts Jesus in this way. Other epistles, not by him, but also early, also show no knowledge of Jesus as he is portrayed in the gospels.

Most theologians nevertheless suppose that, in spite of their strange silences, these earliest Christian writers had the Galilean ministry and the Jerusalem Passion, as we know it from the gospels, in mind. Yet many of these same theologians admit that a great deal of what the gospels say of Jesus—not only in their miracle stories—is mere legend. Such scepticism is no ephemeral fashion but has been progressing since the end of the eighteenth century. As I show in chapter 5 below, really seminal work was done early in the present century, and by now even Catholic scholars are contributing and finding defence of many of the traditional claims a quite hopeless task. Maurice Wiles, an Anglican Canon and a scholar of stature, has conceded that there is an "oddity" in affirming that Jesus is the embodiment of the divine, and at the same time acknowledging that "our knowledge about him in himself is at every point tentative and uncertain."[1] From the Catholic side, Professor Adrian Hastings sees that many who have "much wanted to go on identifying themselves as Christians . . . have found more and more elements of Christian belief apparently untenable". The "unanswered questions" have multiplied and "today seem almost out of control". He adds that, while in past centuries major Christian bodies fought each other savagely over differences which now look "curiously trivial", today Catholics, Orthodox, and Protestants find their large common doctrinal core being eroded away:[2] Burton Mack, Professor of New Testament Studies at the Claremont School of Theology in California, goes so far as to call the gospels' portrayal of Jesus "fantastic", "the result of a layered history of imaginative embellishments of a founder figure" (*Lost Gospel*, p. 247).

Few of Mack's colleagues would go so far as this. Nevertheless, as we shall see, the discrepancy, which has to be admitted, between the portrait of Jesus in the Pauline and in other early epistles on the one hand, and the gospel portraits of him on the other, occasions a good deal of perplexity among some of today's Christian commentators. Others avoid the whole problem by seizing on the very few passages which form apparent exceptions to Paul's silence, or by adducing others which they claim as exceptions but which are quite obviously not. I discuss their defensive tactics in chapter 2 below. It has also been claimed that one need not expect much reference to the doctrines and behaviour of the gospel Jesus in earlier writers who are presumed to have known about him, and this defence is also examined below.

Some say that what matters is not beliefs about Jesus—whether he was, or is, divine or not, and so forth—but the Christian church. This indicates the lengths to which some churchmen are willing to go if only they may be allowed to retain their institution. There is, however, more than one church, and it is hard to see what would constitute a church if no particular beliefs were involved. Others shrug off the difficulty of getting reliable information about Jesus by saying that the same applies to most personages of ancient history. What do we really know about Thales, Apollonius of Tyana, and innumerable others? The only exceptions are great and public figures (such as Julius Caesar, Cicero, or Marcus Aurelius) whose writings are extant or concerning whom there are often other ancient records—literary, numismatic, archaeological. All this is true enough, but if Jesus is to be in any sense our saviour or even our guide, we need more than flimsy or dubious testimony.

If the earliest notions about Jesus were so different from what is said of him in the gospels, it becomes necessary to explain both how the earliest ideas originated and also how it came about that, by the time the gospels were written, he had come to be regarded as a teacher and miracle-worker who died under Pilate. In my first book on Jesus (*JEC*), published in 1971, I argued that the pagan mystery religions greatly influenced the earliest Christian thinking about a supernatural redeemer. By the time I wrote my *DJE* (first edition 1975) I had realized that Jewish antecedents must have been of greater importance. The earliest Christians were Jews, and early Christian documents accept the God of Israel, the Old Testament (OT), Jewish apocalyptic and angelology, and Jewish ideas about the Messiah. I was able to show that what is known as the Jewish Wisdom literature could well have supplied Paul and other early Christian writers with the conviction that a supernatural personage had come to earth, only to be humiliated there, and had then returned to heaven.

I continue to regard this Jewish Wisdom literature as of great importance for the earliest Christian ideas about Jesus. There was an ancient Wisdom myth which explained the underlying goodness of creation and also the undeniable evil in it by combining two ideas: that a Wisdom figure stood at God's side and participated as he created the world (Proverbs 8:22–31), and that when Wisdom sought an abode on earth, mankind refused to accept her, forcing her to wander from one place to another, until finally in despair she returned to heaven (1 Enoch 42:1–2). An alternative and less pessimistic version of the myth is given in Ecclesiasticus, the book from the OT Apocrypha alternatively known as The Wisdom of Jesus Son of Sirach. Here Wisdom is still personified and represented as God's agent in creation. She says "I am the word which was spoken by the Most High" (24:3, NEB), alluding to the opening chapters of Genesis, where God creates the universe by speaking words of command ("Let there be light", and so on). And she still traverses the whole earth, seeking an abode. But in this version the creator finally gives her a home in Israel, where she lives as the Torah, "the covenant-book of the Most High, the law which Moses enacted to be the heritage of the assemblies of Jacob" (24:23).

'Wisdom' is, in Greek, feminine, but Philo, the Jewish sage of Alexandria who died ca. A.D. 50, practically identified her with the masculine 'Logos', the 'word', the highest of God's 'powers' which functioned now independently of him, now as aspects of him. Philo was pleased to discover that Bethuel, which means 'daughter of God', was a name applied to a male in Genesis 28:2. This enabled him to say that "while Wisdom's name is feminine, her

nature is manly", and that she is called feminine only to indicate
her inferiority to the masculine maker of the universe.[3]

The influence of Jewish Wisdom literature on Paul is undeniable: statements made about Wisdom in this literature are made
of Jesus in the Pauline letters. Paul's Jesus, like Wisdom, assisted
God in the creation of all things (1 Corinthians 8:6). At Colossians
2:3 we read of "Christ in whom are hid all the treasures of wisdom and knowledge"—hidden because he lived obscurely. At 1
Corinthians 1:24 Paul actually calls Christ "the power of God and
the wisdom of God". The Swiss theologian Eduard Schweizer,
reviewing all the evidence, concludes that it was from speculations in the Wisdom literature that Paul acquired the notion of
Jesus's pre-existence (his existence in heaven, before he came to
earth).[4] And the article 'Wisdom' in the 1963 revision of James
Hastings's 1904 *Dictionary of the Bible* concedes that Wisdom, as
figured in the Jewish literature, "would seem to have been used in
the NT in some of the finest Christological passages", including
Colossians 1:15ff, Hebrews 1:3 and Jn. 1:1–18. In this latter passage, the prologue to the fourth gospel, we learn that "the
Word (*logos*) became flesh and dwelt among us"; and a great deal
of what is said of the *logos* in this prologue is paralleled in the
Wisdom literature. Dodd was able, a generation ago, to list the
impressive parallels.[5] Many Christians have come to feel uncom-
fortable with all this obvious mythology.[6]

There was also a pre-Christian genre known as the 'wisdom
tale', according to which the righteous man—no particular person
is meant—will be persecuted but vindicated after his death. In the
apocryphal book The Wisdom of Solomon, his enemies have condemned him to "a shameful death" (2:20), but he then confronts
them as their judge in heaven, where he is "counted among the
sons of God" (5:5).[7] Cognate is the martyrological book 2 Maccabees, with its belief in the resurrection of the faithful; and 4
Maccabees adds to this the idea that someone steadfast in the faith
unto martyrdom can benefit others because God will regard his
death as a "ransom" for their lives, an expiation for their sins.[8]
That a martyr's death could function as an atoning sacrifice, to
be followed by his immortality, was, then, a not unfamiliar idea
in Paul's Hellenistic environment, and such influence has been

invoked as an important source of the concept of Jesus's death as a saving event.[9]

I stressed the importance of 'Wisdom' material for Christian origins both in my *DJE* (the second edition of which appeared in 1986) and in my *HEJ* of 1982. In *WWJ* of 1989 I concentrated on the gospels rather than on earlier Christian literature, and tried to show how unreliable they are. I dealt in detail with their birth and infancy narratives and with their passion and resurrection stories, but said little about the teachings they ascribe to Jesus—an omission made good in this present book, where I also show (in chapter 3) that such comments on Christianity as are extant from early pagan and Jewish writers give either no confirmation at all to the claims of the gospels, or none that is independent of Christian sources.

How, then, was it that, by the time the gospels were written, Christians had come to link Jesus's lifetime with Pilate's? I have answered this question as follows. Pauline statements that Jesus lived in an unspecified past, "when the time had fully come" (Galatians 4:4), soon developed into the view that he lived "at the end of the times" (Hebrews 9:26; 1 Peter 1:20). This may originally have meant no more than that his first coming inaugurated the final epoch (however long) of history (the epoch that would culminate in his return to earth as judge); but it was in time taken to mean that he had lived on earth in the recent past. And to Christians of A.D. 75 or later—about the time when the traditions begin to link Jesus with Pilate—death by crucifixion (already attested by Paul, but not given any historical context in his nor in other early epistles) would have suggested death at Roman hands. If Paul envisaged any historical circumstances for Jesus's death, he may well have thought of his "Christ crucified" as one of the victims of earlier Jewish rulers. The Jewish historian Josephus, writing near the end of the first century A.D., tells that Antiochus Epiphanes, king of Syria in the second century B.C., and the Hasmonean ruler Alexander Jannaeus, of the first century B.C., both caused living Jews to be crucified in Jerusalem (Josephus expressly notes that in these cases this punishment was not inflicted *after* execution, as it often was[10]). Both periods of persecution are alluded to in Jewish religious literature (for instance in the Dead Sea Scrolls); and Jannaeus's crucifixion of 800 Pharisees left a strong impression on the Jewish world. Paul's environment, then, would have known that pious Jews had been crucified long ago, although dates and circumstances would probably have been known only vaguely. But for Christians and Jews of A.D. 70 and later, crucifixion was known as a Roman punishment. Titus had executed many in this way during his siege of Jerusalem during the Jewish War. If, then, Jesus died at Roman hands, it would be natural to place the occasion during the Roman occupation of Judea, i.e. some time later than A.D. 6. From such a premiss, Pilate would naturally come to mind as his murderer, for he was particularly detested by the Jews, and is indeed the only one of the prefects who governed Judea between A.D. 6 and 41 to be discussed in any detail by the two principal Jewish writers of the first century, Philo and Josephus. A date much nearer A.D. 70 for Jesus's death would not have been entertained. It is clear from the pre-gospel evidence that the circumstances were not known; and the post–A.D. 70 originators of the tradition of death under Pilate will have been aware that, had the death been much more recent to their own time, they would have known far more about its circumstances than they in fact did. The devastation of Judea in the Jewish War from A.D. 66 will have made it difficult for later writers to have much in the way of accurate knowledge of what happened there in the first half of the century, and hence easy for them to suppose that Jesus's death occurred in that period. By the time of the gospels, traditions blaming Pilate had been filled out and rewritten so as largely to absolve him from guilt, and to place this burden on the Jews. By then, Christians and Jews were in serious conflict, and it would have been natural for Christians to have assumed that such conflict had existed earlier and been responsible for Jesus's death.

If my readers think it is more plausible to take the gospel passion narratives at face value rather than to account for them in this way, I would reply that these narratives are very widely admitted to be highly problematic, as I have shown in my *WWJ*. I am not, in this book, presupposing acquaintance with this or any other of my earlier books, but shall from time to time be giving references to them for readers who might wish to pursue a topic further than it is taken here.

My earlier books have naturally met with a very mixed reception. Numerous scholarly reviewers allowed that I had pointed to important issues and problems, although they could not agree with my conclusions. John Bowden, an Anglican priest who is now Editor and Managing Director of SCM Press, wrote what I can only call a savage review of *JEC* in the Church Times (12th February, 1971). He questioned my qualifications to say anything on the subject at all, declared me "not worth arguing with" and my book "best forgotten". However, to judge from his own *Jesus: The Unanswered Questions* (SCM, 1988), he has in the meantime become considerably less confident about orthodox answers. He there allows not only that the gospel miracle stories include "a high proportion of pious legend" (p. 160), but also that there is "considerable difficulty" in discovering just what Jesus's ethical teaching was (p. 112), let alone in assessing its present-day relevance. His conclusion is that much of the traditional picture of Jesus must go, and he confesses himself quite unable to say what remains (p. 206). On the whole, it was the more conservative writers who were openly scornful of my work, as one would expect from what James Barr has called the "quite total complacency and lack of self-criticism" of conservative evangelicals, whose rejection even of theologics labelled liberal or modernist has always been total.[11] The techniques which inform the comments they have made on my work are indicated in chapter 1 below.

In the gospels Jesus's Passion is prefaced with an account of his ministry; and although we can see, in the way outlined above, how the Passion came to be provided with a specific historical setting, it is not possible to account in this way for what the synoptic gospels say of his Galilean ministry, with its teachings and its miracles. In the Pauline and other very early Christian documents there is at least a Passion which could in time be made specific as to time, place and circumstances; but there are no Jesuine miracles and, although there is much ethical teaching, it is not ascribed to the historical Jesus, as we shall be seeing below. Nor is Jesus linked in any way with Galilee. Accordingly, I have felt obliged, in this present book, as I have not done before, to allow that the obscure Jesus of the Pauline and other early letters is not the only historical or quasi-historical figure from which the very different Jesus of the gospels was developed.

In this connection, I would note that it is very widely agreed that Mark is the oldest of the four gospels, and was adapted in one way by Matthew and in another by Luke. We shall be seeing below repeatedly that the way these two later evangelists manipulate the material they took from Mark is very revealing. John Bowden spells out, with almost brutal frankness, what is here involved when he says that they "altered what they found before them in Mark because they wanted to produce works which were more helpful to their church" (*op. cit*, p. 40. Many commentators try to bagatellize these changes by saying merely that they were made 'for theological reasons'). Now it is also widely agreed that, additionally to their use of Mark, Matthew and Luke drew on a further common source, consisting mainly of sayings of Jesus. It is not extant and has to be reconstructed from the non-Marcan material common to these two gospels; and it is known as Q (German Quelle = source). It does not mention Pilate, nor Jesus's Passion, crucifixion, or resurrection. Recent students of this Q are claiming that they can divide it into chronological layers, and that the earliest of these depict a Jesus who was an itinerant Galilean preacher of the early first century. I discuss this analysis of Q in chapter 6 below. Certainly, Q includes references to place (Galilee) and time (the period when John the Baptist was active) which give its Jesus a particular and specific historical setting that is entirely lacking in the earliest extant Christian literature. The gospels' portrait of his ministry prior to his Passion seems to have been developed from this basis—transforming this Galilean teacher into a supernatural personage. The story of his ministry is then supplemented with the Passion story, set in Pilate's Jerusalem, as this story had been developed from antecedents I have specified above.

My two final chapters address ethical issues raised by the NT, particularly by the gospels. The question of anti-Semitism (chapter 7) continues to give concern now that so much recent experience, in Europe and in Africa, shows so clearly that tribalism of any kind is the curse of mankind. Chapter 8 is concerned with wider ethical matters. Today we hear frequent complaints that 'materialism' is widespread. It is not meant that many now believe that the processes of life are destined to be explained in the same terms as physical phenomena: few are interested in explanations of organic phenomena in any terms. The protest is rather against what is termed 'consumer materialism', which however really means little more than a primary concern for the material interests and welfare of human beings. It does not exclude 'spiritual' interests except what are regarded as the illusory ones alleged by religious propagandists. Art and ethics can be as much the concern of the 'materialist' as of the Christian.

Readers will see that in this book as in previous ones I owe a great deal to the painstaking work of the scholarly and critical theologians, and have not ignored that of their more traditionally-minded and conservative colleagues. I have thought it mostly unnecessary to indicate the clerical or academic status of any of them, but readers will be aware that books issued by SCM (Student Christian Movement), SPCK (Society for Promoting Christian Knowledge), and other well-known theological publishing houses were not written by partisan atheists. Indeed, nearly all my references are to scholars with theological commitments. Even the most sceptical of them manage somehow to soldier on. Adrian Hastings, whom I have already quoted, sees around him "almost infinite unanswered and seemingly unanswerable questions", but nevertheless abides by "that singular cornerstone of Christian belief: the mysterious universality and finality of meaning of Jesus the Christ" (pp. 2–3). Alan Sell, well aware of all the problems, seeks "a truly contemporary theology". It

> will be fired by the Gospel, grounded in the Scriptures, nourished by the Catholic faith of the ages, fertilised by Reformation emphases, tempered by Enlightenment critiques, and applicable today.

This from his 1992 inaugural lecture to a Chair of Divinity in the University of Wales. One can envisage the thunderous applause.

How little even many educated believers, clerical and other, have come to terms with the problems which perplex many NT scholars will be obvious to my readers throughout this book, and is illustrated in some detail in chapter 4. Lecky's *History of the Rise and Influence of the Spirit of Rationalism in Europe*, first published in 1865, shows rather well how beliefs do not depend much on argument, but on example. We believe, in the mass, what we suppose all the others (or the others whom we respect) believe—until we have discovered that this criterion is unsound. Then the first tendency is to disbelieve almost everything. Many people live in one or other of these states, or oscillate between them. Rational belief is, for most people, possible only in a small region of special knowledge which for professional or other reasons they happened to have explored. My hope is that the present book will give its readers some basis for rational opinions about the issues discussed.

1

The Commentator's Task

1. Motivation and Bias

The way motivation affects a commentator's ideas has been the subject of much unfruitful dogmatizing. The German historian Friedrich Meinecke supposed that the historian cannot do his job properly unless he feels love towards his subject-matter—hatred or indifference being equally pernicious. This view was obviously prompted by distaste for the way in which Enlightenment historians had written of Christianity. Thus he complained of Hume's "sober, detached empiricism", of lack of "spiritual depth" in Gibbon and "lack of antiquarian love" in Voltaire.[1] The Jewish scholar Geza Vermes tells us that "religious writings disclose their meaning only to those who approach them in a spirit of sympathy" (*Jesus*, p. 63). This can all too easily be taken to mean that one should be favourably disposed towards their claims, whereas in fact—as I am sure Vermes would agree—what is decisive in the pursuit of truth is solid argument, not sunny dispositions.[2] Some Christian writers go so far as to claim that one must be a Christian believer to investigate Christianity most effectively. N.T. Wright, for instance, is convinced that "serious study of Jesus and the gospels is best done within the context of a worshipping

community,"[3] such as that of his own chapel (at Worcester College, Oxford), to which he dedicates his book. Benedetto Croce
supposed that "I shall vainly scan the pages of the Gospels or the
Pauline epistles if I have no feelings, however quiescent, of Christian love, of salvation by faith".[4] He would perhaps not have
regarded it as vain to read *Mein Kampf* without some feelings,
however quiescent, for Naziism. It is true that we must interpret
the words we read, and can do so only in terms of our own experience. Yet one may learn by observation how people think and
behave, without finding in oneself a proclivity to do the same, as
one may get to know the habits of hyenas without any tendency
to imitate them. Neither sympathy with nor hostility to a given
material, religious or other, need necessarily warp the reasoning
process, but may make the mind work all the harder to produce
results which will stand up to searching scrutiny. Meinecke had to
admit that, even though Voltaire was "concerned only to tear
away the halo from the chosen people", he understood Jewish
history better than some of his predecessors (pp. 101–02). Gibbon's attitude to early Christianity was hardly sympathetic, yet it
is remarkable how few corrections to his account editors of his
work have found it necessary to make. Collingwood, in his
attempt to discredit him, was reduced to arguing that it is inappropriate to annotate his work at all. He complained that Bury's
annotations added new facts "without suspecting that the very
discovery of these facts resulted from an historical mentality so
different from Gibbon's own that the result was not unlike adding
a saxophone obligato to an Elizabethan madrigal. He never saw
that one new fact added to a mass of old ones involved the complete transformation of the old".[5]

Collingwood does not explain the process of 'transforming' old
facts. Bury's annotations may either supplement Gibbon or correct him. In the former case, gaps in Gibbon's story may be filled,
or doubts he expressed resolved; in the latter, his views may be
superseded. But it is hardly necessary to pretend that every additional fact makes the previous story obsolete. As for the saxophone and the madrigal, we think that an Elizabethan poem
sounds better in an Elizabethan setting because this is what we

are used to—although we have no objection to hearing the sonatas of Mozart on a modern pianoforte, or arrangements of old music for modern orchestras. There is of course no real parallel between the setting of old music to modern instruments and the annotation of old history books. Gibbon's *attitude* towards the facts he related was very different from Collingwood's, and that, for Collingwood, was his real fault. One might conjecture that the author of *The Idea of History* was suffering from the effects of an Oxford course in philosophy, and that his troubles arose from taking lectures on Plato and Kant too seriously. This may be part of the mischief, although he was surely not an altogether unwilling victim, as his 'philosophy' seems to offer an escape from the all too intelligible implications of the work of the Enlightenment.

Emphasis on sympathy and commitment may well be a reaction against demands for impartiality and absence of presuppositions. These demands are, however, more justly met with the retort that it is impossible to recount events or doctrines without purpose; even the most detailed account is a selection, and every selection must be guided by some aim. Nevertheless, a single presentment may be useful for more purposes than one. If there is occasion to inquire about something outside the common fields of social or religious history, a work composed with this end in view may not exist, yet the relevant facts may sometimes be collected from the standard histories. It is not necessary to compile a new history of the world every time one has a particular problem to solve.

If selection is inevitable even when mere description of events or situations is being attempted, it is equally necessary in the early stages of a quest for fruitful generalizations. At these stages, progress in any scientific inquiry is possible only by stressing broad tendencies and ignoring disturbing factors. The Periodic Table of the chemical elements would hardly have been established if too much weight had been attached to irregularities and anomalies. Eventually, of course, it is the more careful scrutiny of these exceptions which provides clues for further discovery. But it is of great importance to establish preliminary generalizations, for these give purpose and direction to subsequent research.

Any writing which consistently defends some overall thesis is liable to be regarded as biased; and imputing bias is encouraged by the fact that it is less laborious to explain someone's views in this way than by analysing his reasoning. If an author does have some propagandist aim, we may suspect his accuracy; but the accuracy is what primarily concerns us.

Historians of science have given evidence enough to correct the view that scientific work is normally motivated by pure love of truth. Rudwick, for instance, has shown that one of the principal contenders in nineteenth-century geology—Sir Roderick Murchison—was driven "by a determination to gain all the glory of discovery for himself" and to minimize the achievements of rivals by emphasizing their mistakes. Yet, adds Rudwick, "such morally ambiguous passions are often what sustain scientific activity."[6] Quite so: while the reasoning process may serve to guide us towards our goal, the goal must first exert some kind of attraction before this process can be brought into play. Hume summed this up well when he wrote: "Reason, being cool and disengaged, is no motive to action, and directs only the impulse received from appetite or inclination by showing us the means of attaining happiness or avoiding misery".[7] The immense application and industry demanded of the competent historian or scientist cannot easily be sustained without the impelling force of some emotion.

Citizens of a country and supporters of a political party or a creed often respond with obvious signs of resentment to criticism of that to which they are committed. Self-esteem may well be involved here. An individual whose own achievements do not sufficiently justify the requisite degree of self-esteem seeks to feed the appetite for it vicariously. He expands his conception of self to include his country, his party, his creed, and criticisms of any of these he regards as equivalent to attacks on himself. The habit of relying on such an expanded self for the satisfaction of self-esteem has the disadvantage that one cannot easily contract again to one's normal dimensions when one's country or creed is humiliated. Hence the perennial need for some grounds on which to base a high opinion of them. The phenomenon is particularly clear in the case of militant nationalism, but political and religious militancy frequently illustrate it.

ii. Guidelines for Hostile Writing and Illustrations of Their Use

What I have just said is more likely to be true of the rank and file members than of a creed's or nation's spokesmen and leaders, with whom I am here principally concerned. It is perhaps worth summarizing the guidelines they all too often follow in making hostile comments on an author. I am of course particularly concerned with remarks aimed at one who is critical of religious orthodoxy, and all the guidelines are represented in comments I have seen on my own work:

1. Question his qualifications to say anything on the subject at all ('Does this man know Greek?')

2. Never give the impression of carefully rebutting a rational argument, but speak patronisingly, as of a crude and discredited theory which deserves no more than a brief mention (e.g. his book is 'fun' and one must admire his mental agility and capacity for belief).

3. Affix distasteful labels to him, suggesting his adherence to discredited philosophical or other modes. (Dispose of Strauss and Baur by saying that the Tübingen School of critical theology was 'Hegelian'.[8] 'Negative' is a useful label here, even though the Finnish theologian Heikki Räisänen has noted that "the history of biblical study is full of examples from Galileo through Strauss to Albert Schweitzer which demonstrate that it is the 'negative' results which have most forcefully driven research forwards."[9]

4. Lump him together with discredited commentators, and if he himself has criticized these, make no mention of the fact.

5. Represent his minor errors and slips as indications of total incompetence.

6. Make plausible-sounding objections to his case as if he were himself unaware of them and had not attempted to answer them.

7. Say he relies on certain *a priori* dogmas; for instance, claim that he rejects the New Testament miracles not because he gives grounds for finding the evidence for them in the documents inadequate, nor because he is able, additionally, to account for the narratives without recourse to the idea of supernatural intervention, but because he arbitrarily rules out in advance the idea of supernatural events.

8. Pick on a book he does not mention—the literature on his subject being illimitable—and call his failure to do so 'a serious omission'.

9. Do not produce arguments, but appeal to 'authorities', alleging them to have settled all that is in question. At the same time, complain that he does no more than this, and also that the authorities on which he relies are 'out of date'.

10. State his case in an elliptical way which, while it would not mislead the few who already know his work, will make others suppose that he is defending an untenable, even absurd position. Above all, do not quote him at any length if his arguments are difficult to answer. ("No purpose is served by quoting the maverick and ill-founded views of G.A. Wells".[10])

11. Adduce propositions which, while themselves true, are irrelevant to his case.

Bruce *(Documents,* pp. 15–16) gives a signal example of this final guide-line when he rebuts arguments against the trustworthiness of the New Testament by pointing to its rich manuscript tradition—the mss. evidence for it being "ever so much greater than the evidence for many writings of classical authors". One can only comment that if there had been a Tacitus club in every European town for a thousand or more years with as much influence as the local Christian clergy, sections of the *Annals* would not have been lost. And if, instead of copying again and again the books of the New Testament, scribes had copied works which they regarded as heretical; and if the authorities had also allowed works downright hostile to Christianity to survive instead of suppressing them, then we should have a much clearer picture of what underlay Christianity's successful struggle against opposing forces. Mere possession of Porphyry's work *Against the Christians* became a capital offence under Constantine.[11] It has been repeatedly pointed out that papyrus quickly deteriorates in a humid climate, so that a work was likely to survive only if recopied at intervals; and that this would be done only if it was officially sponsored or if it was both popular and free from official vetoes.

The following example comprises passages which seem to rely heavily on guidelines 1, 2, and 3 in the above list. The author is Carsten Thiede, described on the cover of his book as "a member of Council of Germany's Institute for Education and Knowledge", who lives in Wuppertal with his English wife. He writes in English, and begins:

> Occasionally it has been suggested by ill-informed controversialists that the Gospels in their present state are 'purified' fabrications of later centuries, with an invented picture of a Jesus who never existed like this, if he ever existed at all.

"Ill-informed" implements guideline 1, and the dismissive tone ('controversialists', not 'scholars') guidelines 2 and 3. Worse than ellipsis (guideline 10) is the suggestion that dissent has been but 'occasional' and has characteristically consisted in assigning the gospels to 'later centuries' (plural). But what are Thiede's readers expected to understand from his statement that the gospels have been called "purified" fabrications? He is too contemptuous of the unnamed ill-informed controversialists to whom he ascribes such a view to tell us, but is obviously alluding—clumsily and in garbled fashion—to those NT scholars (particularly Helmut Koester, Professor of Ecclesiastical History at Harvard) who hold that one gospel (canonical Mark) is an abbreviated version, purified from gnostic views, of an earlier gospel of Mark.[12]

Thiede goes on to refer to an essay of 1988 in which an "assistant editor-in-chief of a scientific magazine" (guideline 1 again) "claims that some of the most important elements of the Gospels are inventions; and he is only imitating what others have tried before him". 'Imitation' we all recognize as a low and menial capacity, resorted to by those incapable of creativity and originality (guideline 3). He then adds:

> The most notorious of these [others], perhaps, was G.A. Wells, a pro-
> fessor of German at Birkbeck College, London [guideline 1 with a
> vengeance here], who managed to distort the evidence [guideline 2]
> until he reached the conclusion that Jesus never existed at all [guide-
> line 10]. And the middle ground is occupied by those who make their
> own selections about what they think can be true [a suggestion of
> guideline 7] and what must be wrong, from the virgin birth to the
> empty tomb.[13]

It is very difficult to represent an author fairly by means of a few
select quotations. But if the audience envisaged is sufficiently
naive, there is no need to quote or to give references; all that is
necessary is to present, as here, in one's own way the case
opposed, omitting anything that might arouse the reader's interest or tempt him to read the author in question, and suggesting
by any means that he is arbitrary, unscholarly, unqualified.

Thiede's whole book is a totally uncritical acceptance of patristic traditions, which he represents as "facts reported by early historians" (p. 4). It illustrates how fortresses of theology, long since
abandoned by a majority of serious scholars, continue to be
walled with libraries of 'learning' by their residual defenders. It is
sobering to turn from such confident apologetic to frank
appraisals from perplexed theologians who know of what they
speak.[14] John Bowden well represents them when he says ('Nerve',
p. 82): "There are [today] virtually no new substantial and intellec-
tually attractive statements of traditional Christian belief which
counter successfully the now well-established criticisms of it."

I do not suppose that deliberate malice is commonly the
motive in following any of the guidelines I have specified. The situation is rather this. A scholar makes up his mind on certain
issues over years of intensive study and then comes across a
closely-argued book which puts quite contrary views. To assimilate it properly would require considerable time and effort, and if
he were finally to accept its arguments, he would have drastically
to revise the convictions he has so laboriously built up over a long
period. He thus has a double motive for convincing himself that it
is not worth serious attention.

That motives of this kind have repeatedly been efficacious is
familiar to historians of science. Alfred Wegener's theory of 'conti-
nental drift' may serve as an example. The theory is now regarded

as so obviously true, and of such importance in bringing together apparently disparate phenomena under a single explanatory principle, that surprise has been expressed that it was not given a sympathetic hearing when first propounded. But there need be no surprise, for the audience originally addressed felt (rightly) that they were being asked to discard so much of what they had so painstakingly learned as well-established.

2

'Catholic Truth' on the Historicity of Jesus

The Catholic Truth Society's pamphlet *Did Jesus Exist?* (1986) is mainly devoted to criticism of my book of the same title, the first edition of which had been published eleven years earlier. The pamphlet is written by John Redford, described as "a scripture scholar and Director of the Southwark Diocesan Catechetical Centre". It would be difficult to pack more misrepresentation and inadequate discussion of my views into his twenty-three pages. I know it is difficult to give a fair and accurate statement of views with which one is completely out of sympathy and which one is therefore likely to find fanciful; but Redford typifies those commentators who seem so confident from the start that a work is nonsense that they can neither apprise themselves of its actual arguments, nor study it with any suspension of full belief in the premises on which they base their own views.

i. The Earliest References to Jesus

According to Redford, I argue that Paul, the earliest extant Christian writer, "was not talking about an actual human being Jesus of Nazareth, but about a dying and rising God". Paul and his readers, says Redford, knew quite well that Jesus had lived on earth as a man, so that, from my premises, he will have to be regarded as someone who tried to play a "confidence trick" on his audience by deceiving them into believing the contrary.

This, even as caricature, is grotesque. My argument was that Paul was concerned to stress how utterly Jesus—in his view a supernatural being (not a god) who had existed before the creation of the world—had humbled himself in condescending to take on human form and thereby to be born as an ordinary Jew. I quoted (*DJE*, p. 97) Paul's statement (Galatians 4:4) that Jesus had been "born of a woman under the [Jewish] law". I noted (mostly in a sub-section expressly entitled 'The Jesus of Paul') that Paul insisted that Jesus had been sent into the world by God to redeem it, had been born there as a descendant of David, as the scion of Jesse to govern the gentiles predicted by Isaiah, had died there by crucifixion, had been raised three days later, and had subsequently (but not immediately after his resurrection; see below, p. 57) appeared to various persons, including Paul himself. I stressed (p. 25) that "it did matter to Paul that Jesus had a human history". Hence it is quite beside the point when Redford thinks to countervail me by insisting that Paul gives "the clearest reference to the actual, and not mythical death of Jesus", and that "it is impossible . . . even to contemplate that Paul did not believe that Jesus existed."

It is perhaps worth noting in passing that a supernatural birth from a virgin mother, as alleged in Matthew and Luke, would run quite counter to Paul's argument that Jesus had come to earth in complete lowliness. For Paul, Jesus was "declared to be the Son of God with power" by dint of his resurrection (Romans 1:4). But for pious souls this was not enough. They thought he must have been certificated as Son of God even during his lifetime, and so there arose the legend recorded at the beginning of Mark's gospel: the heavens opened at his baptism, the Spirit descended on him like a dove as he stepped from the waters, and a heavenly voice declared "Thou art my beloved Son". But even this did not satisfy piety, and so Matthew and Luke, as later evangelists, make him actually be born of the Holy Spirit. Thus the stories of his virgin birth are to be understood as having originated by way of competition with those of his resurrection and his baptism: all alike determine the precise moment of his achieving the dignity of Son of God. Even some Catholic scholars—for instance Meier (*Marginal*, p. 213)—now admit that Matthew and Luke's birth and infancy narratives "seem to be largely products of early Christian reflection on the salvific meaning of Jesus Christ". Others, of course, continue to insist, as Alistair Hunter, a liberal Church of Scotland minister, has complained, that "the virgin birth and the incarnation must be accepted as historical facts *even in the face of wholly antagonistic evidence,* because the doctrine of the nature of Jesus demands it." (The italics are original.)[1] There are obviously still people who suppose that 'facts' required by their pet theory must be true facts.

Let us return to Redford. What I have denied is not that Paul believed in a historical Jesus, but that he believed Jesus to have lived the life ascribed to him in the gospels (written after Paul's time), where he figures as a teacher and miracle-worker in Pilate's Palestine, and therefore as a contemporary, or near-contemporary of Paul. Redford claims that "Paul speaks of the historical Jesus only *twenty* years after his death". He thus uncritically accepts the gospels' dating of this death, and is perfectly entitled to this opinion, but not to state it against me as an established fact known to Paul when precisely what I have called in question is that Paul understood Jesus to have lived and died at that time.

It is tiresome to have to set out, once again, the relevant data, but it is the only way to deal effectively with misrepresentation. Not only the Pauline letters, but all early Christian epistles—a substantial body of material[2]—fail to confirm what is said of Jesus in the gospels. They do not portray his life as mythical, but do not set it in any historical context. A passage typical of their attitude is Colossians 1:15, where he is called "the image of the invisible God, the first-born of all creation, for in him all things were created, in heaven and on earth". Statements like this do not read like allusions to a near-contemporary, particularly when coupled, as they are, with no specification as to where and when he was active on earth. These early letters never refer to his trial before a Roman official, nor to Jerusalem as the place of his execution. They include no allusion to a place of birth or residence— he is not here called 'of Nazareth'—nor to activity such as miracle-

working in Galilee or Judea. When Paul wants a practical example for his correspondents to follow, he normally, as Nineham has
noted, quotes himself and his fellow-missionaries, and does not
appeal to the behaviour of Jesus.[3] Nor could one gather from
these letters (Pauline and other) that Jesus had been an ethical
teacher or had taught in parables. They are indeed full of ethical
admonitions, but betray no awareness that Jesus had (if we
believe the gospels) already taught on similar lines. For instance,
Paul had a strong ascetic tendency, saying "it is good for a man
not to touch a woman", and wishing that all men were of like
mind with himself on this matter. He adds: "He that giveth his
own virgin daughter in marriage doeth well; and he that giveth
her not in marriage shall do better" (1 Corinthians 7:1, 7, 38). The
logion of Mt. 19:12 ("There are eunuchs which made themselves
eunuchs for the kingdom of heaven's sake. He that is able to
receive it, let him receive it") would have given him invaluable
support. And Jesus's statement that marriage belongs to the old
aeon, not to the new ("when they shall rise from the dead, they
neither marry nor are given in marriage, but are as angels in
heaven", Mk. 12:25) would have helped Paul not only here in 1
Corinthians 7, where he says he has "no command of the Lord"
(verse 25) concerning whether it is better to remain unmarried,
but also in chapter 15 of the same epistle, where he insists (verse
42–44) that the dead will be raised in a "spiritual" body, not in a
"natural" one (see below, pp. 57f). Again, Paul tells his Christian
readers to "bless those that persecute you", bids them "judge not",
and urges them to "pay taxes". Surely in such instances he might
reasonably be expected to have invoked the authority of Jesus,
had he known that Jesus had taught the very same doctrines, as
according to the gospels he had. It seems much more likely that
certain precepts concerning forgiveness and civil obedience were
originally urged independently of Jesus, and only later put into
his mouth and thereby stamped with his supreme authority, than
that he really gave such rulings and was not credited with having
done so by Paul, nor by other early Christian writers.

It will not do to argue that epistles, as a genre, cannot be
expected to show interest in Jesus's human life; for epistles of
somewhat later date—written when the traditions embodied in

the gospels had become current—do allude to it.[4] The ethical
teaching ascribed to him in the gospels enters second-century
Christian writings in a way that Christian commentators themselves find singularly abrupt. Canon Harvey, for instance, holds
(*Commands*, pp. 23–25, 31) that "for the most part . . . the first
Christian communities were not aware of any new or distinctive
ethic that was attached to their profession of faith in Christ"; that
"the source for Paul's moral teaching can almost always be identified as the inheritance that any serious-minded person would
have received from the traditional wisdom of his time"; and that
Jesus's uncompromising ethical commands in the gospels—Harvey has the Sermon on the Mount particularly in mind (compare
below, pp. 191f)—are either likewise absent altogether from other
canonical epistles or "make only an occasional and usually unac-
knowledged appearance"; whereas the Christian literature of the
second century shows, in this respect, "a startling difference. It is
as if the distinctive ethic of Jesus, as we find it in Matthew and
Luke, has now begun to make its impact and has impressed a
new moral character on the Christian community."

When significance is ascribed to these discrepancies between
the earliest Christian literature on the one hand and the gospels
and later epistles on the other, some Christian commentators
react with barely disguised scorn, saying for instance—I quote
Graham Stanton—that "as every student of ancient history is
aware" (What an ignoramus that fellow Wells must be!) "it is an
elementary error to suppose that because something is unmentioned it therefore did not exist or was not known about".[5] Of
course silence does not always prove ignorance, and any writer
knows a great many things he fails to mention. A writer's silence
is significant only if it extends to matters obviously relevant to
what he has chosen to discuss. Apart from being much concerned
with ethics, Paul was not indifferent to miracles: on the contrary,
he believed in their importance as a means of winning converts.[6]
It is, then, striking that he never suggests that Jesus worked them,
and even declares—in a context where he is resisting demands
for (miraculous) "signs"—that he can preach only "Christ crucified", and that he knows only "Jesus Christ and him crucified"
(1 Corinthians 1:22–23; 2:2). Again, Paul and other early Christian

writers were very concerned about Jesus's second coming, his
'parousia': would it be preceded by obvious catastrophes, or occur
without warning? On these points, 2 Thessalonians (probably not
written by Paul, although it claims to be from him) contradicts
the doctrine of the genuinely Pauline 1 Thessalonians—I give the
relevant details in *HEJ*, p. 50—but neither appeals to any teaching of Jesus on the subject, such as that detailed in chapter 13 of
Mark. This is very hard to understand if Jesus had in fact given
such teachings, and supposedly only a decade or two before Paul
wrote. Stanton says it is unreasonable to expect "precise historical and chronological references . . . in letters sent by Paul to
individual Christian communities to deal with particular problems." I am not pointing to lack of precision, but to total silence
concerning what the gospels say of Jesus's teachings and behaviour even when reference to them would have been of crucial help
apropos of the "particular problems" Paul was addressing. And,
as I have said, once we come to epistles which can be dated later
than the gospels, we do find the kind of allusions so noticeably
absent from earlier ones (and not only from the Paulines).

If we believe the gospels, there is a great deal in Jesus's teaching and behaviour that would have been relevant to disputes in
which Paul was embroiled. One of the major issues confronting
Paul was: should gentiles who accepted Christianity be required
to keep the Jewish law? One would never suppose, from what he
says, that Jesus had views on whether the law should be kept, as,
according to the gospels, he had. In Galatians (2:11ff), Paul takes
issue on this matter with Peter (Cephas)—one of the leaders of
the Christian community at Jerusalem ca. A.D. 50. Paul does not
suggest that Peter had been a companion of the historical Jesus,
any more than he himself had been; and although he is very anxious to discredit Peter, he does not attempt to do so by mentioning—here or elsewhere—Peter's denial of Jesus, which is so
prominent in the passion narratives of the gospels. The situation
to which Paul refers in Galatians is that Peter had deferred to the
Jewish law by refusing to eat with gentile Christians when he vis-
ited Antioch. Yet Paul does not support his indictment of this—
to him—unchristian behaviour by mentioning Jesus's table-
fellowship with publicans and sinners. Admittedly, these were not

gentiles, but appeal to the precedent of table-fellowship with them would make it hard to deny a like attitude to gentiles. And appeal to the clear dominical word of Mk. 7:15—which had been spoken publicly, to "the multitude" (verse 14)—would have enabled Paul to decide the whole controversy. Jesus says there:

> There is nothing from without the man that going into him can defile him: but the things which proceed out of the man are those that defile the man.

Mark explains that the first of these two statements declares all foods to be clean, and he makes Jesus explain that, by what "comes out of the man", we are to understand evil thoughts and evil behaviour (verses 19–21). But Paul does not appeal to this ruling either here in Galatians, or when discussing whether Christians may eat food that had been consecrated to heathen deities (1 Corinthians, chapter 8). As Furnish (*Jesus*, pp. 57–58) has noted, had such a radical saying as Mk. 7:15 been part of the pre-synoptic Jesus tradition, it is hard to understand why there had been such conflict about clean and unclean foods in the early church. In more general terms, it really is astounding that words or behaviour of Jesus critical of the Jewish law—if they be authentic or even if they then existed as mere creations of early Christian communities—do not seem to have been available in Pauline congregations, such as those in Antioch or in Galatia, which were founded on the basis of a mission to gentiles that dispensed with this law; for it is obvious from what Paul says that the Antiochan community which witnessed Peter's offensive behaviour was as little able as Paul himself to counter it with an appeal to words of Jesus and could supply him with no such words with which to fortify his case against the Galatians zealous of the law whom he was addressing. All that Paul can allege in order to establish the freedom of the gentiles from the law is to say that Jesus's crucifixion has put an end to it. As in the earliest Christian documents generally, it is not to Jesus's manner of life, nor to his teaching, but only to his death—in circumstances completely unspecified—that appeal is made in support of an important doctrinal matter. That this is so in the case of Paul has often been conceded,[7] but it is true not only of him. As Canon Harvey concedes, in the epistles generally "Jesus is a model for moral conduct, but the appeal is to his redemptive activity, not to particular episodes in his life" (*Commands*, p. 180).

Of course, attempts have nevertheless been made to establish that Paul, after all, did know Jesus's teachings. Romans 14:14 ("I know and am persuaded [πέπεισμαι] in the Lord Jesus that nothing is unclean of itself") is often claimed as implying knowledge of the ruling recorded at Mk. 7:15. But it would be strange if Paul should allude to this dominical saying only in this somewhat peripheral context,[8] and not in his central arguments about the law. Räisänen has examined this and other of Paul's statements introduced in the same way (e.g. Galatians 5:10, RSV: "I have confidence (πέποιθα) in the Lord that you will take no other view than mine") and notes that in each case the 'confidence'—expressed by the same Greek verb—refers to convictions and insights he has won from fellowship with the risen and exalted Christ. He is convinced "as a Christian" (the NEB rendering) of these matters. He is saying how deeply committed he is to their truth, not that his commitment is based on a saying of Jesus. Räisänen argues that acceptance of gentiles into Christian congregations without circumcision, and contact with them without regard to biblical food laws, will have begun from spontaneous conviction that nothing should be allowed to stand in the way of fellowship between believers in Christ; but that later the need was felt for some theological justification of this. Mk. 7:15 can thus be understood as an attempt to justify a practical step taken in the gentile mission long before. He supports this view of the true sequence by noting that, even in Acts, words of Jesus play no part in the controversy as to whether a law-free Christian mission is allowable, not even at the Jerusalem conference on the matter in chapter 15. There, Paul and Barnabas tell how God had shown, by signs and wonders, his approval of their mission to gentiles; i.e. this mission had begun spontaneously, but now some justification of it had come to be felt necessary. Here this takes the form not of a dominical saying, but of Peter's recall of a vision where he had been told that he was free to eat food he had regarded as profane and unclean, and so had concluded that God was thereby showing him that association with gentiles is permissible (10:14–15, 28–29). The story presupposes that Peter was not aware of any ruling by the historical Jesus to the same effect. Acts and Luke were written by the same author. "No wonder", says Räisänen, that "Luke omitted Mk. 7 in his gospel!"[9]

Paul's silences are, then, significant silences, and examples of them can be multiplied.[10] Although he is not the only early Christian writer to be thus silent, he occupies such a prominent place in the canon that it is his silences that cannot always be overlooked. D.B. Taylor has recently called them both "striking" and "amazing" (Mark, p. 3. He mentions, as a possible exception, "the ambiguous instance of 1 Corinthians 15", which I discuss below, pp. 57ff). Even Stanton, in his early (1974) book Jesus of Nazareth in New Testament Preaching (Cambridge: Cambridge University Press), having written of Paul's "rich portrait" of Jesus's character, and having claimed that "what happened between the birth and death of Jesus and what Jesus taught were both deeply rooted in Paul's whole theological thinking", nevertheless goes on to allow, in a discreet footnote, that "the almost complete absence of references or allusions in the epistles to the gospel traditions remains puzzling", and "there is no fully adequate explanation" (pp. 109–110, 115n.). S.G. Wilson has surmised, with his characteristic candour, that the whole topic is often "instinctively avoided because to pursue it too far leads to profound and disturbing questions about the origin and nature of Christianity."[11] But the way the whole problem is so often simply ignored is well illustrated in Vermes's latest book on Jesus. Having noted that the only point on which students agree is that much of the teaching ascribed to him in the gospels did not originate with him at all, but is later tradition put into his mouth, Vermes is nevertheless confident that he can sift this material so as to extract "the real message of the real Jesus" (Religion, pp. 6, 146). His insouciance concerning chronology emerges when he insists on treating the Pauline letters and the fourth gospel together as both ruled out by the other three gospels (p. 215) even though Paul pre-dates them, whereas the fourth gospel is probably a little later than they. Vermes has earlier written of "the metamorphosis of Jesus the Jew into the Christ of Christianity in the works of Paul, John and the rest of the NT writers" (Jesus, p. 13). It is strange to speak of earlier writers 'metamorphosing' the portrait of later ones.

On what, then, were the earliest hazy ideas in these epistles about Jesus's incarnate life based, and how did they come to be replaced, by the end of the first century, with the idea of a teacher and miracle-worker who died under Pilate? I have indicated how I answer both these questions in the Introduction to this book (and also much more fully in *DJE* and *HEJ*). Concerning the first of these questions, the humiliation on earth and exaltation to heaven of a supernatural personage, as preached by the earliest Christian writers, were certainly well represented in the Jewish background, particularly in the Wisdom literature;[12] and statements made about Wisdom in Jewish literature are made of Jesus in the Pauline letters.[13] The religion of one day is largely a reshuffling of ideas of a yesterday, and to this Christianity is no exception. I have also noted above, as another relevant factor, that Paul and other early Christians must have heard of actual crucifixions of holy men (documented by the first-century Jewish historian Flavius Josephus and alluded to in Jewish literature of the intertestamental period) that had taken place in Palestine one and two centuries before this time. Such knowledge will surely have seemed to Paul, and to other early Christians, confirmation of what he interpreted the Wisdom literature as telling him: that Jesus, a redeemer ('Jesus' means 'Yahweh saves') had come to earth and been killed long ago. This dating is actually represented in Jewish thinking, for (as I noted in *DJE*, pp. 198f) some traditions on which the Talmud drew persistently place Jesus among these ancient victims by dating him somewhere in the second century B.C.

Redford's version of what I have said on these matters is that "Paul invented the idea of the shameful death of a fictitious Messiah from texts of the Old Testament Wisdom literature"—presumably as part of his 'confidence trick'. But I argued that Paul sincerely believed that the evidence (not restricted to the Wisdom literature) pointed to a historical Jesus who had lived well before his own day; and I leave open the question as to whether such a person had in fact existed and lived the obscure life that Paul supposed of him. (There is no means of deciding this issue.) Redford adds: "For Wells, therefore, Paul never spoke about the life of Jesus because in reality Jesus never existed outside Paul's imagination." In fact, as I said (*DJE*, p. 97), Paul has so little to say of this life because he was convinced that it was lived obscurely: in coming to earth Jesus "emptied himself" of his supernatural form, and humbly assumed "the form of a servant" (Philippians 2:7). His life culminated in a shameful and ignominious death on the cross "in weakness" (2 Corinthians 13:4). So obscure was he that, until he manifested his true power at the resurrection, no one knew who he was: had they known the truth, "they would not have crucified the Lord of glory" (1 Corinthians 2:8). There could be no greater contrast than this with the wonder-working teacher of the gospels, whose "fame spread throughout all Syria".[14] Another Catholic caricaturist of my views, Ian Wilson, says I have written "no less than three seemingly erudite books . . . , essentially arguing that because Paul's letter [sic] can be demonstrated to have been written before the gospels, the gospel writers must simply have invented a human Jesus to fit Paul's imaginings".[15] The first-century Christian evidence I have adduced covers more than the letters of Paul, and a very significant factor is that in many respects the Jesus of the gospels (human or otherwise) does *not* fit Paul's imaginings.

The early epistles are, then, not merely silent about gospel material; they view Jesus quite differently from the gospels. Scholars have repeatedly recognized this discrepancy as perplexing and have been unable to explain it satisfactorily. Fridrichsen, having noted the "rather curious but indisputable fact that Jesus's miracles are very rarely mentioned outside the four gospels", noted also that, for Paul, "all of Jesus's life between the incarnation and death is summed up in the idea of *humiliation*"[16] (author's italics). Wrede had already said the same,[17] and they both refer for justification to (among other passages) Philippians 2:6ff, which I have just quoted. More recently, Harvey allows, referring to this same passage, that one would not really expect the Jesus who "emptied himself" of his supernatural status, in order to "humble himself" by obediently suffering death on Earth, to have been "at the same time capable of performing supernatural feats." But as the gospels tell us that this is precisely what he did, we must, so Harvey insists, accept their record as "a firm historical datum", just as we accept from them that Jesus was a teacher, in spite of "the virtual silence of the epistles" on that matter also.[18]

One reason why the ideas of the gospel writers were so different from those of Paul is that the post-Pauline Jewish War with Rome meant the dispersal and reduction to insignificance of the Jerusalem Christianity known to him. These events represented a decisive break in continuity—a break which will have made it very difficult indeed for Christian writers in the final decades of the first century to have reliable ideas about earlier Palestinian Christianity, and about the basis of its doctrines. The extent of the disruption caused by the war is emphasized by the NT scholar Burton Mack:

> The war lasted the better part of ten years, from the riots and skirmishes of 66 c.e., through the battles that raged around and within Jerusalem for four years, to the fall of Masada in 73 c.e. Reading the history of the war written by Josephus, one gets the impression that the internecine conflicts within Judea and Jerusalem were as devastating to the social order as the armies of the Romans were to the city walls and defenses. When it was over, the temple was in ruins, Jerusalem was a burned wasteland, and many of the people of Judea had been uprooted and scattered throughout Palestine, Transjordan, and the cities along the coast. It was a bloody end to the second temple-state, and there was no official leadership left to put its pieces back together. There were, as a matter of fact, hardly any pieces left. (*Lost Gospel*, p. 171)

The first writers, apart from Mark, to link Jesus with Pilate were the author of 1 Timothy and Ignatius of Antioch, both active either late in the first century or early in the second,[19] in Christian communities remote from Palestine,[20] and so with only hazy ideas about it and its pre-war circumstances. Mark himself even gets its geography seriously wrong (see below, p. 25). The communities of these authors, and of their addressees, will have included gentiles and had largely abandoned Jewish practices.[21] Mark even found it necessary to explain Jewish customs to his addressees, who presumably lived at some distance from Palestine; he did so inaccurately, and may himself have been a gentile.[22]

Paul certainly wrote his letters before Jerusalem was

destroyed in A.D. 70, for in them he refers to a Christian community there which was obviously untroubled at his time of writing.
From what he says it is clear that the Jewish and Roman authorities were permitting Christians to practise their religion there.
This in itself tells against the view that the founder of the faith
had been executed there only a decade or two earlier as a result of
Jewish or Roman hostility; for it is hard to believe that Jerusalem
Christians who were proclaiming that Jesus had risen from the
dead, and was about to return in order to end the present dispen-
sation, would have remained unmolested by authorities who had
recently found it necessary to contrive his execution. With the
gospels, the situation is different, and they include passages
which betray awareness that the city had been destroyed when
they were written. A well-known example is Matthew's insertion
of two verses (22:6–7) in the parable of the marriage feast which
represent the Jews as—I quote J.T. Sander's comment—"the natural enemies of Christianity, who got what they deserved when
Rome destroyed Jerusalem" (*Schismatics*, p. 26). Luke shows similar awareness of the catastrophe of A.D. 70, evidenced in his
rewriting of Mk. 13 (cf. *HEJ*, pp. 113ff). The case that his gospel is
dependent on the Jewish historian Josephus has recently been
restated and pressed by Mason (*Josephus*, pp. 211ff, 224). This
would mean that he wrote in A.D. 95 or later.

As for Mark, I have argued (*HEJ*, pp. 107ff) that it was
written around A.D. 90, and Anderson's recent study of its
references to persecution of Christians (compare below, pp. 146ff)
has pointed to such a date. It is usually dated between A.D. 65
and 75, but scholars are showing an increasing preference
for the later part of this decade (Brown, *Death*, p. 4n.). Morna
Hooker, in her commentary in Black's NT series (London, 1991,
 p. 8), thinks that Mk. 13, where Jesus is represented as setting
out the future right up to his second coming, was written with
knowledge of the events of A.D. 70. Others have argued that the
parable of the wicked husbandmen (12:1ff) betrays such knowledge even more clearly. Jesus here tells of a man who planted
a vineyard, let it out to tenants and went away. He sent a series
of servants to collect its produce, but the tenants maltreated
and even killed them. Finally he sent his "beloved son", but

the tenants killed even him, knowing quite well who he was; whereupon the owner "will come and destroy the husbandmen and will give the vineyard unto others." The description in the opening verses is taken from the Greek (Septuagint) version of Isaiah 5:1–3, where Israel is figured as God's vineyard. The owner in the parable is clearly God, the son is Jesus (who is thus represented as openly declaring himself God's son), the tenants are the Jewish leaders he is addressing, who will kill him and who realize that Jesus is casting them in this role of his murderers (12:12). The series of rejected servants are the OT prophets, "sent" by God but ignored or persistently maltreated by Israel; and the "others" to whom the vineyard is to be given can only be the Christian community. The whole is clearly a conscious literary construct, an allegory fashioned by the church with the death of Jesus in retrospect. It is a "tightly constructed story . . . literally packed with invitations to think of Israel's epic history from a Christian point of view" (Mack, *Myth*, p. 169n). As Jesus is made to predict not only his own murder, but also God's "destruction" of those responsible for it, it is reasonable to read this as an allusion to the fate of Jerusalem in A.D. 70, widely regarded in early Christianity as God's punishment of the Jews for killing him (compare below, pp. 51ff).

Stanton *(loc. cit.* in note 5 above) urges against my views: "If the gospel traditions about Jesus were largely invented about A.D. 100"—I do not in fact put even the gospels and certainly not their underlying traditions quite as late as this—"Why is it so difficult to find the convictions and emphases of Christians of that period in the gospels?" In fact, however, 'convictions and emphases' pointing to a post-A.D. 70 situation are discernable in them, namely this evaluation of the destruction of Jerusalem, and also anticipation that Christians will be persecuted for their faith. That the fourth gospel makes Jesus actually preach Christology (see below, p. 104) is also relevant here, as is its author's awareness that Christians had been excluded from the synagogue (compare below, pp. 182f and *HEJ*, pp. 126–27).

1 Thessalonians 2:15–16, which declares that "the Jews killed the Lord Jesus", for which crime "retribution has overtaken them for good and all" (NEB) reads like a reference to the Christian

view of Jerusalem's fate. For this (and other) reasons—summarized by Brown, *Death*, pp. 378–381—numerous theologians have set the passage aside as a post-Pauline interpolation. Furnish, for instance, says that "there are good reasons to think that it is from a later hand" (*Jesus*, p. 70). One of Redford's particularly clumsy attempts to discredit me is what he says apropos of my acceptance of these arguments, namely:

> To sustain his thesis that Paul was not talking about Jesus as a real human being, Wells has to expunge 1 Thessalonians 2:15 ("the people who put the Lord to death") from the genuine text of the letter. But there is no reason for this textual surgery except for the problems that not doing it causes one who denies that Jesus existed.

Quite apart from the fact that I have not propounded the 'thesis' that Paul was not talking about Jesus as a real human being, my overall argument is unaffected by whether this passage is genuine or not; for to say that 'the Jews' killed Jesus still does not give the death any historical setting. If Paul, who regarded Jesus as a Jew, as 'a servant to the circumcised" (Romans 15:8), thought of his execution as having occurred a century or more before, he might well have supposed that 'the Jews' were the culprits. The numerous Christian scholars who have excised the passage were certainly not impelled to do so because they were anxious to deny Jesus's historicity.

It is vital to Redford's position that the gospels be regarded as based, even though indirectly, on eyewitness reports, because this, he thinks, allows him to explain Paul's silences: "Paul did not talk much about Jesus's life on earth simply because it did not form part of his experience", which was "of Jesus risen from the dead". (As before, similar silences in other early epistles, including Hebrews, 1 Peter, and James are ignored). This, he says, is why "Paul says that we know Jesus 'according to the flesh' (2 Corinthians 5:16) no more, but only according to the Spirit." What Paul actually says here is (in literal translation):

> From now on, we know no man according to flesh: if indeed we have known Christ according to flesh, we no longer know him (so).

The opening phrase does not mean that Paul is no longer interested in anybody's biography (as Redford's argument would require), nor that he has no personal acquaintances. As many exegetes agree (Furnish, *Jesus,* pp. 17–18), the reference is not to 'Christ in the flesh' (the earthly Jesus); for 'according to flesh' qualifies the verb 'known', not the noun 'Christ', and the meaning is that he no longer has an 'unspiritual' conception of Christ, and no longer judges anybody by worldly standards.

Redford cannot brush aside the evidence that Mark, the earliest extant gospel, is a collection and redaction of bits and pieces of earlier tradition of different provenance. Yet he tries to turn this admission to account by claiming that at least the first three of the four gospels originated thus and that this is the only way to account satisfactorily for their many "similarities and differences"—it would be indecent to speak of 'contradictions' in this connection. (That term can be reserved for use in discussions about the Koran or the Dead Sea Scrolls.) In fact, however, many of the differences between Mark and Matthew, and between Mark and Luke, are due, as we shall see, to conscious manipulation of Mark's narrative by these later evangelists, each of whom adapted it to the needs of his own theology. Although, then, even Mark's gospel has to be admitted to be derivative, Redford mentions what he calls the majority view that this gospel "originated from John Mark, a companion of the apostles mentioned in Acts 12:12 and elsewhere". In this context he refers for support to Kümmel's standard *Introduction.* However, even in the English translation of the obsolete edition of this book on which Redford relies, Kümmel regards this majority view as no more than "thoroughly possible" ('quite possible' would render the German better) and allows that it presents "difficulties", such as that Mark "does not appear to know the Palestinian geography clearly". (Mk. 7:31 puts the Decapolis to the west of the Sea of Galilee when it actually lies to the east, and places Sidon south, instead of north of Tyre). In a later edition (earlier than Redford's pamphlet and accessible to him in English translation had he bothered to consult it) Kümmel is decidedly less confident: the majority view that John Mark is the author is now said to be "scarcely reliable"; the author is "unknown to us" and "obviously has no personal knowledge of Palestinian geography, as the numerous geographical errors show".[23]

Having thus bolstered his case by drawing on a work which does not give its author's most mature view on the relevant issue, Redford proceeds to call my view of the gospels "the nineteenth-century understanding of them". What this means is not entirely clear (except as implying that I am hopelessly out of date), but it is said in a context where he is combating the "extreme view" of "the Tübingen school" that Mark was written as late as A.D. 120 and John some sixty years later. Redford must know that such unacceptable dating is no part of my argument, and that I do not date any of the four later than "near the end of the first century" (*DJE*, p. 3). He declares that "no serious difficulties"—of the kind that my arguments raise—arise when one supposes that all four were written "by the close of the first century"—as if I did not subscribe to this dating. He adds: "The Christian claim that these documents go back to the original witnesses of Christianity receives daily confirmation by the scholars' proceeding on that assumption." He must know that many Christian scholars who do so proceed are thereby unable to authenticate a good deal of gospel material. Stewart Sutherland has justly noted that 'little agreement is to be found between specialist scholars about the historical content of Jesus's life beyond the barest of bare outlines."[24]

ii. The 'Brethren of the Lord'

As the substance of the gospels is so much better known than that of the epistles, it is difficult for the reader of the latter to peruse them without—consciously or otherwise—interpreting them from his knowledge of the former. One must constantly remind oneself that, as the gospels did not exist when Paul wrote, one has no right to assume, prior to investigation, that the traditions which came to be embodied in them were known to him, even when appearances suggest this, as in a few cases they do. The most striking example is Paul's reference to "the brethren of the Lord" (1 Corinthians 9:5) and to "James the brother of the Lord" (Galatians 1:19), whom he here designates as one of the leaders of the Jerusalem church. We immediately think of those

persons designated brothers of Jesus in the gospels, without paus-
ing to ask whether Paul had in mind members of a fraternity, of a
small group of Messianists not related to Jesus, but zealous in the
service of the risen one.

Even in two of the gospels, Jesus is made to call followers who
are not his blood relatives "brethren". "One is your teacher, and
all ye are brethren" (Mt. 23:8). Later in this gospel, the women
running from the empty tomb were intercepted by him, and "took
hold of his feet and worshipped him", whereupon he instructed
them: "go tell my brethren that they depart into Galilee, and there
shall they see me" (Mt. 28:8–10). The sequel shows that the disciples, not Jesus's family is meant; for the eleven "went into
Galilee", where they saw and worshipped him (verses 16–17).
Again, in the fourth gospel, Jesus says to the women, in the same
circumstances: "Touch me not, for I am not yet ascended unto the
Father; but go unto my brethren, and say unto them, I ascend
unto my Father . . . " (Jn. 20:17). Theologians have given strong
evidence that John did not know the other gospels directly (his
gospel has no passages of any length in common with them), but
at times drew on sources very similar to theirs and reworked
them so as to express his own theology. The parallel here with
Matthew may therefore well be due to a common source, a resurrection narrative in which Jesus made some statement about his
"brethren". Each evangelist has adapted the underlying tradition
differently. Matthew makes the women touch Jesus to show that
he is risen in body, not a ghost to be dismissed as a hallucination;
John makes him say: do not cling to me and so hinder my ascension. But both include the word 'brethren' in the sense of disciples, and this word was presumably in the source from which
both drew. If it there meant Jesus's blood brothers, we have to
suppose that both evangelists, independently of each other,
changed its sense so as to make it mean a group of disciples, and
this seems unlikely. The natural conclusion is that, already in the
source, it meant a group of disciples; and this would be evidence
for an early (pre-gospel) use of the title 'brethren' as meaning a
group serving the risen Lord. It is relevant to note that Paul's
phrase is 'brethren of the Lord'. He does not speak of 'brethren of
Jesus'.

I have discussed the NT references to Jesus's family in some detail in *HEJ* chapter 8. As I note there, Luke-Acts (both books written by the same author) never names the blood brothers of Jesus, even though the author will have known from Mark that one of them was called James. Also, the author does, in Acts, represent a certain James as leader of the Jerusalem church, but he never suggests that this person was Jesus's brother. In sum, Paul writes of "James the brother of the Lord", who was one of the Christian leaders at Jerusalem; and Luke (in Acts) writes of a James who is not more specifically defined, but who led the church at Jerusalem and had (chapter 15) negotiations with Paul, which obviously represent Luke's version of the negotiations between James and Paul mentioned in Galatians. In none of these texts is it necessary, in my view, to regard James as Jesus's brother. But this would be an easy and natural inference for anyone who tried to harmonize them with Mark or Matthew.

iii. Words of the Lord

Redford makes much of the fact that Paul occasionally refers to 'words of the Lord' which are similar to what Jesus is made to say in a few gospel passages; and he argues that this makes it likely that "Paul knew of a body of teaching going right back to Jesus". He makes no mention of the fact that I have been able to show that a substantial number of Christian scholars have come to regard at least some of these as words of the risen, not the earthly Jesus, given to early Christian communities by Christian "prophets" speaking in the name of the risen one. Paul's phrase 'the word of the Lord' is the same as in his Greek Bible was used with reference to prophetic oracles. Hence he may well mean that "he is conveying an oracle which has been formulated '*in the name* of the Lord' by some Christian prophet—or even by himself" (Furnish, *Jesus*, p. 64, his italics). As Eugene Boring notes, "it was in conjunction with the conviction of the early church that the Last Times had dawned that prophets emerged within it": for "it was widely accepted in the first-century Judaism that the Spirit (= the Spirit of Prophecy) was essentially the eschatological gift, so that when prophets reappeared, this itself would be a sign of the dawning End." He adds that "this view was the common denominator of both those circles that affirmed the presence of the prophetic Spirit (e.g. Qumran) and those that denied it (many streams of rabbinic tradition)".[25]

In time, such Christian prophets and their audiences would naturally suppose that Jesus must have spoken during his lifetime in the manner they thought his spirit spoke to them. I would claim that this accounts for what correspondence there is (and it is far from complete) between the few 'words of the Lord' recorded by Paul and what Jesus is made to say in the gospels.

That Paul did receive communications from the risen Jesus is clear from his telling of thrice having asked the Lord—presumably in prayer, as he never met the historical Jesus—that the "thorn in his flesh" (some kind of physical malady) be removed, and of receiving the answer: "My grace is sufficient for thee, for my power is made perfect in weakness" (2 Corinthians 12: 7–9). Here, says E.P. Sanders, is "a direct quotation of the heavenly Lord"; and if such sayings were repeated by Paul or other Christians, without specification of their provenance, it could easily come to be supposed that Jesus had made them during his incarnate life (*Historical Jesus*, p. 62). It is thus not surprising that even some of the sayings ascribed in the gospels to Jesus before his crucifixion bear clear marks of having originated as dicta of the exalted Christ. "Where two or three are gathered together in my name, there am I in the midst of them" (Mt. 18:20). Omnipresence belongs to the risen Christ, and this assurance of it is given in the context of what is to be done by "the church" to discipline its members, and therefore belongs to the time when the church had become an organized body. The same is true of Paul's statement (1 Corinthians 14:34–37) that it is "a commandment of the Lord" that "the women keep silence in the churches".

Paul gives a "word of the Lord" at 1 Thessalonians 4:15–17 as his authority for the assurance that those Christians who have already died before Christ's second coming (his parousia) will not forfeit its benefits: "We who are left alive" when he comes will be "caught up in the clouds" with the resurrected dead "to meet the Lord in the air". There is no teaching to this effect in the gospels, and the issue it addresses can hardly have become a burning one until Christians became alarmed at the failure of the parousia to occur when deaths were depleting their numbers. Hence this 'word' will have been spoken by the risen Lord to the early church.

Paul's other references to 'words of the Lord' are all in 1 Corinthians (7:10; 9:14; 11:23–26 and 14:37). This is the only one of his letters which includes a discussion of Christian prophecy (chapters 12 to 14). Eugene Boring observes (p. 74) that "this itself should suggest some relationship between Christian prophecy and the tradition of Jesus's words." I have already quoted 14:37 which requires silence from women in church, and 9:14 is not important in the present context;[26] but the other two passages have significant parallels in the gospels. Redford notes the following similarity:

1 Corinthians 7:10–11	*Mark 10:11–12*
Unto the married I give charge, yea not I but the Lord, that the wife depart not from her husband (but if she depart, let her remain unmarried, or else be reconciled to her husband); and that the husband leave not his wife.	Whosoever shall put away his wife and marry another committeth adultery against her; and if she herself shall put away her husband and marry another, she committeth adultery.

I shall refer later to the variant ms. readings of Mark at this point. Jesus has just attempted (three verses earlier in Mark) to confute Pharisees by arguing for indissolubility of monogamous marriage from the Greek (Septuagint) version of their scriptures where the Hebrew original would have less clearly supported him (compare below, p. 193). This does not suggest an authentic dialogue. Moreover, he could not, as Mark alleges in the verses quoted above, have told a Palestinian audience that a wife should not seek divorce, since in Palestine only men were allowed to do so. But Paul could appropriately urge such a ruling on the gentile Christian communities to which he appealed; and if he told them it was commanded by the Lord he would have meant a directive given by some Christian prophet speaking in the name of the risen one—an obvious way of supporting a ruling which he was anxious to inculcate. When at a later stage it was supposed that Jesus must have said the same during his lifetime, the doctrine was, however inappropriately, put into his mouth as an address to a Palestinian audience. (I said all this in *HEJ*, p. 23 and *DJE*, p. 28, but Redford simply ignored it.)

It is clear from Paul's discussion of prophecy in 1 Corinthians that it was in church where the prophets came forward with their 'revelations'. There, "two or three prophets" might speak, while the others "weigh what is said"; and "if a revelation is made to another sitting by", then the first should be silent, "for you can all prophesy one by one" (14:28–31). Paul takes a very positive view of the "spiritual gift" of prophecy, and prefers it to the practice of 'speaking with tongues', that is, making utterances which are not immediately intelligible and which have to be interpreted (14:9), although he includes both the ability to speak in this way and the ability to interpret such speech in his lists of 'spiritual gifts' (12:10). Obviously, the straightforward statements of prophets were less likely to disrupt order than unintelligible pronouncements, and Paul is concerned that "all things should be done decently and in order" (14:40). Nevertheless, even prophecy could be disruptive, and he has to warn against aberrations. He wants the Corinthians to understand that no one speaking by the Spirit of God ever says "Jesus be cursed!" and no one can say "Jesus is Lord" except by the Holy Spirit (12:3). There was a 'Christ party', a sub-group among the Corinthian Christians (1:12), and it has been suggested that their prophets may have been responsible for the dictum, 'Jesus be cursed' because they did not share even Paul's minimal interest in the historical Jesus, but felt inspired solely by the exalted Christ.[27] Be this as it may, Paul is obviously protesting against what he regards as some kind of abuse of the gift of prophecy. In 1 Thessalonians he argues that what the community itself regards as abuse of the gift must not be allowed to discredit it altogether: "Do not despise prophesying, but test everything" (5:20). Obviously, a medley of doctrine would inevitably result from gatherings at which "all" could prophesy, "one by one". But this is one of the bases on which the churches' Christologies were built.

Paul himself repeatedly speaks of 'revelations' which he feels impelled to pass on to the community. Examples from 1 Corinthians include:

2:13   We impart this in words not taught by human wisdom,
       but taught by the Spirit.
7:40   In my judgement a widow is happier if she remains as
       she is, and "I think I have the Spirit of God".
14:37 What I am writing to you is "a command of the Lord".

Other NT authors show how widespread the phenomenon was
in the early church. Ephesians (which I with many others regard
as post-Pauline) tells that gentiles have equal status with Jews in
Christianity, and that, although this was not previously known, it
has "now been revealed to Christ's holy apostles and prophets by
the Spirit" (3:5). The book of Revelation refers to prophets as integral to the church (22:9), and delivers logia of the risen Lord to his
church through his spokesman, the author (22:16 and 20). Acts
locates prophets in the church at Antioch (13:1) and elsewhere
(15:32; 21:10), and many messages are said to be imparted by the
Spirit (16:6–7; 20:23; 21:4). Likewise in the fourth gospel the disciples are told that "the Spirit of truth" will come to them in due
course and tell them "the things that are to come" (Jn. 16:13), and
that "the Holy Spirit" will teach them everything (15:26).

Other NT authors follow Paul in warning against abuses of
prophecy. 1 John urges the faithful to "test the spirits, whether
they are of God, because many false prophets are gone out into
the world", propounding the pernicious 'docetic' view that Jesus
had only a phantom body, not a real body of flesh while he was on
earth (1 Jn. 4:1–3). Matthew's Sermon on the Mount warns
against "false prophets which come to you in sheep's clothing but
inwardly are ravening wolves" (7:15). The verse is not included in
Luke's equivalent of this material (6:43–49), and Matthew has
surely introduced it into a list of general exhortations to the community because such prophets were bothering his church. They
apparently belonged to a rival Christian group, for he allows that
they may well call Jesus "Lord", may well "prophesy", "cast out
demons" and "do many mighty works" in his name; but he will
reject them at the final judgement because of their "lawlessness"
(ἀνομια, 7:22–23). It may be that they preferred reliance on
doctrines revealed by prophets to following the strict code advocated in the Sermon.

The most striking instance of words of the Lord recorded by Paul is provided by Jesus's eucharistic words ("this is my body", and so forth). Paul expressly says that they came to him through a personal revelation from the (risen) Christ: he "received" them "of the Lord" (1 Corinthians 11:23). In the first three gospels similar words are spoken by Jesus at the Last Supper. Atempts to show that Paul's version of them reached him from human tradition which went back to the accounts of persons actually present on that occasion have been effectively rebutted by the Jewish scholar Hyam Maccoby.[28]

Although Matthew follows Mark fairly closely, there are major discrepancies between the gospels, and between them and Paul, as to these eucharistic words. In Luke (chapter 22) they are introduced with the following unparalleled passage:

> (15) And he said unto them, With desire I have desired to eat this passover with you before I suffer; (16) for I say unto you, I will not eat it until it be fulfilled in the kingdom of God. (17) And he received a cup, and when he had given thanks he said, Take this and divide it among yourselves.

Luke continues with a logion that is not in Paul and which (worded slightly differently) is placed after the meal by Mark and Matthew:

> For I say unto you. I will not drink from henceforth of the fruit of the vine until the kingdom of God shall come (verse 18).

These discrepancies suggest that this logion was originally an independent saying which the synoptic evangelists (or their sources) have linked in different ways with the eucharistic words.

Luke follows this with the eucharistic words proper:

> And he took bread, and when he had given thanks he brake it and gave to them, saying, This is my body (verse 19a).

All three synoptics and Paul too have "this is my body". These enigmatic words seem to be basic to the whole tradition. Paul adds to them "which is for you: this do in remembrance of me" (1 Corinthians 11:24)—an obvious attempt to elucidate or comment on the enigma and to represent Jesus as instituting the eucharist

as a rite. Some mss. of Luke supplement "this is my body" in a
similar way, adding:

> which is given for you: this do in remembrance of me. And the cup
> [he took] in like manner after supper, saying, This cup is the new
> covenant in my blood, even that which is poured out for you
> (22:19b–20).

The RSV and the NEB relegate these words of the so-called
'longer' Lucan text to the margin; for scholars (for example
Ehrman, *Corruption*, p. 197) have argued from the ms. evidence
that the shorter text is original, so that Luke's account originally
said nothing about the atoning effect of Christ's body or blood.
This shorter text was felt to be unsatisfactory also because it
referred to the cup (verse 17) before the bread (verse 19a). The
longer text rectifies this by its supplementary reference to a further cup; and by adding also "this do in remembrance of me" it
makes Jesus, as does Paul, institute the eucharist as a rite. These
words of institution are absent from Mark and Matthew, but
otherwise the longer Lucan text brings Luke broadly into line
with them—although they have adapted the words about the wine
so as to parallel those about the bread: "this is my body" is
followed in Mark and Matthew by "this is my blood" (not "this
is the new covenant in my blood", as in Paul and in the longer
text of Luke); and Matthew additionally labours the atonement by
saying not that Jesus's blood is "poured out for you" but
"is shed for many unto remission of sins" (compare below, p. 98
on the significance of this). Thus only Paul unequivocally ascribes
to Jesus both the eucharistic words, and the institution of the rite.

The fourth gospel has nothing at all corresponding to all this
in its passion narrative, but makes Jesus declare earlier, in
Galilee:

> (6:51a) I am the living bread which came down out of heaven; if any
> man eat of this bread he shall live for ever: (51b) yea and the bread
> which I will give is my flesh, for the life of the world . . . (53) . . .
> Except ye eat of the flesh of the Son of man and drink his blood, ye
> have not life in yourselves. (54) He that eateth my flesh and drinketh
> my blood hath eternal life; and I will raise him up at the last day . . .
> (58) This is the bread which came down out of heaven . . . , he that
> eateth this bread shall live for ever.

Some commentators set verses 51b to 58 aside as one of the final editorial insertions in this gospel. They argue that the editor wanted to change the topic from eating bread to consuming Jesus's flesh and blood, which he regarded as essential to salvation; and that at verse 58 he skilfully works back to 'bread', the starting point of his insertion (verse 58 picks up the wording of verse 51). His purpose (compare Haenchen, *JE*, pp. 326ff), was to introduce two doctrines foreign to the fourth gospel prior to its final redaction, namely the expectation of a resurrection on "the last day" (verse 54), and the restriction of such hopes to those who partake of the eucharistic sacrament. Whether these verses were added later or not, it remains true that John omits any account of the institution of the eucharist at the Last Supper.

In sum, the gospels give us: eucharistic words without institution of the rite (Mark, Matthew); a minimum of such words without institution (Luke's shorter text); fuller eucharistic words with words of institution (Luke's longer text); and no such material at all at the Last Supper, but something resembling it earlier (John). Maccoby comments (p. 94) that this is not what one expects to find in the gospels if Jesus in fact spoke eucharistic words and instituted a rite at the Last Supper. A eucharistic practice was by no means uniquely Christian. Something similar was practised both among the Jewish Qumran sectarians and in the pagan mystery cults.[29] Once such a practice had been established among Christians, it would be natural for them to suppose that Jesus had ordained it.

Finally, I would note that Paul, introducing the eucharistic words which he "received of the Lord", tells (according to the RV) how "the Lord Jesus took bread in the night in which he was betrayed" (1 Corinthians 11:23). This rendering suggests that Paul knew of Judas's betrayal. But he never mentions Judas, and the Greek verb he uses here ($\pi\alpha\rho\alpha\delta\iota\delta\acute{o}\nu\alpha\iota$) signifies 'handed over', 'delivered up'. To render it as 'betrayed' or even as 'arrested' (NEB) is to interpret him from the gospels. Mack, with many other commentators, observes that Paul is referring not to a betrayal, but to the martyr's fate, and that he nowhere mentions a third party involved in the 'handing over', the subjects of the verb being either Jesus himself (Galatians 1:4 and 2:20, Jesus "gave himself for our sins", "gave himself up for me") or God (explicitly in Romans 8:32, "He spared not his own Son but delivered him up for us all"; and understood as the subject of the passive in Romans 4:25, "He was delivered up for our trespasses"). "It was Mark who supplied another human subject (Judas) when he decided to make the meal part of the historical narrative of the passion" (*Myth*, p. 299; compare *HEJ*, p. 26 and references; *DJE*, p. 25 and references).

iv. The Inconsistent Voices of the New Testament

In an article entitled 'The Authority of the Christian Faith', the late Richard Hanson declared it "impossible to deny that Paul knew the salient facts about the character of Jesus". This is carefully, not to say cunningly, worded in that it suggests to the reader knowledge of the substance of what the gospels say, while in fact (as the next sentence shows) not committing the writer to ascribing to Paul any more than knowledge of "a Christ of gentleness, humbleness, compassion and resolution, who deliberately accepts the way of the cross".[30] Hanson obviously had in mind such passages as 2 Corinthians 10:1, where Paul mentions the "meekness and gentleness (NEB magnanimity) of Christ"—as if this established acquaintance with biographical details, when in fact it may well mean that Jesus was meek and magnanimous because he condescended to come to earth in human form at all (the doctrine of other Pauline passages). Again and again when Paul refers to Jesus's ethical qualities, the reference is either to his incarnation or to his death, neither of which is given a historical context.

Hanson's statement typifies the common assumption that any proposition in the epistles—Pauline and other—which in some way resembles a teaching or attitude in the gospels may justly be regarded as an 'echo' of the latter. That there was an influence in the opposite direction—that, for instance, teachings regarded as important were in time put into Jesus's mouth—is well-known, but commonly disregarded when relating epistles to gospels. It seems difficult, even for the scholar who knows that the former mostly pre-date the latter, to remain uninfluenced by the supposition that, because epistles are addressed to the post-resurrection church, their authors must have known of what the gospels claim to have been pre-resurrection situations. For the lay reader this supposition is further encouraged by the fact that, in our printed Bibles, he comes to epistles after he has read the gospels, and by the further fact that some epistles name as their authors persons who bear the same names as personal disciples of Jesus in the gospels. He will, for instance, suppose that 1 Peter was written by the Peter he knows from the gospels. Kümmel's standard handbook would however inform him that this epistle is "undoubtedly pseudonymous", "shows no evidence at all of familiarity with the earthly Jesus", with his life or his teaching, and that a Galilean fisherman could not have written such "cultivated Greek", with "many rhetorical devices" and with all the OT quotations and allusions deriving from the Greek version of these scriptures, not from the Hebrew originals.[31] The lay reader will at best be familiar with overall depictions of the NT and of early Christianity—synthesizing accounts where—as Räisänen has recently complained—the landscape "is no longer historical but overtly theological", and where it commonly happens that "an acute analyst turns into a pious preacher".[32]

"Our acceptance of any historical fact", says Redford "is to some extent an act of faith", in that it is dependent on acceptance of testimony, not on direct experience of the fact. He adds: "I have no doubt whatsoever that Napoleon existed; but only because countless historians inform me that he did, and I have no reason whatsoever to disbelieve them". There is here an implied parallel with the evidence for Jesus; and if his existence ca. A.D. 30 were as well attested as that of Napoleon in 1815, the whole matter could indeed be regarded as settled. That 'countless historians' allege certain events to have occurred is not in itself decisive. Most of them might be uncritically following predecessors. What really matters is the undesigned coincidence of independent testimony. There are so many early and independent sources of information about Napoleon which show an overall consistency that it is much easier to account for them by accepting what they say than by supposing a universal conspiracy to deceive posterity.[33] I have tried to show that, in the case of Jesus, the twenty-seven books of the NT, when considered in chronological order, give no such consistent picture. It simply bedevils the whole issue if one begins by assuming that the authors of all twenty-seven must have had substantially the same conceptions of the Jesus of whom they speak, and must all have believed him to have lived when the gospels say he lived, so that the early epistles, written only a generation or so later than this dating of his lifetime, must either be taken as confirming at any rate the broad outline of what the gospels say of him, or be set aside as "hoaxes". This is John Macquarrie's word in his well-known survey of Christology *Jesus Christ In Modern Thought* (London: SCM, and Philadelphia: Trinity, 1990, p. 348); for he believes that these are the alternatives with which we are faced. One can see from this the kind of thinking which has led Redford to impute to me the view that Paul was playing a 'confidence trick'.

I am reserving my criticism of what Redford says about pagan and Jewish testimony concerning Jesus to the next chapter, where we shall see that there is no pagan or Jewish evidence that is independent of Christian tradition and which could function as external confirmation of it.

3

Pagan and Jewish Attitudes to Jesus

i. Suetonius, Pliny, and Tacitus

"If Jesus did not exist", asks Redford, "why on earth did not someone say so in those early days?" As a matter of fact, Justin Martyr did have to defend Christianity, in the debates between Jews and Christians, against the charge that Christians had "invented some sort of Christ" for themselves and had accepted "a futile rumour" (*Dialogue with Trypho*, 8, a work dated around A.D. 135). However, with his objection "in mind", Redford turns to what is said about Jesus by Roman historians, and notes that the few who mention him do not deny that he existed. On p. 15 of *DJE*, I made the following comment on this fact:

> Today Christianity has been so important for so long that one is apt to assume that it must have appeared important to educated pagans who lived A.D. 50–150; and that if they fail to discuss Jesus's historicity or the pretentions of his worshippers, their silence must be attributed to their consciousness that they were unable to deny the truth of the Christian case. In fact, however, there is no reason why the pagan writers of this period should have thought Christianity any more important than other enthusiastic religions of the Empire. Dio Cassius, who wrote a history of the realm as late as ca. A.D. 229; makes no mention at all of Christians or of Christianity, and alludes but once to its then great rival, Mithraism. Because Christianity so long remained insignificant, except among the lower classes, its

major pagan critics—Lucian (died around A.D. 200), Celsus (died
ca. 178), Porphyry (d. 303) and the Emperor Julian (d. 363)—all
wrote long after the gospels had become established, and gathered
from these gospels that Jesus was a teacher and wonder-worker of a
kind perfectly familiar to them. As they could thus assign him to a
familiar category, they had no reason to doubt his historicity.
Porphyry seems to have been close to the standpoint of those modern
writers who hold that, although Jesus existed, we can know nothing
of him; from the contradictions between the gospel passion narratives he infers that the evangelists are in general unreliable, and he
calls them "inventors, not narrators" of events.

The historian T.D. Barnes observes that "most inhabitants of the
Roman Empire in A.D. 100 were either unaware of or uninterested
in the Christians in their midst. Even in Rome, where there had
certainly been Christians since the reign of Claudius, the varied
epigrams of Martial and the satires of Juvenal make no identifiable allusion to the new religion, though both authors deride
Jews and Judaism." He adds that there is likewise nothing in the
speeches of the much-travelled Greek orator Dio Chrysostom
(who survived until after A.D. 112), nor in his contemporary
Plutarch.[1] For Redford, however "Jesus of Nazareth had become
world-famous" by A.D. 80! He might learn from his Catholic colleague J.P. Meier that, "as hard as it is for devout Christians to
accept, the fact is that Jesus was simply insignificant to national
and world history as seen through the eyes of Jewish and pagan
historians of the 1st and early 2nd centuries A.D. If he was seen at
all, it was at the periphery of their vision" (*Marginal*, pp. 7–8. This
is one reason why Meier calls Jesus "a marginal Jew").

Redford mentions statements by Suetonius, the younger Pliny
and Tacitus (all from the early second century). These writers do
not, as he implies, mention 'Jesus', but refer to him only as
'Christ'. The historian Suetonius may fairly be interpreted as saying that under the Emperor Claudius (who died A.D. 54) there
were disturbances in Rome between Jews and Christians concerning the claim being pressed by Christians that Jesus was the
Messiah. But no more about the 'historical' Jesus need have been
included in this Christianity of Claudius's day than what extant
Christian writers (Paul and others) were saying before the gospels
became established later in the first century; and this much does

not confirm their portrait of Jesus as a preacher and wonder-worker in Pilate's Palestine.

As for Pliny, Redford claims he was "describing Christian worship to sceptical Romans". This is meant as a hint that he must have researched Christianity pretty thoroughly. In fact he was not concerned to counteract scepticism, but wrote (A.D. 112) as governor of a province asking his emperor (Trajan) whether he was right to leave Christians unmolested provided they were prepared to conform to Roman religious rites and to forswear Christianity. It is clear from what he says that his only knowledge of these people was what he had extracted from them under interrogation, namely that their convictions amounted to "a perverse and extravagant superstition", involving (among other things) reciting "a form of words to Christ as a god". Whether the 'Christ' they worshipped had been on earth as a man will have been of no interest either to him or to Trajan. What worried them was that Christians were holding meetings which, because of Christian unwillingness to make due obeisance to the emperor, might have been seditious; they were not concerned about whether there was any historical basis to Christian doctrinal niceties.

More important for Redford than either Suetonius or Pliny is what Tacitus wrote (ca. A.D. 120) about the burning of Rome in Nero's time (A.D. 64), and about the belief that the fire had been started by order of the emperor himself. "To scotch this rumour", says Tacitus, Nero substituted as culprits and punished with the utmost refinements of cruelty "a class of men loathed for their views, whom the crowd styled Christians". In order to give his educated readers some idea as to who these people were—he evidently did not expect them to know already—Tacitus adds that Christians "derive their name and origin from Christ who, in the reign of Tiberius, had suffered death by the sentence of the procurator Pontius Pilate". Tacitus himself will have known this much of them because, as governor of Asia (the western third of Asia Minor) ca. A.D. 112, he will have had the same kind of trouble with them that Pliny was experiencing as governor of Bithynia at that very time. Meier allows that he "might have had judicial contacts with Christians similar to those reported by Pliny", who was "a close friend" of his (*Marginal*, p. 91). Tacitus continues:

For a while this dire superstition was checked; but it again burst
forth and not only spread itself over Judea, the first seat of this
mischievous sect, but was even introduced into Rome, the common
asylum which receives and protects whatever is atrocious. The con-
fessions of those who were seized discovered a great multitude of
their accomplices, and they were all convicted, not so much for the
crime of setting fire to the city as for their hatred of the human race.
(*Annals*, xv, 44)

Attempts were made at the end of last century and early in this
one to set aside the whole passage—including, of course, the
mention of Christ's death under Pilate—as a Christian interpolation. They are quite unconvincing,[2] and understandably recent
commentators no longer even mention them. However, Tacitus's
statement that Christ was executed under Pilate is no more than
what Christians themselves (familiar as they were by then with
the gospels' version of Jesus's life and death) were at the time
alleging; and he could easily have drawn his information, directly
or indirectly, from them.

Redford, however, thinks it likely that Tacitus made an independent inquiry and consulted "official documents" which informed
him of Jesus's crucifixion. I noted (*DJE*, p. 14) against this that, had
he done so, he would not have given Pilate an incorrect title. An
inscription found in 1961 records the dedication by Pilate of a
building in honour of Tiberius and shows that he was 'prefect', not
procurator, of Judea. I pointed out that C.H. Dodd conceded that
the title used by Tacitus is an anachronism, for provincial gover-
nors of equestrian status bore the title 'procurator Augusti' only
from the time of Claudius (from A.D. 41). That Tacitus used the
term current in his own lifetime suggests, then, that he did not
obtain his information from records or archives. He cannot be
directly citing any official record. The same conclusion is also supported by his failure to name the executed man. He says nothing of
'Jesus' and uses the title 'Christ' as if it were a proper name. Hostile
to Christianity as Tacitus was, he was surely glad to accept the
Christians' own view that their religion was of recent origin, since
Roman authorities were prepared to tolerate only ancient cults.[3]
Finally, if, as is surely the case, Tacitus was concerned simply to
give some indication as to who Christians are, he would not

thereby have been led to ferret out 'official documents' (if indeed such existed) on an alleged execution in Palestine nearly 100 years earlier. C.F. Dupuis, a perceptive eighteenth-century French commentator on this passage in Tacitus, compared what it says about Christ with what a French historian might say for the benefit of his readers if he had occasion to mention an Indian sect that had established itself in France, namely that these people were called Brahmins after a certain Brahma who had lived in India at a certain time past. Such a statement would clearly not imply that he had done antiquarian research on the matter. It is quite arbitrary of Redford to say that Tacitus "would have known if Jesus had not existed". E.P. Sanders's verdict is fully justified: "Roman sources that mention Jesus are all dependent on Christian reports" (*Historical Jesus*, p 49). And these reports were themselves not widely known. Walsh's recent article summarizes the relevant facts: "Pliny evidently knew next to nothing not only about the sect but about his own government's policy towards the sect. Tacitus had to inform his readers of the very basics. Trajan and Hadrian betray no knowledge." He adds that, even after 165, the satirist Lucian of Samosata, who mocked Christian simplicity in his *De morte peregrini*, was obliged to provide his readers with rudimentary (though somewhat inaccurate) information about the Christians.[4]

ii. Thallus and Phlegon

The relevant article in a standard Christian religious encyclopaedia notes curtly that "Thallus cannot be considered as witnessing" to events in Jesus's life.[5] Nevertheless, conservative scholarship continues to adduce him (and to censure me for not doing so) because, as Bruce concedes, there is no other "certain reference made to Christianity in any extant non-Christian Gentile writing of the first century" (*Documents*, p. 114). In fact, however, it is doubtful whether Thallus referred to Christianity at all, and whether—if he did so—he was writing early enough to do more than merely reproduce what he found in Christian tradition.

According to Bruce, Thallus wrote "about A.D. 52". The only evidence Bruce gives for this dating is that "he has been identified with a Samaritan of that name who is mentioned by Josephus

(Ant. xviii, 6, 4) as being a freedman of the Emperor Tiberius" (p. 113). In a later book Bruce admits that this identification is "doubtful".[6] In actual fact, the mss. of Josephus have to be amended to yield the name 'Thallus' at all here. The unamended reading is given in the Loeb edition and translated there as "there was in addition a certain man of Samaritan origin" (ἄλλος Σαμαρευς γένος: the emendation converts ἄλλος to Θαλλος).[7] All that Josephus says of this person is that he once loaned a large sum of money to Agrippa; and so, even if the emendation is correct, it is hazardous to identify him with Thallus the historian.

Thallus's writings have not survived, but are alluded to by later writers. Julius Africanus, a third-century Christian, wrote concerning the darkness at the crucifixion that "Thallus calls this darkness a solar eclipse". From this reference, says Bruce, Maurice Goguel inferred "(a) that the gospel tradition, or at least the traditional story of the Passion, was known in Rome in non-Christian circles towards the middle of the first century; and (b) that the enemies of Christianity tried to refute this Christian tradition by giving a naturalistic interpretation to the facts which it reported" (*Documents*, p. 113).

Africanus adds that it was quite unreasonable of Thallus to attribute the crucifixion darkness to a solar eclipse because there is a full moon at Passover, and so the moon cannot then lie between the sun and the earth. Jacoby notes that it is not certain from what Africanus said that Thallus made any mention of Jesus or of Jewish history at all, and may simply have recorded the eclipse of the sun in the reign of Tiberius, for which astronomers have calculated the date 24 November A.D. 29; it may have been Africanus who introduced Jesus by retorting—from his knowledge of Mark—that this was no eclipse, but a supernatural event.[8] That this may be so is conceded by R.T. France who, having studied both Bruce's argument and my reply to it in *DJE*, comments: "We do not know whether Thallus actually mentioned Jesus's crucifixion or whether this was Africanus's interpretation of a period of darkness which Thallus had not specifically linked with Jesus." France also rejects the confident statement that Thallus wrote "about A.D. 52", and says that "his date of writing is not known", so that "there can be no certainty that, if he *did* refer to Jesus explicitly, this reference may not have been drawn from Christian sources."[9] Jacoby holds that he wrote as late as the second century.

The passage I have quoted from Africanus continues with a reference to Phlegon, the chronicler who was a freedman of Hadrian (who died in A.D. 138), and who may have actually discussed Jesus. Whether there is any allusion to Jesus in the passage given in Africanus is another matter. It reads:

> Phlegon tells us that in Tiberius Caesar's reign, at the time of the full moon, there was a total eclipse of the sun, from the sixth hour to the ninth. It is plain he speaks of this [namely of the darkness at the crucifixion].

R.M. Grant justly regards these words as "a late interpolation by someone with more piety than intelligence"; for we cannot accept that, having just found fault with Thallus for calling this darkness an eclipse of the sun, Africanus then went on to cite Phlegon, without any censure at all, as calling it just that, and as adding, what he has just before stated to be an absurdity, that it occurred at full moon. Furthermore, what Phlegon actually said has been preserved by Eusebius, whose quotation shows that Phlegon made no reference at all to full moon, nor to a three-hour duration of the eclipse. He quotes Phlegon as saying:

> In the fourth year of the 202nd Olympiad [A.D. 32/33] there was a great eclipse of the sun, surpassing all that came before it. At the sixth hour the day was turned into such complete darkness that the stars were seen in the sky; earthquakes in Bithynia overturned many buildings in the city of Nicaea.[10]

There is no reason to think that Phlegon referred in this context to events relating to Jesus. Jacoby comments that, in spite of the dating (A.D. 32/33), he can only have had in mind the total eclipse for Nicaea on 24 November 29. He adds that this, and the earthquake in Bithynia, were reported by both Thallus and Phlegon "simply as facts. The positioning of them in the year of Christ's Passion by Christian chronographers . . . was particularly easy to effect, as 29/30 and 32/33 fall in the same Olympiad."[11] (That there was an earthquake at the moment of Jesus's death is reported only by Matthew, 27:51–54.) Passages in Origen (given by Grant, pp. 98–99) claim that Phlegon did elsewhere mention Jesus; but that a mid-second-century writer should do so is not significant, for such testimony is too late to be decisive.

iii. The Talmud

Redford declares that the Talmud accepted Jesus's existence as a historical fact, and would have spread information to the contrary "with glee" had it been available. He makes no mention of what modern Jewish scholars have said that bears on this. I was able to show (*DJE*, p. 12) that they date the earliest references to Jesus in rabbinical literature as not earlier than the beginning of the second century; and I noted that, if Jesus's fame had in fact "gone through all Syria" in the late 20s or early 30s (Mt. 4:24), and if he had experienced the kind of repeated altercations with Jewish orthodoxy alleged in the gospels, the absence of earlier references becomes very hard to explain. I also observed that, when rabbis[12] did begin to mention him, they are so vague in their chronology that they differ by as much as 200 years in the dates they assign to him. Christianity was obscure before A.D. 70, and the rabbis had problems enough concerning the reformulation of their own faith after the destruction of the temple in that year, so it is not surprising that they long said little about Christianity, which was rapidly becoming a gentile religion. Vermes (*Religion*, p. 8) notes: "With sporadic and questionable exceptions, no rabbinic awareness of the gospels . . . can be proved. Even negative reactions to the New Testament are rare and belong to a relatively late period." Such comments as are made about Jesus, says Sandmel (another Jewish scholar), "derive from hearsay about what is in the gospels" and ascribe his miracles "to evil sorcery rather than to benign supernaturalism."[13] Belief in miracles was, in antiquity, part of the way in which everyday reality was comprehended. Hostile commentators would therefore meet allegations that a particular person worked them by denigrating them as mere magic, not with a denial that he worked any (still less with a denial of his existence). This is the attitude to Jesus's miracles which is ascribed to his enemies even in the gospels. ("By the prince of the devils casteth he out the devils", Mk. 3:22.)

In sum, by the time rabbis came to mention Jesus at all, he had come to be represented by Christians themselves as a teacher and wonder-worker—a kind of person as familiar to the rabbis as to his pagan critics. Vermes, who regards the first three gospels as fundamentally reliable, has nevertheless said: "In an age and society in which the combination of sanctity and the miraculous was considered normal, Jesus's talents and activities fitted the image of the holy man" (*Jesus*, p. 27). Brown concedes that, apart from the testimony of Josephus (which I discuss below), "we have practically no Jewish evidence from the period 60–100 that would tell us how Jews looked on Jesus, his followers, and their claims about him" (*Death*, p. 526n.) Brown's fellow-Catholic, Meier, agrees that "in the earliest rabbinic sources, there is no clear or even probable reference to Jesus of Nazareth", and that "when we do finally find such references in later rabbinic literature, they are most probably reactions to Christian claims, oral or written" (*Marginal*, p. 98). Nor is there any mention of Jesus, or indeed of any NT character, in the Dead Sea Scrolls, although certain scholars have claimed to see Jesus and John the Baptist disguised under symbolic names in these texts "This", says Meier, "simply proves that learned fantasy knows no bounds" (p. 94).

Finally, I would ask whose historicity *was* questioned in antiquity, when both pagan historians and Christian Fathers accepted pagan saviour gods as historical personages? (Herodotus says Attis was the son of a king of Lydia and that Horus, son of Isis and Osiris, was a ruler of Egypt. Clement of Alexandria regarded pagan saviour gods as "mere men" and Firmicus Maternus called Osiris and Typhon "without doubt" kings of Egypt). Can one expect much in the way of critical scepticism when, even in modern times, Wilhelm Tell long passed as a real person?

iv. Josephus

Strangely, Redford makes little of the two mentions of Jesus in the extant mss. of Flavius Josephus's *Antiquities of the Jews*. He speaks of "a reference", not of two, implies (wrongly) that it occurs in Josephus's other major work, the *History of the Jewish War*, and says that some scholars think it "was inserted later by a Christian scribe, not by Josephus himself". If he fails to invoke Josephus against me, his omission is more than rectified by his Catholic colleague J.P. Meier, who writes:

> It is significant that the 'Testimonium Flavianum' is quickly and facilely dismissed without detailed examination by G.A. Wells in his popular and somewhat sensationalistic *Did Jesus Exist*? Obviously, Wells's desire to maintain the thesis that Jesus never existed demands such a treatment of Josephus, who would otherwise destroy Wells's whole argument before it could really get started. Wells's presentation descends to simple affirmation, supported not by argumentation but by citation of generally antiquated authorities, in the case of the James passage [i.e. the shorter of the two], which is declared to be a brief marginal gloss from a Christian, which was later incorporated into the text. Wells's book, which builds its arguments on these and similar unsubstantiated claims, may be allowed to stand as a representative of the whole type of popular Jesus book that I do not bother to consider in detail. (*Marginal*, p. 87)

The 'Testimonium Flavianum' is the longer of the two passages in the extant manuscripts of Josephus's *Antiquities* which mentions Jesus (Book 18, sections 63–64), and states not only that Pilate had him crucified after he had been indicted by the Jewish authorities, but also that he was perhaps more than a mere man, that he was the Messiah, that on the third day after his death he appeared to his followers, and that this "and countless other things about him" had been foretold by "the prophets of God". Only the most naive commentators can still suppose that an orthodox Jew could have written such obviously Christian words. If Josephus had believed all that this passage imputes to him, he would not have restricted his comments to this brief paragraph (and to a single phrase in the other, shorter passage). Hence the most that can be claimed is that Josephus here made *some* reference to Jesus, which has been retouched by a Christian hand.

This is the view argued by Meier as by most scholars today, particularly since S. Pines drew attention to a less obviously Christian version of the 'Testimonium' which is quoted in Arabic translation in a tenth-century Christian work. (I have discussed this version, and the intemperate use made of it by J.H. Charlesworth in my *Belief and Make-Believe*, pp. 143–48.) Meier nevertheless allows (p. 59) that there are some "respectable defenders" of the position that the passage as a whole is a Christian interpolation. It occurs in a context where Josephus is relating the misfortunes of the Jews, some of which occurred when Pilate was governor of Judea. If Josephus had not mentioned Jesus when speaking of Pilate, Christians would have regarded this as an omission which needed to be rectified. The passage seems not to have existed in the first centuries of Christianity, for, as Sandmel wryly notes, "although Church Fathers quoted Josephus frequently, and this paragraph would have suited their purposes admirably, yet they never quoted it" (*We Jews*, p. 18). It is first quoted by Eusebius in the fourth century. Feldman names two Fathers from the second century, seven from the third, and two from the early fourth, all of whom knew Josephus and cited from his works, but "do not refer to this passage, though one would imagine it would be the first passage that a Christian apologist would cite" (*Josephus*, p. 695). He adds that, even after Eusebius, three fourth-century Fathers and five from the fifth century (up to and including Augustine) often cite Josephus, but not this passage. In the early fifth century, only Jerome does. Thus after Eusebius a century elapses before it is again referred to, and this suggests that some time elapsed before all or most copies of Josephus's *Antiquities* came to include it. (Our earliest manuscript copies containing this part of that work date from the eleventh century.)

One third-century writer who could not have known the passage is Origen for, although he believed that Josephus had made some mention of Jesus (see below, p. 54), he regretted (in the same context) that Josephus did not accept that Jesus was the Messiah; whereas the 'Testimonium Flavianum' expressly affirms that he was the Messiah. That Christian writers did in fact interpolate the works of Josephus was shown about 100 years ago when fifteenth-century manuscripts of a Russian translation of his *The Jewish War* were discovered containing information about John the Baptist, Jesus, and his disciples.

One reason for thinking that the whole of the 'Testimonium' has been interpolated is that it breaks the thread of the narrative at the point where it occurs. But Meier dismisses this objection with the sole comment (p. 86) that anyone interested in such a line of argument should consult H. St. John Thackeray's *Josephus the Man and the Historian* (New York: Jewish Institute of Religion Press, 1929). Thackeray is actually far from dismissive on this issue, pointing out that the framework in which the paragraph is placed consists of an account of a series of riots or disturbances (θόρυβοι) which caused the Jews distress: it is preceded by two θόρυβοι occasioned by Pilate and followed by two or three more occasioned differently, whereas it has in itself nothing to do with θόρυβοι. This objection to the authenticity of the 'Testimonium' is sometimes misunderstood as implying that all Josephus's stories about Pilate must have been written in unbroken sequence, so that, if the 'Testimonium' is excised, all that follows it in the same chapter must also be regarded as interpolated, as Josephus returns to Pilate only at the beginning of the next chapter. In fact the objection is that the 'Testimonium' occurs in a context which deals with disturbances bringing misfortune to the Jews, not all of which are attributed to Pilate. Mason (*Josephus*, p. 165) has recently restated the objection as follows:

> Josephus is speaking of upheavals, but there is no upheaval here. He is pointing out the folly of Jewish rebels, governors and troublemakers in general, but this passage is completely supportive of both Jesus and his followers. Logically, what should appear in this context ought to imply some criticism of the Jewish leaders and/or Pilate, but Josephus does not make any such criticism explicit. He says only that those who denounced Jesus were "the leading men among us". So unlike the other episodes, this one has no moral, no lesson. Although Josephus begins the next paragraph by speaking of "another outrage" that caused an uproar among the Jews at the same time, there is nothing in this paragraph that depicts any sort of outrage.

Thackeray allowed that this objection—that the passage does not fit well with its context—"carries great weight" and had been "powerfully advocated by Norden" who regarded it as conclusive. Yet he finds it "not insuperable", for "Josephus was a patchwork writer, as appears from this very passage, in which he, or probably an older authority, has strung together, not in chronological order, two unconnected sets of riots, one relating to the Jews in Palestine, the other to two religious disturbances in Rome, one of which has nothing to do with the Jews" (pp. 140–41). This surely overlooks the fact that Josephus is well aware that the latter is a digression, and that he both introduces and terminates it as such, saying, after he has narrated it: "I will now return to relating what happened about this time to the Jews at Rome, as I told you I would"; whereupon he returns to his proper theme, the misfortunes of the Jews, and tells how 4,000 of them were banished from Rome. When a writer digresses, and confesses to doing so, this does not make him a "patchwork" writer from whom we must expect any kind of irrelevancy.

J.N. Birdsall has noted, in support of the view that the whole of the passage has been interpolated, that an ancient Table of Contents of the *Antiquities,* known in several mss. and in the Latin version, omits any reference to it. Admittedly, he adds, it omits mention of other passages as well, including the adjacent passage which Josephus himself stamped as a digression. (It is hardly surprising that a digression should be omitted from a summary!) Yet the omission of the passage about Jesus "is surely significant in the light of the undisputed fact that the transmission of Josephus was almost entirely at Christian hands, and all the mss. are late, giving plenty of time for an entry to be inserted".[14] Josephus was so popular with Christians partly because he reiterated the superiority of biblical ethics to Graeo-Roman morality and religion, but—as Mason has recently stressed (*Josephus,* pp. 10–16)—far more because he gives such detailed description of the appalling suffering during the siege and destruction of Jerusalem in A.D. 70 which Christians regarded as God's decisive punishment of the Jewish people for their rejection of Jesus. That the 'God of love' had thus carefully arranged the slaughter of a later generation that had played no part in Jesus's death rapidly became a commonplace among Christian writers.

Mason himself finally decides that the 'Testimonium' is not wholly interpolated, since "Christian copyists were quite conservative in transmitting texts. Nowhere else in Josephus's voluminous works is there strong suspicion of scribal tampering", and "to have created the *testimonium* out of whole cloth would be an act of unparalleled scribal audacity" (pp. 170f). This seems to overlook the considerable interpolations (which Mason agrees to be such) in the Old Russian translation of *The Jewish War,* and there are extensive Christian interpolations in other Jewish writings of the period, now known as the OT pseudepigrapha. Mason has observed how remarkable it is that "the Gospel authors unanimously and without equivocation know that the Roman governor at the time of Jesus's death was Pontius Pilate", even though they are much vaguer about the Jewish leaders whom they represent as the chief culprits in his condemnation: "Mark does not even name the chief Jewish official: Matthew seems to have researched or recalled that his name was Caiaphas; Luke implies that he was Annas; and John [wrongly] makes Caiaphas an annually appointed high priest but places Jesus's significant trial before Annas" (pp. 130f). Pilate, then, is so prominent a name in Christian thinking (from the time of the traditions represented in the gospels) about Jesus's death that, as I have said, if Josephus had written of Pilate without mentioning Jesus, Christian scribes would have seen this as an omission to be rectified.

The shorter of the two Josephan passages has been more widely accepted as a reference to Jesus genuinely from Josephus's hand. Festus had just died (A.D. 62), and Albinus, sent by the emperor to replace him as governor of Judea, had not yet arrived; so an intemperate high priest named Ananus who, as a Sadducee,[15] was "more rigid in judging offenders than all the rest of the Jews", took the absence of a governor as an opportunity to get rid of miscreants. He

> assembled the Sanhedrin of judges and brought before them the brother of Jesus, him called Christ, whose name was James, and some others. And when he had formed an accusation against them as breakers of the law, he delivered them to be stoned. (Book 20, section 200)

Some apologists have argued that to call Jesus "him called Christ" is too dismissive a phrase for a Christian interpolator to have used of Jesus. But he is described with these very same (Greek) words at Mt. 1:16; and at Jn. 4:25 the coming Messiah is also designated with them—in both cases without pejorative implication. Admittedly, 'called' (λεγόμενος) can in certain contexts be dismissive, in the NT as elsewhere (for instance, the 'so-called' gods in contrast to the only God, 1 Corinthians 8:5), but it does not invariably have negative implications, neither in the NT nor in Josephus, where it frequently means 'to be named' (of places, for example "a village called Arbela", *Ant.* 14:415) or 'to have the surname' (of persons: the third of the Ptolemies "was called Euergetes", *Apion* 2:48).

Meier thinks the reference to Jesus in the passage must be original because a Christian interpolator would have called James 'the brother of the Lord', not 'the brother of Jesus'. But an interpolator might well have been aware that an orthodox Jewish writer could not plausibly be represented as calling Jesus 'the Lord'. We do not have to assume that *all* interpolators went to work with more piety than sense. Meier adds that the reference is likely to be genuine because it is a "short matter-of-fact statement" (p. 58). This, however, is what it will have been if it originated as a marginal gloss, as I argued in *DJE* (p. 11)—a suggestion that Meier has so scornfully rejected. Josephus, I said, probably wrote of the death of a Jewish Jerusalem personage called James, and a Christian reader thought he must have meant James the "brother of the Lord" who, according to Christian tradition, led the Jerusalem church about the time in question. This reader accordingly noted in the margin: 'James = the brother of Jesus, him called Christ', and a later copyist took this as belonging to the text and incorporated it. Other interpolations are known to have originated in precisely this way.

Of course, this will be a more plausible hypothesis if there are positive reasons for doubting authenticity. One such is that in Josephus's entire work the term 'the Christ', meaning the Messiah, occurs only in the two passages where mention is made of Jesus, with no attempt to explain what it means to the pagan readers to whom Josephus was appealing. When he applies a Messianic prophecy to Vespasian, he is careful not to call it such, but "an ambiguous oracle" in the Jewish scriptures which Vespasian fulfilled when he was declared emperor in Judea. When he tells that Theudas led a multitude to the Jordan ca. A.D. 44–46, promising to conduct them over dryshod like Joshua before Jericho, he does not call him a Messianic agitator or pretender, but a "charlatan" who claimed to be a "prophet". This is likewise how he describes the Egyptian who, a decade or so later, led a

crowd as far as the Mount of Olives, promising that the walls of
Jerusalem would fall down at his word.[16] As Brown notes (*Death*,
p. 475), although "Josephus describes all sorts of historical figures
(prophets, would-be kings, priests, agitators) in the 1st century
A.D., he never calls one of them a Messiah". That he habitually
takes such care to avoid the term makes its sole and unexplained
use in the two Jesus passages suspect.

Other grounds for regarding the shorter of these two passages
with suspicion have been adduced by Juster. After mentioning the
stoning of the offenders, it states that moderate persons, incensed
at Ananus's action, sent messengers to Albinus (still on his way)
to tell him that Ananus had no authority to convene the Sanhedrin without his consent, and readily convinced him of this.
Juster asked sardonically: Did a Roman governor need to be told
what his rights were? Was there no one to stand in for him when
he was absent to prevent any usurpation of his authority? And
how about those Jews hastening to say they had no right to act?
Why, he adds, they are the same as those who say the same thing
to Pilate in the fourth gospel: "It is not lawful for us to put any
man to death" (Jn. 18:31). Scholars are divided as to whether
there was in fact any such restriction of the Sanhedrin's
authority.[17] But the truth on this matter does not affect Juster's
argument, which is that Josephus mentioned an execution of a
Jew, possibly named James, by order of the Sanhedrin, and that a
Christian, aware that the fourth gospel had declared that body to
be without competence to make any such order, adapted Josephus's text so as to reflect this.[18]

That there has been some tampering with the passage is suggested by the fact that Origen, who refers to Josephus's account of
the death of James, claims to have read something rather different
on that subject in his text of Josephus from what now stands there.
Writing in the third century, he said that, according to Josephus, the
fall of Jerusalem and the destruction of the temple were God's punishment of the Jews for their murder of James "the brother of Jesus,
him called Christ" (*Contra Celsum*, i, 47). If a text of Josephus had
contained any such statement, it could only have been as a result of
Christian interpolation. It was the nearest Christians could plausibly get to making Josephus take the Christian view that the fall of

Jerusalem was God's punishment for the killing of Jesus. Schürer regarded the passage as an interpolation that has not survived in our manuscripts, but which shows that Josephus was subject to interpolation at this point (where James is introduced), so that the reference to "Jesus, him called Christ" in our manuscripts falls under suspicion.[19] Moreover, whereas in this extant passage James is said to have been killed on the basis of a sentence of court, Hegesippus and Clement of Alexandria—both Christian writers of the second century—say that he was killed in a tumult instigated by scribes[20] and Pharisees, without prior legal proceedings: he was thrown down from the wing of the temple and finally dispatched with a fuller's club.[21] Those who wrote this can hardly have known of the passage about James as it now stands in Josephus.

Meier stamps Tacitus and Josephus as two, as indeed the only two pagan and Jewish "independent witnesses to Jesus's existence, ministry, death and ongoing influence" (pp. 91, 93). By 'independent' he means that their information is not drawn from nor a reaction to Christian documents known directly or indirectly (p. 104 n30). Strangely, he nevertheless allows that quite possibly Tacitus was simply "repeating what was common knowledge about Christians at the beginning of the second century" (p. 91). He even says that it is "doubtful" that Tacitus "represents an independent source" (p. 140), and that it is quite likely that Josephus "had met or heard about Christians" in Rome after the Jewish War. But he thinks it difficult to accept that Josephus "drew directly on oral statements of Christians" (p. 67), because, in the text of the longer passage as reconstructed by himself (with all obviously Christian material deleted)—a text for which there is no textual evidence—there is no mention of the resurrection (which is certainly mentioned in the actual text that we have).

Meier concludes that "all opinions on the question of Josephus's source remain equally possible because they remain equally unverifiable" (p. 68). This hardly warrants calling his testimony "independent". Even if he did make some (perhaps uncomplimentary, or at best neutral) reference to Jesus that has been reworked in the longer passage into the present eulogy by a Christian hand, the date of the work in which both passages occur (A.D. 93) makes it too late to be of decisive importance for the historicity of Jesus;

for at least some of the gospel accounts, placing Jesus in Pilate's Palestine, were in written form by then, and Josephus could, like Tacitus, have taken his information from what Christians were by then saying. This would be quite in accordance with his largely uncritical attitude to his sources in this late work where—as is noted in the new English edition of Schürer's book (p. 58 of the volume cited in note 19 above)—they are often employed "not only negligently, but also—at least where it is possible to check them— with great freedom and arbitrariness", with only "occasional" evidence of any critical attitude towards them.

Some of my critics have supposed that, according to me, the sparsity of early pagan and Jewish references to Jesus is in itself sufficient evidence that he did not exist. This is not, and never has been, what I have argued. I am concerned simply to discredit the widespread belief that non-Christian testimony establishes his existence beyond all reasonable doubt, and makes any further discussion of the matter unnecessary. The importance of the pagan and Jewish testimony has repeatedly been exaggerated because the Christian notices are so obviously shot through with legend.

Few today will read any detailed discussions of this non-Christian material, but many will accept the assurances given in brief and misleading summaries of it, typified in John Macquarrie's 1990 prize-winning book (as cited on p. 38 above, p. 349), where we are told that Pliny, Suetonius, Josephus, and the Talmud "afford evidence that Jesus existed from writers who were either indifferent to Christianity or even hostile", and also show that he died by crucifixion in the reign of Tiberius "since this is mentioned even in the barest references, like that of Tacitus".

v. A Modern Jewish Scholar Concedes the Historicity of the Resurrection

Conservative Christianity greeted an orthodox Jewish scholar, Pinchas Lapide, with considerable acclaim when he recently confronted the hesitancy of many Christian scholars and conceded the historicity of Jesus's resurrection. His book is, however, most

striking mainly because he is so well aware of the cogent objections that Christian scholars have themselves made, rather than
for its responses to them. Let us first study what the NT has to say.

Paul is the earliest witness who has testified to Jesus's resurrection, in his statement (1 Corinthians 15) that Jesus died, was
buried and rose again three days later. He gives no indication of
where or when this is supposed to have happened, but appears to
be simply reciting a creed he took over on his conversion to
Christianity. He follows this by a list of persons to whom the risen
Jesus had recently (within the last few years) appeared. Many
commentators (including Redford) suppose that Paul here
implies that not only these appearances, but also the crucifixion
and resurrection were recent, and that "some of the witnesses of
the resurrection" were still alive when he wrote. In fact, however,
although he places the resurrection three days after the death, he
does not indicate when the death occurred. It is only the appearances that he says are recent, and someone who sees a ghost does
not necessarily suppose that it is the wraith of a recently deceased
person.

Paul's list of appearances is but a list, and gives no details of
how, when or where these encounters took place or what happened; and its items correlate very poorly with the records of
appearances in the gospels, where we find the risen Jesus anxious
to show that he is no tenuous ghost (as sceptics who dismissed
resurrection appearances as hallucinations might be tempted to
think): "See", he says to his disciples, "a spirit hath not flesh and
bones as ye behold me having" (Lk. 24:39). This "flesh and bones"
were presumably solid enough to support clothes, as no one supposes that the gospels would have us believe that he manifested
himself naked. Yet according to the same gospels, his body was
such that it enabled him to arrive within closed doors and vanish
at will. For some purposes, then, his body is represented as solid,
for others not. Paul, for his part, had clearly not believed that
Jesus rose in physical body and then consumed broiled fish (Lk.
24:41–3); for he declared, in a context where he was discussing
Jesus's resurrection, that "flesh and blood cannot inherit the kingdom of God" (1 Corinthians 15:50). He believed that the dead are
raised not in physical body, but "in glory" (verses 42–43), and with

their lowly bodies changed to be like Jesus's "glorious" one (Philippians 3:21). Paul would surely have rejected as blasphemous any claim to have witnessed the risen Lord eating, or to have eaten and drunk with him, as at Acts 10:41–43 Peter claims that he and his fellows had done, chosen as they were as "witnesses" by God and "commanded to preach to the people". (The wording suggests that one factor in the origin of this tradition about eating and drinking was the desire to show that the apostles were in a position to testify that the earthly and the risen Jesus were one and the same person.) Paul never suggests that Jesus tarried on earth after his resurrection, and never places any interval between his rising and his being at the right hand of God (Romans 8:34; Colossians 3:1; 1 Thessalonians 1:10). He seems to have assumed that the risen Jesus ascended to heaven immediately, with a body of radiance; and so he will naturally have supposed that the subsequent appearances he lists were made by a descent from heaven—as is the case even in the accounts of the appearance to Paul himself in the Acts of the Apostles, where Paul's life and ideas are portrayed very differently from the account in his own epistles.

What we have here is developing tradition. The earliest Christians, we may conjecture, simply asserted that Christ died and was raised, and embodied these convictions in preaching formulas such as 'The Lord is risen'. The next stage was to offer supporting evidence by listing recipients of appearances, as is done in 1 Corinthians. The next stage was to give actual descriptions (not mere listings) of the appearances, as in the canonical gospels. Finally, in the apocryphal Gospel of Peter, there is a description of the resurrection itself.

I noted in *DJE* (p. 32) that if, as I believe, Paul did not regard the resurrection as a recent event, then the recent appearances would have been taken as evidence that the general resurrection of the dead, and the final judgement of both living and dead, were soon to come. Christ was risen: that meant that all would rise. But now that he was not only risen, but had begun to appear to men, the final events which would bring the world to an end could not be long delayed.

Lapide allows that the NT "remains the only source for the resurrection", that the relevant narratives contain "much legend", and that nowhere else in the canon are "the contradictions so glaring".[22] Nevertheless, he holds that "legends *can* also be bearers of truths, which by no means deprive the kernel of the narrative of its historicity" (p. 93). It is a common assumption that there is always a 'kernel' of historical fact underlying any miracle story in the gospels. The historian Michael Grant, for instance, declares that Jesus did not feed 5,000, but "must have done *something*"[23] (Grant's italics). Lapide thinks we may assume that at least some of the contradictions in the resurrection narratives are "based on errors in the translations" of semitic originals. But our Greek gospels do not appear to be translations; much of Matthew and Luke is an adaptation of the Greek gospel of Mark, and there is no reason to believe that their resurrection narratives, absent from Mark, are based on anything 'semitic'. The whole idea of Aramaic originals underlying the early Christian writings has been shown to be baseless (see below, p. 163).

Lapide also allows that the only persons who encountered the risen Jesus were believers, or people who subsequently became such. But he thinks this no objection, on the ground that, had Jesus appeared to a large number of non-Christian Jews, his resurrection would have simply been incorporated into the Jewish creed, which would have remained exclusive (pp. 117–18), so that faith in the God of Israel would not have been carried to the gentile world, as it was by Christianity. Such a development cannot have come about "as the result of blind happenstance" (p. 142), but only from divine guidance.

Lapide also thinks that Jesus's resurrection must be admitted to be unoriginal: there were pagan "deities, heroes, philosophers and rulers who, all long before Jesus, suffered died and rose again on the third day" (p. 40). But he surmises that God may have intended the true resurrection of a just person to eliminate such idolatry and to carry knowledge of the true God "to the four corners of the earth by means of the Easter faith" (p. 122).

Another possible objection is that resurrection of the dead was an idea already familiar to Jews as well as to pagans (pp. 46ff), and so Jesus's disciples could readily have come to think that death was not the end for him (p. 65). His resurrection even became a "theological imperative" for them, for "where was the

justice of God if this righteous one . . . had to fail so miserably?"
(pp. 88–89). Their confidence in God's loving-kindness was reinforced by their "faith in Jesus as the proclaimer of salvation" sent
by him (p. 135). Lapide will have us believe that all this was not
just wishful thinking: "If desertion by God and suffering mortal
tortures are the end of a great hope-filled person, how can people
continue to hope for goodness and justice amidst a world that
remains both inhumane and alienated from God?" (p. 146). He
must surely be aware that many hopes and beliefs have managed
to survive the apparent *coup de grâce*. And is not the suffering of
innumerable hope-filled persons, past and present, a familiar fact
which we have learned to accept without supposing that there
must necessarily be some compensatory gain?

Having answered objections in this way, Lapide offers, as positive evidence:

   i. The gospels do not describe the actual resurrection, a lack
     of embellishment which enhances their trustworthiness.
  ii. Fiction would not have made women the first to find the
     tomb, for rabbinic Judaism considered women incapable
     of giving valid testimony.
 iii. That they wanted to anoint the body shortly [sic] after the
     burial proves that neither they nor the disciples expected
     any resurrection. (pp. 95–96)

The last of these arguments contradicts the admission that the
resurrection was, for the disciples, a "theological imperative". The
motive of the women—to anoint the body—is excluded by the
narratives of Matthew and John—for different reasons. In the
fourth gospel the anointing had already been effected before bur-
ial, and in Matthew the sepulchre is guarded, so that the women
expect only to be able to visit it, not to enter it (28:1). And to pro-
pose to anoint a body more than a day after death in a Mediterranean climate is not a very credible motive. The women are the
first to arrive at the tomb because in Mark (and in Matthew) the
disciples are represented as fleeing and deserting Jesus at Gethsemane. By making him die alone, without human support, Mark
brings out the magnitude of the burden he bore in his isolation.
Furthermore, it is the appearances of the risen one, not the
emptiness of the tomb, that testify to the resurrection, and these

are represented as unexpected even though Jesus had repeatedly predicted his resurrection when addressing the disciples (Mk. 8:31; 9:31; 10:32–34). In any case, the empty tomb entered the tradition only with Mark (Paul shows no knowledge of it), and his motive for having the women keep silence about it ("they said nothing to anyone", Mk. 16:8, corrected by Luke 24:9 to "they told all these things to the eleven") may well have been that he (or his source) knew that the whole story of the angel at the tomb was previously unknown and had not been part of the original Easter proclamation. The canonical gospels represent an advanced, but not the final stage in developing tradition, and that a later, apocryphal work goes even further than they do, with a fantastic description of the resurrection itself, constitutes a difference in degree rather than in kind.

Lapide does not see that those Christian theologians who deny that Jesus rose from the dead have found that any more positive view brings them up against insuperable difficulties. He supposes instead that they are in some way ashamed of the resurrection's "material facticity" (p. 130). He has a motive of his own in accepting it, namely that a denial would imply that Christian churches "are based on fraud or self-deception", and this would undermine the honesty of the Jewish-Christian dialogue that he is very anxious to promote (p. 144). It is apparently not necessary, in the interests of such dialogue, for Jews to accept the incarnation, nor "Jesus's Messiahship for the people of Israel", nor "the Pauline interpretation"—the very earliest extant—of the resurrection (p. 153); for these he rejects. His acceptance of the resurrection is a parallel to the argument of a Muslim scholar—in the interests of Islamic-Christian harmony—that in the Koran there is no denial that Jesus was crucified, when in fact there very obviously is.[24]

Finally, Lapide confesses to uncertainty: "the exact nature of the occurrence" cannot be comprehended (pp. 127f). The "Easter experience" was "undefinable" and cannot be further explained (p. 90). Like all miracles, the resurrection "escapes scientific proof" and even "any exact description" (p. 126. Why this? Many supposed miracles have been described with precision). The appearances were "purely Jewish faith experiences", and "where the power of faith is involved, Jews have a power of imagination that sometimes borders on the supernatural" (pp. 124f). So in the end, we must have faith in faith. On such an attitude, a Christian theologian has recently made the following apposite comment:

> 'Faith' . . . in most contexts looks rather like a fraud word meaning simply, 'We insist on the truth of these claims, though we have no demonstrable or examinable grounds for making them'. Provided everyone remains agreed on what 'faith' is to consist of, the practical difficulties can be contained. But when the day comes (and history shows it is never delayed for very long) that people start to disagree about faith, the resulting quarrel is inordinately fanatical for the very reason that there is no calm and rational way of deciding it; sadly also in a totally unreasonable quarrel, the least reasonable opponent is generally the victor. The history of the Christian church is perhaps the best illustration of all time of this sobering truth. (D.B. Taylor, *Mark*, p. 55)

Vermes considers the considerable Christian acclaim of Lapide's book somewhat ridiculous, and "wonders whether the ghost of deep insecurity which haunted the Christians of antiquity in the face of Jewish unbelief has been wandering until this day, waiting for a Dr. Lapide to lay it to rest".[25] But Lapide's appeal to faith is naturally welcome to Christian theologians who understand the resurrection on a similar basis. Meier speaks for many of them when he says that the risen Jesus is one of the "ultimate realities" affirmed by faith "beyond what is merely empirical or provable by reason", and that access to this risen Lord "is given only through faith". He implies that this access is direct, unmediated by ideas: "Primarily faith affirms and adheres to this person . . . and only secondarily to ideas and affirmations about him" (*Marginal*, pp. 197–98). It is presumably because I lack faith that I believe that this 'person', or indeed anything at all, can be known to me only through my ideas, through my sense organs and brain, and that I have no direct access to reality any more than the rat or the rabbit.

Although Lapide is an extreme example, numerous Jewish scholars from the nineteenth century to today have been more ready than some of their Christian counterparts to accept much in the gospels as historically accurate. Sandmel explains why:

A Jew versed in Scripture and in Talmud who enters into the pages of the Synoptic Gospels finds himself in familiar territory. . . . Scripture is cited in ways like the citations in the Talmud . . . , the parables of Jesus either duplicate or overlap rabbinic parables, and the 'conflicts' which Jesus has with Pharisees and chief priests bring to mind both the animated discussions of the Talmud, and recall intra-Jewish conflicts between Pharisees and Sadducees.

Sandmel himself endorses this attitude to the extent of saying that "for someone like me, the Gospels . . . so recreate the Jewish scene that the recreation must be the result of knowledge and reflection on it, and it cannot be regarded as merely fictional". Yet he allows that "there is scarcely an item in them that does not bristle with problems", and that Jews impressed by what is recognizably Jewish in the gospel accounts are in danger of expressing judgements which are not "weighed in the light of the accumulated Gospel scholarship". He warns that "the broad congruency of some item in the Gospels with Jewish practice does not in itself establish historical reliability": Mark may well speak of a Sanhedrin, but this "can fall short of confirming that Jesus stood trial before it". He notes too that, correlatively to undue Jewish willingness to countenance what is said in the gospels, Christians have often been "inordinately eager to cite some Jewish opinion in support of a Christian contention". He mentions Christian acclaim of Klausner's influential (but in his opinion unreliable) book on Jesus as a signal example (Sandmel, *We Jews*, pp. 65–66, 92, 119, 122–23). In view of these remarks, it would be fair to say that modern Jewish acquiescence does not settle even the question of Jesus's historicity.

4

Hard-Line
Protestantism:
The Case of
J.W. Montgomery

i. Protest Against Critical Theology

In February 1993 I was opening speaker in a debate on the reliability of the NT organized by the Lawyers' Christian Fellowship at
the Inns of Court School of Law. The speaker opposing me was
Dr. J.W. Montgomery, Professor of Law and Humanities at Luton
University, described in a book he published in 1975 as "the
author of more than thirty-five books in English, French, Spanish
and German", and "internationally regarded both as a theologian
and as a lawyer". In the American journals (one Catholic and one
Lutheran) in which he has recorded his assessment of the debate
and his appraisal of my published work on early Christianity he is
introduced as "the Rev. John Warwick Montgomery, a Lutheran
and practising barrister".[1] Both his speech and mine at the debate
were tape-recorded, and the organizers kindly supplied copies of
the tape to the speakers and, on request, to the audience; hence I
am able to state accurately what was said on the occasion. I am
focusing the whole of this chapter on Professor Montgomery not
so much on account of his professional eminence as because his
standpoint is typical of the very traditional approach to Christian
doctrines which still has a strong following today, as we shall see
from, for instance, the like-minded writers to whom he is able to
appeal.

In his published assessment of our debate Montgomery declares that I have "gorged" myself "on an indigestible diet of German [and other] critical scholarship", and accuses me of dependence on "the Bultmannian and post-Bultmannian efforts to apply existential anti-objectivism to the study of Christian origins". In fact none of the arguments on which I rely have the slightest connection with existentialism. (Remember how people tried to discredit Strauss by saying he relied on Hegel!) And I have expressly pointed out—at the debate as elsewhere—that such "anti-objectivism" as there is in the positive programme with which some theologians (including Bultmann) compensate their demolition work (for example, by maintaining that we can still accept the resurrection as an article of faith, even though it never happened) is a forlorn attempt to retrieve positions which they themselves have shown not to be sustainable by straightforward historical inquiry. In stamping my views as subjective and hence arbitrary, Montgomery is implying that his own are objective and hence reliable. The lawyer must establish his own credibility in the course of discrediting his opponent.

One of the "Bultmannian principles" to which Montgomery says I am beholden is "the unproved and unprovable assumption that miracles do not occur". It is a common ploy to accuse an adversary of arguing from presuppositions instead of from evidence. To say that a preconceived attitude has been imposed on the truth is what most theologies have said of other theologies for centuries; and as this is indeed how arguments are so often based, the charge is apt to be uncritically regarded as just. In fact, however, I have never worked from the *a priori* supposition Montgomery imputes to me. That everything happens in accordance with certain conditions is the basis of science (at any rate in the case of macroscopic phenomena), but until we have reached the stage of being able to specify the conditions for all possible states and processes, the acceptance of this principle is an act of faith. It is because investigation has hitherto led to an ever-widening region in which regularity can be observed that we are apt to assume that eventually it will be found to prevail universally. All our principles are on the same footing: they are reached by induction and can never be accepted absolutely.[2]

As for the NT, if we are to accept its miracles, we need more cogent evidence than the kind of mutually exclusive and uncorroborated narratives found there. The evidence is particularly weak where Christian doctrine requires it to be strong, namely apropos of the virgin birth and the resurrection. Another objection is that, in the course of early Christian tradition, miracles have been multiplied or enhanced: those in the fourth gospel are more stupendous than the ones in the synoptics.[3] All alike have countless analogies in classical antiquity and cannot be regarded as more credible than these. And many of them—pagan and Christian—are narrated according to a stereotyped form. Käsemann (*Essays*, p. 50) notes that miracles of healing include such motifs as: i. the insistence on the long duration of the illness and the previous unsuccessful striving after a cure (for example Mk. 5:25–26, apropos of the woman with an issue of blood); ii. an action which demonstrates the success of the healing (as when Peter's mother-in-law, cured of her fever by Jesus, is immediately able to wait upon him, Mk. 1:31) or the astonished cry of witnesses, which serves the same end—or both, as when the paralytic takes up his bed and walks, to the astonishment of all (Mk. 2:12). Nineham (*Mark*, p. 94) instances, as a close pagan parallel, Lucian's story that "Midas himself, taking up the bed on which he had been lying, went off into the country". And Käsemann (*loc. cit.*) observes that "the adaptation of pagan motifs becomes particularly obvious when the woman with the issue of blood is healed through the mere grasping of the virtue-laden garment of Jesus, or healing power is ascribed in the setting of Acts to Peter's shadow or Paul's handkerchief." All these reasons, and not philosophical bias, are why numerous theologians, to Montgomery's disgust, are unable to accept the miracles in the canonical documents.

Montgomery also contrives to give the impression that I have merely uncritically accepted the evaluations of such theologians and have ignored both the conservative defence and the evidence of the primary texts. I have in fact devoted considerable space to the conservatives,[4] and if it has been insufficient, the present volume does something to make good that defect. As for my ignoring the primary texts, he tried to bolster that charge at the debate by quoting my final reference to one of the more sceptical theologians (John Bowden) at the end of my *WWJ* as if this book had been merely a recital of such pronouncements and not a detailed examination of the NT itself. And by omitting an important clause from his quotation,[5] he gave the impression that the scepticism of such theologians is itself not based on close study of the primary sources at all. This is in fact what he supposes to be the case: he insists that there is no "factual evidence" that would tell against the inerrancy of the Bible (*Crisis*, p. 21).

This book *Crisis* shows quite clearly how Montgomery has reached this standpoint. Bultmann and many other NT critics felt unable to stop work once their purely historical investigations had undermined the credibility of scripture, and so they introduced philosophemes (often drawn from existentialism) to repair the damage. (I illustrated Bultmann's technique in this matter in *JEC*, pp. 47–49.) Montgomery can see that their philosophemes are nonsense (he quotes some of the quite ridiculous ones on p. 31), but he does not realize that this philosophical salvage work is quite independent of the historical-critical investigations, the negative results of which prompted it. Hence he supposes that, if we sweep aside the philosophemes, the critical work goes away with them, leaving us with an inerrant Bible.[6] In other words, finding fault with the Bible has depended on donning existentialist (or other equally arbitrary philosophical) spectacles, and once these are discarded we find that there are no errors or contradictions in it at all: all the alleged or apparent ones have been shown to be not such, either long ago or by the work of recent apologists and harmonizers.[7]

It comes as no surprise to find that this very same standpoint is that of the Fathers of the church to whom Montgomery is so much beholden. Irenaeus supposed all heresy to be a distortion of scripture occasioned by following some particular false teacher (some second-century equivalent of Bultmann, presumably), and deriving ultimately from undue deference to some particular form of philosophical reasoning[8] (some precursor of Montgomery's *bête noire*, existentialism). Apologetic technique has not changed much over the centuries.

Montgomery nevertheless has to allow that even the harmonizers may leave some residual difficulties unresolved. The position he recommends to readers is:

Harmonization of scriptural difficulties should be pursued within
reasonable limits, and when harmonization would pass beyond such
bounds the exegete must leave the problem open rather than, by
assuming absurd error, impugn the absolute truthfulness of the God
who inspires all Holy Scripture for our learning. (*Crisis*, p. 103)

Someone who takes this view has no right to complain that other
persons harbour *a priori* principles.

Montgomery even wants "a moratorium on the use of any and
all modern theologians, whether liberal or conservative" because
their scholarship is not "neutral". (That he himself is in Holy
Orders was not disclosed at our debate.) Hence he objected to
the use I have made of the critical work of Raymond Brown
and Joseph Fitzmyer (both Catholic priests!) on the ground that
theologians "have a professional axe to grind." But one would
expect any such bias to make them supportive rather than
critical of NT claims. To write as many of them do is surely
'against interest' (the phrase lawyers use to describe a certain
kind of *un*likely behaviour)—at any rate against their interests
as clergy and preachers, and in accordance only with their quite
different interests as scholars, which impel them to write what
will stand up to critical scrutiny from their peers. The fact that
I have been able to show that much in my account has the back-
ing of NT scholars is surely not to be adduced as weakening my
position.

The scholarship Montgomery allows includes not only that of
lawyers, but also of "secular historians" and "literary specialists". I
have commented on attempts by the latter to defend the Bible in my
What's in a Name? It is in any event quite gratuitous to suggest that
a writer who is not a cleric or a theologian can be taken as "neutral"
in what he says on religion. Is Gibbon's account of early Christianity
to be accepted as neutral? Most commentators from other profes-
sions have pronounced on religion precisely because they had
strong views on it. And they, no more than the theologians, speak
with one voice. Among classical scholars, Sherwin-White says one
thing about the accuracy of the Acts of the Apostles and Sir Moses
Finley says the opposite.[9] Lawyers, as Brown shows in his comprehensive study of the Passion, have been particularly drawn to
Jesus's trial, have usually disclaimed religious motives and pro-

fessed purely legal interests, yet have mostly taken the accounts in the four gospels at face value and tried to harmonize them; whether or not they treat the material critically, "the most divergent results emerge from their studies" (*Death*, pp. 329–331). Jean Imbert, a French Professor of Law (also a committed Catholic) finds that nothing in these gospel accounts transgresses historical reality, that the evangelists here as elsewhere complement each other without contradiction, each one adding some new detail not described by a predecessor, but sometimes—particularly in the case of John—finding it unnecessary to record what a predecessor had already made clear. A much more negative view of the same material is taken by W. Fricke, a German lawyer writing a few years later.[10]

Sir Norman Anderson, writing as "an academic lawyer" in support of the historicity of the resurrection, claims that "lawyers are traditionally trained to weigh evidence and see where it leads, rather than to reach some hypothetical conclusion and then impose it on the evidence".[11] Of their training I cannot speak, but their practice has seemed to some (and not only to Dickens) to be to make the best of their client's case and the worst of his opponent's. The best conditions for right judgement seem to be a situation where our interest does not lie on one side or the other, but merely in ascertaining what the facts are; where we do not care what the truth is, but are very anxious to know it. Sir Norman will have difficulty in convincing some of us that this is the position of the courtroom advocate. My own experience of lawyers turned scholars is that they are apt to retain the courtroom technique of being mainly concerned to say what they hope their audience will accept by way of discrediting opponent witnesses. I am not saying that their scholarship is insincere. They naturally suppose that the technique they daily employ is appropriate in other contexts.

Quite apart from pleas from interested parties, it may be said—as a generalization on the psychology of belief—that people are apt to acquire a strong prejudice in favour of any view, however cheerful or however gloomy, which they themselves have originated or defended. It may have been adopted reluctantly, but once someone has associated it with himself, with his own reputation, he gets a special liking for it that has no connection with its intrinsic merits. We all need to be on our guard here, and

because a certain group or class of persons has no obvious immediate professional interest in a given matter, they are not to be
assumed to be immune from danger.

The way Montgomery tries to exploit non-theological evidence
is illustrated when he adduces the 1961 discovery at Caesarea of
an inscription naming Pilate prefect (not, *pace* Montgomery,
procurator: see above, p. 42) of Judea as "archeological support
for the historicity of the gospel accounts". That Pilate was governor there in the early first century has long been known from
ancient non-Christian literary evidence, and the inscription confirms no more than that. Whether he had any dealings with a historical Jesus, and if so, whether he tried to act in a kindly manner
and yielded only finally to Jewish malice in condemning him, as
the gospels would have us believe, is quite another matter. Philo
and Josephus represent him as devoid of kindliness and
detestably cruel towards his subjects.

However, nothing that scholars turn up is, for Montgomery,
decisive, although it was remarkable how often during the debate
he purported to settle a disputed issue simply by appealing to
authorities—representing, for instance, Imbert's conservative harmonization of the gospel accounts of Jesus's trial as definitive, and
citing what he said was W.F. Albright's claim that every one of the
NT books was written by a baptized Jew before A.D. 70. (Albright,
conservative enough as he was, in fact claimed less than this.)[12]
What Montgomery wants is "strict reliance on the *primary
sources*—the first- and early second-century historical materials
themselves" (his italics). These, he said at the debate, have come to
us exactly as they were written, without distortion. Any textual
critic knows that this is an exaggeration. There is considerable
manuscript variation in what Jesus says on divorce, and whether
Luke has a doctrine of atonement depends on which manuscripts
of his account of the Last Supper are to be taken as giving the original reading (compare above, p. 34). The International Greek NT's
apparatus of Luke provides what the Birmingham theologian D.
Parker reckons to be "upwards of 30,000 variants for that Gospel,
so that we have, for example, 81 in the Lord's Prayer." He adds:

> We do not possess *the* Greek New Testament. What we have is a mass
> of manuscripts, of which only about three hundred date from before

A.D. 800. A mere thirty-four of these are older than A.D. 400, of which only four were at any time complete. All these differ, and all at one time or another *had* authority as the known text.[13]

Ehrman's recent and thorough discussion of the NT text leads him to conclude that, during the earliest period of its transmission, it "was in a state of flux" and "came to be more or less standardized in some regions by the fourth century, and subject to fairly rigid control (by comparison) only in the Byzantine period" (*Corruption*, p. 28). He adds in a note that this is the view of a wide range of scholars. His reviewer J.K. Elliott, himself a textual critic, has underlined the importance of this book.[14]

In any case, the reliability of the text is largely irrelevant to my arguments, few of which are based on anything other than the received text as printed in the RV. Montgomery's insistence that the oldest known fragment of an ms. of the NT (the John Rylands papyrus P[52], comprising five verses of Jn. 18) is to be dated as early as A.D. 100 is likewise irrelevant (as well as optimistic[15]) as I date all four gospels at ca. A.D. 90 (sixty years later than the dates they ascribe to events in Jesus's life) and I see no reason why they should not have been copied at an early date. My principal arguments concern the claims of these documents, not their manuscript attestation, and Montgomery agrees that these claims need to be evaluated. But he believes that this can be done without scholarly help, and that scripture can, indeed must, be allowed to "interpret itself" (*The Law*, p. 87). This is the position one expects a Lutheran cleric to take, for the Reformation Protestants insisted on it as the obvious way of eliminating the need for a pope or a church to say what scripture means. If it were a feasible way of reaching unambiguously convincing results, we should not have so many Christian denominations—there are said to be 20,800 in a Christian Encyclopaedia published in 1982[16]—quite apart from the very many conflicting scholarly appraisals.

ii. The Testimony of Papias

The specific example that Montgomery gives in support of his principal charge against me is that I dismiss Papias's testimony "not on the basis of the testimony itself, but because post-Bultmannian German scholarship—in this case Conzelmann—questions it." Papias, Bishop of Hierapolis in Asia Minor, is of some concern to Christian apologists, as he is the first writer to mention written gospels (Mark and Matthew) by name, and is our earliest source of information for the tradition that, although Mark had not kept company with Jesus, he wrote his gospel on the basis of what he was told by Peter. His books survive only as quotations in later writers, and the date of writing cannot be precisely determined: Barrett (*John*, p. 106) gives reasons that ca. A.D. 140, with a margin of at least ten years on either side, is as likely as any alternative dating. In his *Ecclesiastical History* of ca. A.D. 325, Eusebius quotes (iii, 39) a passage where Papias says he inquired about Jesus from anyone "who had followed the presbyters", who were themselves pupils of the immediate disciples of the Lord. (I give the relevant section of this passage in note 20 to this chapter.) So the sequence through which the tradition passed was: Jesus—his disciples—the presbyters—their followers—Papias. A few lines later Eusebius declares that Papias himself "actually heard" two of the presbyters. But this contradicts what he has just quoted Papias himself as saying, and is in any case only half-heartedly alleged; for he adds: "At least (γοῦν) he [Papias] mentions them frequently by name and gives their traditions in his writings." As Barrett (*John*, p. 109) notes, this is no proof at all of personal acquaintance.

From his informants Papias gathered a good deal of what Eusebius calls "mythical matter", and this included the ascription to Jesus of the teaching that "there will be a millennium after the resurrection of the dead when the kingdom of Christ will be set up in material form on this earth." A full generation later than Papias Irenaeus recorded (ca. A.D. 185) that the presbyters had heard—from the apostle John himself—how Jesus had taught that "in those days vine will be produced, each one having a thousand branches, and in each branch ten thousand twigs" etc. (*Against Heresies*, v, 33). Papias, he adds, "bore witness to these things in writing". This view of Messianic times is in fact merely a late Jewish legend, represented for instance in chapter 29 of the Syriac Apocalypse of Baruch (of ca. A.D. 100); and its ascription to

Jesus shows how readily oral tradition could come to credit him with having taught whatever was available by way of popular or sectarian religious belief.

Papias stresses that he preferred what he heard from his informants to what he read in books; and the information he thus gathered included grotesque stories about Judas: his body became so swollen that even his head could not pass where a wagon passes; the place where he died remains uninhabited because of its foul stench, and no one can pass it without holding his nose. This is not reliable reporting traceable to eyewitnesses, but morbid fantasizing inspired by loathing of the supposed traitor. The Catholic editor of the fragments that are extant from Papias's books says, introducing them, that "on the whole they do not make pleasant reading".[17] What Papias really shows is: how fanciful oral tradition about Jesus and his associates can be, and how wrong is the common assumption that reliance on it came to an abrupt end once the now canonical gospels had been written.

Irenaeus, exaggerating the continuity of Christian tradition, went so far as to call Papias "a hearer" of the apostle John. Eusebius, however, records (*loc. cit.*) that Papias "makes plain in the preface of his treatises that he had in no way been a hearer and eyewitness of the sacred Apostles." Montgomery goes even further than Irenaeus and claims that Papias "informs us of the primary-source authorship of all four Gospels, as told to him personally by John." In fact, Papias makes no mention of the gospels of Luke and John in any extant passage and it is unlikely that he ever mentioned them at all; for Eusebius promises (*op.cit.*, iii, 3) to record what ecclesiastical writers had said about canonical and 'disputed' books, yet gives no extracts from Papias about these two gospels.

The way in which uncritical tradition about Papias proliferated is evident from the so-called Anti-Marcionite prologue to the gospel of John which is contained in some mss. of the Vulgate and has been dated at ca. A.D. 400.[18] It alleges that Papias was a "dear pupil" of the apostle and even that he wrote John's gospel from John's dictation. The author of this prologue obviously had no real knowledge of the second-century situation. What Papias himself said in the passage quoted by Eusebius (again see note 20 to this chapter) is that he tried (at some time previous to his time of writing) to extract from the pupils of the presbyters what the presbyters themselves *were saying* that John (and other immediate disciples of the Lord) *had said*. The two contrasting tenses imply that, whereas the presbyters were still alive and still testifying when Papias made his inquiries, John and the other immediate disciples were not. And Papias's concern to find out what John had *said* does not suggest that he believed John to have written a gospel.

On the basis of a tradition handed down by Irenaeus, but with no earlier support, the church came to believe that the apostle John survived until Trajan's reign (A.D. 98–117). This tradition allows John to have lived long enough to have been personally known to Papias—even at the time when Papias wrote his books if their date can be shifted from ca. A.D. 140 to the very beginning of the second century. So we are not surprised to find the very conservative R.H. Gundry claiming to have "established the date of Papias's writing as during the period 101–108 CE".[19] Gundry also supposes that the presbyter who (indirectly) informed Papias was none other than "the apostle John". Papias does include a 'John' among the two presbyters he names, but Eusebius noted, by quoting Papias himself, that this John is distinguished from the apostle John. Unfortunately, Papias avoids the term 'apostle' and calls the members of both groups he has carefully distinguished—the apostles and the presbyters—"disciples of the Lord". This invites confusion which conservative commentators have been quick to exploit.[20]

Much of this is clearly stated in my first book on Christian origins (JEC, 1971), quite independently of Conzelmann. From what Montgomery says one might think that Papias's reliability had remained unquestioned prior to "post-Bultmannian German scholarship". But even Eusebius regarded him as a bit of a noodle ("a man of very little intelligence, as is clear from his books"). On any showing, even Gundry's, he wrote in the second century: his information (*pace* Gundry) was very indirect and his belief that Jesus preached the millennium grape story absurd. All this does not inspire confidence in what he says about the origin of the two gospels he does mention, namely Mark and Matthew. If, as he claims, Peter had supplied the substance of a canonical gospel, even though not writing it down himself, it would still be in essence his and would never have been assigned to someone who was not even one of the twelve. More reasonable would be to suppose that, first, the work was assigned to someone called Mark—a common name in early Christian literature[21] and, Nineham notes, "the commonest Latin name in the Roman Empire", so that "the early Church must have contained innumerable Marks" (*Mark*, p. 39). Then, in order to give this gospel a quasi-apostolic origin, it was argued that this Mark was dependent on Peter, who is a very prominent disciple in it.[22] This dependence will have been suggested by the fact that someone called Mark is favourably associated with Peter in the first of the two epistles (not suspected to be pseudonymous) ascribed to Peter (1 Peter 5:13 mentions "my son Mark"); for "the early Church was in the habit of assuming that all occurrences of a given name in the New Testament referred to a single individual" (Nineham, *loc. cit.*).

That the author of Mark depended on Peter for his information can only be oral tradition, for no such claim is made in this gospel itself, which in any case assigns a much less prominent role to Peter than he plays in the gospels of Matthew and Luke. Did Peter think it not worth mentioning to Mark that he had walked on the water (Mt. 14:28–31), that he will be the rock on which the church will be built and had been entrusted with the keys of the kingdom of heaven (Mt. 16:17–19), had been advised and promised a miracle by Jesus concerning payment of the temple-tax (Mt. 17:24–27) and had sought his advice concerning how often an erring brother is to be forgiven (Mt. 18:21)? And did he also fail to tell Mark of his miraculous draught of fishes which first led him to follow Jesus (Lk. 5:3–9), for none of these incidents are recorded in Mark. They could of course be set aside as mythological expansions of genuine information about Peter preserved there; but such dismissal of Matthaean and Lucan material would not appeal to Montgomery.

If one turns from post-Marcan to pre-Marcan references to an apostle named Peter, one might note that, according to Paul, the very first appearance of the risen Jesus was to Cephas (1 Corinthians 15:5), usually equated with the 'Peter' mentioned in a single

Pauline passage (Galatians 2:7–9).[23] If he had been a personal disciple of Jesus—not my view (cf. above, p. 00), but the generally
accepted one, and certainly Montgomery's—and if he was responsible for the substance of Mark's gospel, did he not think this
experience worth mentioning?

If Peter is ultimately behind Mark's portrait of him, then he
was very negative about himself: he is called "Satan" for his
unwillingness to believe Jesus's plain speaking about the forthcoming Passion and resurrection (8:31–33); his boast after the
Last Supper that, whatever others may do he will not be found
wanting, is followed by inability to keep even brief watch in Gethsemane (14:37) and then by ignominious denial of his master
(14:66–72). Apologists maintain that only Peter himself could
have reported so negatively. But Mark portrays all the disciples
negatively for what, as we shall see (chapter 5 below) have been
called "dogmatic reasons". Matthew and Luke adapt Marcan references to Peter so as to present him more favourably (compare
below, p. 98f). I give numerous instances in this book of where
they adapt other Marcan material equally freely; and they would
surely not have done this if Mark had been accepted as based on
Peter's first-hand experience.

Finally, since the beginning of the twentieth century much of
the narrative of Jesus's ministry in Mark has come to be seen not
as the account of an eyewitness, but as individual and originally
independent stories about Jesus collected by the evangelist—little
narratives which earlier had a separate existence in the teaching
and preaching of the early church. This also will occupy us in
chapter 5.

As for what Papias says about Matthew, all that is extant is
usually translated: he "collected the oracles (τὰ λόγια) in the
Hebrew language and each interpreted them as best he could."
What this means is unclear; the Greek may mean 'translated'
rather than 'interpreted'; the 'logia' may mean the sayings of Jesus
rather than a gospel, and 'the Hebrew language' Aramaic. Beare
observes that "not many take Papias seriously, and those who do
interpret him in different ways" (*Matthew*, p. 22). Some hold that,
if he was referring to a gospel at all, he will have had in mind one
or other of the Semitic gospels (only fragments of which survive)

which were based on our Greek Matthew, but which he took for the original.[24] Whatever he means does not fit our Greek Matthew, which is no translation but an adaptation and expansion of the Greek gospel of Mark. Hence Kümmel declares that we must concede that the report that Matthew was written 'in the Hebrew language' is "utterly false, however it may have arisen" (*Introduction*, pp. 120–21). He adds that all that remains of the tradition passed on by Papias is the name 'Matthew' as that of the author, taken as referring to the Matthew included in the synoptic lists of the twelve apostles. But here again the dependence of this gospel on the Greek gospel of a non-disciple makes it "completely impossible to accept that it originated from an eyewitness and member of Jesus's most intimate circle", and today "only a scattering of scholars" still maintain such a view.

Kürzinger has urged that what Papias says about both Mark and Matthew needs to be taken together and key words in it interpreted from the meaning they bear as rhetorical terms in Greek use at that time. When referring to Mark, Papias makes it clear that by λόγια he understands words about Jesus's deeds as well as his sayings ("the things said or done by the Lord"); and so the immediately following statement that Matthew ordered (συνετάξατο) the λόγια refers to the narrative gospel of Matthew, not to a sayings collection. Kürzinger also challenges the rendering that Matthew wrote 'in the Hebrew language'. He notes that there is no definite article in the Greek here, which he takes to mean 'in Hebrew manner' (style), meaning the style of Hebraic writing in Greek such as the Septuagint; whereas Mark had not been able to put his gospel into proper literary form (οὐ μέντοι τάξει, said of Mark, is meant to contrast with συνετάξατο, said of Matthew) because he could record only what Peter happened to say. On this view, all that Papias affirms when he contrasts the two evangelists is the superior literary quality of Matthew over Mark's less coherent account of Jesus's ministry. The clause generally rendered 'each interpreted them (the λόγια ordered by Matthew) as best he could' does not, then, mean that everybody did their best to understand Matthew's Aramaic, but that 'each (of the two evangelists) presented (the Greek verb here and the corresponding noun mean in rhetoric to record, present, convey something in language) the λόγια (in Greek!) as he was able'—that is, Mark without literary refinement because of his dependence on Peter.[25]

Altogether, in arguing for the reliability of the NT, Montgomery relies very heavily on patristic allegations—from Polycarp (martyred around 155), Papias, and Irenaeus. He regards such statements, reproduced by Eusebius in the fourth century, as reliable evidence that the first gospel was written by Matthew, a tax-collector who became a companion of Jesus. What Eusebius in fact records is that Origen learnt of this in the third century "by tradition" (op. cit., vi, 25).

It is, of course, very convenient, if highly questionable, for the modern apologist to include patristic traditions among the 'primary sources' to which we are to be beholden. But anyone who reads the Fathers rapidly discovers that they have—to use Montgomery's phrase—'a professional axe to grind'. The titles of all four gospels are not original but were added by patristic guess-work in the second century (see WWJ, p. 5). In the old but still valuable Encyclopaedia Biblica, Schmiedel concludes his discussion of the Fathers' views concerning the origin of the gospels by saying that it is vain to look to them for trustworthy information on the subject.[26] Papias's followers brought Mark even closer to Peter than he had suggested. Irenaeus was still content with supposing that Mark wrote after Peter's death, but Clement of Alexandria put the composition of the gospel in Peter's lifetime, although he says it was written without Peter's co-operation. Jerome dropped this proviso and outdid his predecessors by calling Mark not only Peter's interpreter but also the first bishop of the Church of Alexandria.[27] The Fathers made equally strenuous efforts to assign a similar indirect apostolic origin to Luke, the other of the four canonical gospels not already credited to an apostle by its title. Thus Irenaeus and Tertullian declared Luke to have committed to writing the gospel preached by Paul (who, as we saw, in fact preached next to nothing about Jesus's incarnate life). Origen, so Eusebius recorded (op. cit, vi, 25), supposed that when Paul mentioned "my gospel" (Romans 2:16) he meant not the doctrines he preached but the gospel of Luke. Eusebius himself noted, as a current view, that Paul's phrase 'according to my gospel' implies that "he was actually accustomed to quote from

Luke's gospel" (*op. cit.* iii, 4). In classical Greek the word 'gospel' (εὐαγγέλιον) meant the reward given to a bearer of good tidings, and later came to mean the glad message itself. This is what it means throughout the NT—not a written document but 'good tidings' about the salvation of the world.[28] In this sense Paul says that the Lord has ordained that "they which proclaim the gospel should live of the gospel" (1 Corinthians 9:14).

Montgomery's claims, here as elsewhere, are characteristic of a whole body of scholarship which may appropriately be called 'conservative evangelical', and which evidences the recent worldwide upsurge of fundamentalism within Christianity as in other faiths. It is typified by Gundry's commentary on Mark, already mentioned, and by Wenham's *Redating*, both of which uncritically accept early patristic evidence about the origins and authority of the gospels. Wenham (p. 223) even takes "the gospel"—in Paul's mention of some unspecified person whose reputation is high because of his "services to the gospel" (2 Corinthians 8:18)—as an allusion to Luke and to his written gospel, and so is able to date it (and the other two synoptics) earlier than the Pauline letters.

iii. Paul, the Pastoral Epistles, and the Gospel Jesus

Montgomery was unimpressed by the significance I have ascribed to Paul's silences on the life and teachings of Jesus. (On similar silences in other pre-gospel epistles he did not comment.) Paul, he argued, was indifferent to Jesus's life and teachings because he was interested solely in the fact that Jesus had come to earth to die on the cross for the sins of the world and to rise again from the dead. So we are to believe that Paul, anxious as he was to inculcate numerous ethical principles (such as 'judge not' and 'practise forgiveness'), knew that Jesus had taught them, yet was indifferent to the fact; that both Paul and the Christians who strongly opposed him in a truly furious quarrel on the question of obeying the Jewish food laws knew yet ignored the rulings Jesus had supposedly given on this and on other details of the Jewish law; that Paul's convictions on the second coming left him indifferent to eschatological statements which Jesus had made which eventually came to be recorded in the gospels; and finally that what Jesus had supposedly said on all such fundamental issues was of no interest also to all other pre-gospel epistle writers.

It would surely follow from Montgomery's view of Paul's attitude that he would at least be explicit on the Passion; and yet we find that his knowledge of it does not extend even to giving it a historical setting—unless, of course, we regard the Pastoral epistles as genuinely Pauline, and so are able to ascribe to him the knowledge that Jesus stood before Pilate (1 Timothy 6:13). This, of course, is what Montgomery does. He said at the debate:

> A few years ago, Macgregor and Morton subjected the Pauline epistles to computer analysis, taking Romans and Galatians, which are accepted by everybody, as a model, and then fed the literary style of the other epistles into a computer to determine whether they were written by the same person. The conclusion was that they were not; they were written by six or seven different people.

He then ridiculed this work, saying that Harvard students took Macgregor and Morton's book, used the preface and the first chapter as a stylistic base, and fed the style of the remaining chapters into a computer. This gave them the result that the book was written by six different people (Laughter from the audience). He concluded that "it is extremely dangerous to use literary style as a basis for determining authorship, and unfortunately that is virtually the history of German critical scholarship dealing with the New Testament, the scholarship with which Professor Wells is so well acquainted."

This wording even suggests that German critical scholarship has "virtually" restricted itself to stylistic criteria in all that it has said critically of the NT, not only on the question of authorship. Even the latter claim would be a gross distortion. In the case of the Pastorals, their ascription to Paul has been put in doubt by the convergence of a whole series of arguments: they attenuate his theology, do not fit the chronology of his life, and the church organization presupposed in them is likewise later. Whereas Paul had argued with opponents, the author of the Pastorals simply abuses them. Typical is 1 Timothy 6:3–4 where anyone who adheres to different teachings is denounced as conceited, under-standing nothing, and given to a morbid craving for controversy and for disputes about words. The manuscript attestation of the Pastorals is also relatively poor. They are absent from Marcion's collection of the mid-second century, and from the collection in the Chester-Beatty papyrus P[46], dated ca. A.D. 200. Whereas obvi-ously genuine Paulines begin to be quoted by later writers from ca. A.D. 95, there is no certain allusion to the Pastorals until about eighty years later, after which they are cited regularly. In the light of this and other evidence (compare *HEJ*, pp. 89–98), all but the most conservative commentators allow them to be post-Pauline. Letters continued to be written in Paul's name even after the Pas-torals; for instance, a third epistle to the Corinthians, and an exchange of letters between Paul and Seneca which was accepted as genuine by Jerome and Augustine. As Hahneman notes, "the history of the Pauline corpus up to and including the fourth cen-tury is one of continual expansion."[29]

The computer analysis which Montgomery had in mind was done by A.Q. Morton and J. McLeman, not by Morton and G.H.C. Macgregor. The two latter had written together on Luke-Acts and on the fourth gospel, but Macgregor had died by the time Morton and McLeman published their *Paul, the Man and the Myth* (Lon-don: Hodder and Stoughton, 1966), and this is presumably the book the Harvard students analysed. Whatever the book, it was absurd to take anything as brief as a preface as part of a model for the kind of analysis where, as Morton and McLeman stress, length is of crucial importance. (The preface of their 1966 book covered 1½ pages, and its first chapter only 8½ pages.) They did not themselves take any of the epistles "as a model". What they found was that, in all their tests, not only Romans and Galatians but also 1 and 2 Corinthians formed a single group. Concerning the multiple authorship of the remaining epistles ascribed to Paul, they are far from dogmatic (pp. 93–94), and they are well aware of the dangers of appeal to style over questions of author-ship (pp. 23–30). The summary of this work that Montgomery has given in print is carelessly inaccurate.[30]

Anthony Kenny has given evidence that "a much more thor-ough study than Morton's of the most common words and grammatical features in the Pauline corpus does not at all isolate the four major Epistles as a single group"; and he concludes, while paying tribute in his preface to Morton's pioneer work, that "the Pauline problem is not to be solved by regarding only the first four Epistles as the work of a single hand", and that "what is to be said of the authorship of the Epistles is in the end a matter for the Scripture scholar, not the stylometrist".[31] Together with the majority of commentators, I have included Philippians, 1 Thessalonians and possibly also Colossians among the genuine Paulines, and have accepted the reasons which numerous scholars have given for excluding Ephesians, 2 Thessalonians, and the Pastorals. Kenny's dispassionate book might have served Montgomery better than an inaccurate account of Morton's work and the "jolly little story" of the Harvard prank, even though Kenny does not claim to have settled the authorship problem. But scorn is often more effective than scholarship in debate.

iv. Eyewitness Testimony?

A. GOSPELS

It is a cardinal doctrine of conservative Protestantism that the canonical gospels and the epistles ascribed to Peter and John were written by 'apostles' or at any rate by persons close to apostles. Donald Lamont gives it the following forthright expression:

> Without entering into the irrefutable argument for the complete authority of the Bible in matters pertaining to God and His redemption of sinful man, I would criticize in the strongest terms the folly of those who, however scholarly they may be, have made it their business to tamper with the apostolic witness to Jesus in the days of his flesh. That witness is single, unmistakable and consistent.[32]

Montgomery holds that the NT writers "consistently maintain" that their "accounts of Jesus . . . are primary-source records produced by eyewitnesses" (*The Law*, p. 44), that such claims are made "throughout the New Testament" (*Crisis*, p. 41) and that at the debate he was able to cite "the internal claims of the gospels to be written by eyewitnesses" or their close associates. I shall show in this section that this is a gross exaggeration, that only the latest of the relevant material—2 Peter and two passages in the fourth gospel—makes such claims, reflecting the anxiousness of the church to authenticate its sacred material.

Nothing in the first three gospels indicates who wrote them. Mark, the earliest of them, gives but a flimsy account of the Galilean ministry (as we shall see in chapter 5), and this contrasts very obviously with the fullness of detail in the same gospel concerning Jesus's final days in Jerusalem. Wellhausen commented that this discrepancy would not be there if Mark's material derived from the original disciples.[33]

The prologue to the third gospel is often adduced in support of eyewitness authorship, but this would never have happened had it been properly understood; for the author here says that he is writing even later than "many" (not said to have been eyewitnesses) who have already written about Jesus, and claims only to have scrutinized the evidence so that he can, in his own gospel, "trace the course of things accurately from the first", from their inception (Lk. 1:1–4). He of course does not deny—any more than do the vast majority of modern theologians—that the traditions he records *originated* from eyewitnesses, but he does not place himself among them or their associates. He says they delivered their reports to "us", in other words the Christian community, not to 'me'.

As, then, the authors of the three synoptic gospels do not claim eyewitness basis for their reports, support has to be sought from the Fathers—from what Papias says concerning Mark and from what others say concerning Luke and Matthew. Origen's comments on Mt. 9:9, paralleled in Mk. 2:14, are relevant here.

At Mk. 2:14 Jesus calls a tax-collector named Levi to be a disciple:

> And as he passed by, he saw Levi, the son of Alphaeus, sitting at the place of toll, and he saith unto him, Follow me. And he arose and followed him.

Bultmann described this and the similar pericope of the calling of four other disciples (1:16–20) as unquestionably "ideal scenes", meaning that their author imagined them in order to portray what people should ideally do, namely give up everything and follow Jesus.[34] The author of the gospel traditionally ascribed to Matthew thought it better (at 9:9) to replace Levi—an unknown personage who is never again mentioned—with a name from Mark's (and his own) list of the twelve, namely Matthew, who in Mark's list is simply called "Matthew" (3:18), but in Matthew's "Matthew the publican" (10:3), meaning the tax-collector. Origen (see above, p. 78) supposed quite gratuitously that, in replacing Levi with Matthew at 9:9, the author of the gospel here introduced his own name—a view still seriously argued. R.H. Gundry holds that Matthew's employment as a tax-collector necessitated a good command of Greek and instilled in him the habit of jotting down information, so that he was better suited than "the unlettered disciples" to take notes which "provide the basis for the bulk of the apostolic gospel tradition".[35] Wenham (*Redating*, p. 113) quotes this view approvingly; Thiede likewise follows Gundry and envisages "Levi-Matthew taking shorthand notes of the speeches of Jesus, as verbatim as possible, in the original Aramaic, and occasionally in Greek. Even the length of the Sermon on the Mount would not have caused any problems for a shorthand writer."[36]

Gundry is aware of the objection that "an eyewitness such as Matthew the apostle would never have depended on Mark" (p. 184), as the author of canonical Matthew in fact did. He answers by suggesting that Matthew utilized the gospel of Mark because "he wished to preserve the unity of the apostolic gospel tradition", and that Mark's gospel itself derives from the preaching of Peter who "perchance used Matthean 'notes'."

A direct eyewitness basis is claimed in chapters 19 and 21 of the fourth gospel. The pericope Jn. 19:31–37 tells that soldiers broke the legs of the two victims crucified with Jesus, but did not do the same to him, as they saw that he was already dead. However, one of them pierced his side with a spear, "and at once there came out blood and water". The failure to break his legs and the spear thrust into his side are then said to have fulfilled OT texts, namely that not a bone of the righteous man (Psalm 34:20) or of the paschal lamb (Exodus 12:46) shall be broken, and that "they shall look on me, on him whom they have pierced" (Zechariah 12:10, NEB). This naturally raises the suspicion that the whole incident, unknown to the other gospels, has been concocted as edifying fulfilment of these 'prophecies'. But no OT passage was available to authenticate the issue of blood and water, and so this is said to have been reliably reported by an (unnamed) eyewitness:

> And he that hath seen hath borne witness, and his witness is true; and he knoweth that he saith true, that ye also may believe. (19:35)

"He that hath seen" presumably designates a person who had beheld the effusion of blood and water. It is not said that he was the author of the gospel. Probably the claim here is that the author learnt of this effusion from this reliable witness. The following "he knoweth that he saith true" seems to refer to the same witness. If we were to take it as referring to the author, we should have to make it mean 'his witness is true and *I* know that he is speaking the truth'. Barrett rightly implies that this would be a forced interpretation, and notes too that the whole incident of the effusion is "of doubtful historicity" (*John*, pp. 118, 557–58). That water, together with blood, should issue from the side of someone already dead would be miraculous, as a comprehensive article on the subject in a Berlin medical journal conceded in 1963.[37] Some have said that the water was pericardial fluid; but not more than about half a thimble of fluid could come from the pericardium. Fluid from a pleural effusion has also been invoked. But the lungs are at sub-atmospheric pressure, so that if there is fluid in the pleural cavity, a perforation will cause air to go in, not fluid to come out. To remove the fluid, it has to be sucked out under pressure. Even if water did issue with Jesus's blood from a single wound, it could hardly have done so in a way that made it possible for an observer to distinguish the two. The water and the blood are probably meant as an allusion to the sacraments of baptism and eucharist,[38] and the purpose of verse 35 which authenticates their issue from Jesus's body is pretty clearly to combat docetism—the doctrine, expressly criticized in the first of the epistles ascribed to John (see above, p. 32), that Jesus lived on earth with only a phantom body.

I showed in *HEJ* (pp. 189–190) that the whole pericope Jn. 19:31–37 is an insertion not worked into its context with complete consistency, and that it is not only absent from the other gospels, but also includes a detail which is excluded by Mark and which does not harmonize even with the next section of the gospel in which it stands.

The other passage in the fourth gospel which invokes eyewitness testimony outdoes 19:35 by claiming "the disciple whom Jesus loved" as both witness of and writer of "these things" (21:20 and 24), meaning surely the whole gospel. This claim of an eyewitness basis must have greatly facilitated its acceptance in the canon; so different is it from the others that it would otherwise never have been included. If it is accurate in its account of the life of Jesus, the others must be very inaccurate indeed. It alone mentions this beloved disciple, and in its previous chapters he has figured as a kind of superior counterpart to Peter. Although Peter was present at the Last Supper, it was the beloved disciple who "was at the table reclining in Jesus's bosom" (13:23). At the crucifixion, where Peter is not so much as mentioned, it is to the care of the beloved disciple that Jesus entrusts his mother (19:26–27); and when both men go to the tomb, it is he who is first said to believe in the reality of the resurrection (20:8). As all three of these incidents have parallels in the other gospels where he plays no part, the fourth gospel has here presumably drawn on source material similar to theirs, but reworked it so as to introduce him. (This is particularly clear in the case of the visit to the empty tomb; cf. *HEJ*, pp. 128f.) Altogether, this gospel gives prominence to disciples unknown to the synoptics—Nathaniel, Nicodemus, as well as the beloved disciple. It leaves him anonymous, but the late second-century church thought that, although he obviously cannot have been Peter, he must have been one of the two others closest to Jesus in the synoptics, namely the sons of Zebedee, James and John. Only these three witness the raising of Jairus's daughter (in Mark), the Transfiguration (in all three synoptics) and the Gethsemane agony (in Matthew and Mark). However, in the fourth gospel, where alone the beloved disciple figures, there is no mention of any of these incidents. This would be quite extraordinary if the beloved disciple were really James or John. Some commentators have bluntly called him "a creation of the evangelist".[39]

The two sons of Zebedee are not mentioned at all in the fourth gospel until its very final chapter 21, which is almost universally agreed to be a later appendix. Of the two, James was, according to Acts, martyred early, and so the choice of authorship of the gospel naturally fell on John—but only near the end of the second century. Although this fourth gospel had been in existence since the beginning of that century, little notice was taken of it, except by gnostic 'heretics', until ca. A.D. 180, when suddenly mainstream Christians—in particular Irenaeus and Clement of Alexandria—begin to describe it as the work of the apostle John, written in his old age. Irenaeus claims that his own teacher, Polycarp, had known this John personally; but here, as elsewhere, Irenaeus was influenced by the natural tendency of Christian controversialists to exaggerate the continuity of Christian tradition.[40] As for Clement, he felt he needed to explain the lateness with which the fourth gospel was accepted, and also the fact that it is so very different from the other three. Hence he said that, as they had already made plain the "external facts", John, "last of all", and "being urged by his friends and inspired by the Spirit, composed a spiritual gospel".[41] In sum, when these two major Christian scholars wrote, the history of the fourth gospel in the second century had been—notwithstanding their confident testimony—"no plain tale of unquestioned reverence unhesitatingly accorded to a book known from the beginning to have been written by an apostle" (Barrett, *John*, p. 125). By the time they wrote, apostolic authorship was becoming an essential criterion for acceptance, and the identification of the author with the apostle John "may well have arisen simply as a means of claiming apostolic authorship for a work that was actually anonymous" (Lindars, *John*, 1990, p. 21).

That the final chapter 21 of the fourth gospel, where the eyewitness claim occurs, was written by the author of chapters 1–20 is maintained only by the most conservative commentators. The whole of this final chapter comes after a direct address to the reader clearly meant as a solemn conclusion to the gospel:

> Many other signs therefore did Jesus in the presence of the disciples, which are not written in this book: but these are written, that ye may believe that Jesus is the Christ, the Son of God: and that believing ye may have life in his name (20:30–31).

Just before this solemn end, the risen Jesus has instructed the disciples to go out as missionaries ("as the Father hath sent me, even so send I you"), and has given them the Holy Ghost so that they can forgive sins, or withhold such forgiveness (verses 21–23). But in the appended chapter that follows they seem to have forgotten this, and are represented as having returned to their old profession (long since abandoned) as fishermen in Galilee. There follows a story about a miraculous catch of fishes which is so similar to Lk. 5:1–11 (itself without synoptic parallel) that the two must be related. In Luke the incident gives the fishermen their motive for abandoning their trade and following Jesus, while here at the end of the fourth gospel it is a resurrection appearance to them. It seems, then, that there was an underlying tradition very differently manipulated by the two writers. Next in the appended chapter 21 comes a rehabilitation of Peter: his earlier threefold denial is counterbalanced by threefold affirmation of his love for Jesus, who thereupon gives him leadership status with the injunction "feed my sheep", and prophesies for him the glory of martyrdom. From the way he has been depicted in earlier chapters, he really does need the kind of recognition that he is here accorded. The chapter continues with a veiled forecast of his martyrdom— the writer may have known a tradition that he had been martyred—and a dialogue about the future of the beloved disciple where Jesus alludes to the belief, quite uncharacteristic of the fourth gospel, that some of the disciples might remain alive until his second coming (verses 22–23). Jesus, says Dodd (*op. cit.* in note 49 below, p. 431), is here made to subscribe to a "naive conception of his second Advent . . . unlike anything else in the Fourth Gospel". This whole appendix is brought to an end with a verse which tries to achieve an even more grandiose allusion to unrecorded further deeds of Jesus than that which concluded chapter 20:

> And there are also many other things which Jesus did, the which if they should be written every one, I suppose that even the world itself would not contain the books that should be written. (21:25)

This merely amounts to "an exaggerated literary conceit which is not to be taken seriously" (Lindars, *John*, 1972, p. 642), and which shows what a mistake was made in adding material to the original ending of the previous chapter.

B. EPISTLES: 1 JOHN; 2 PETER AND JESUS'S SECOND COMING

Turning now to epistles, we find that 1 Jn. begins with the words:

> That which was from the beginning, that which we have heard, that which we have seen with our eyes, that which we beheld and our hands handled, concerning the Word of life. . .

Montgomery claims that Jesus is here designated "one whom we have seen, heard and touched".[42] But by 'that which' (neuter, not masculine in the Greek) the author seems to mean not Jesus, but the truth about his life and work. This interpretation is required by 'concerning' (near the end of the verse). 'Concerning the Word of life' probably means 'concerning the message which gives life', that is, the Christian message; and a distinction is made in the next verse between the 'we' who know this message and the 'you' to whom it is now being imparted.[43] The author is not to be uncritically equated with the author of the fourth gospel, for this epistle differs markedly from that gospel in doctrine; and its text, as opposed to the title it has been given, is anonymous (see *HEJ*, pp. 98–101).

2 Peter does unambiguously claim (at 1:16) to be the work of an eyewitness of Jesus on earth, and its author says he was present at the Transfiguration "on the holy mountain". The epistle purports—in its text and not just in its title—to be the work of "Peter, an apostle of Jesus Christ"; and so for Montgomery it is to be accepted as the work of the Galilean fisherman who accompanies Jesus in the gospels. However, Bauckham notes, in his survey of relevant research, that "since the beginning of this century . . . , the pseudepigraphical character of the work has come to be almost universally recognised." He thinks it may have been written about A.D. 80–100, although he allows that many date it later, and as the very latest of all the NT books,[44] so that not surprisingly, it shows some knowledge of what is represented in the gospels. It is later than 1 Peter, to which it alludes (3:1), and which itself is certainly pseudonymous (see above, p. 37). Donald

Guthrie, a scrupulously fair though conservative commentator, allows that it was "neglected" until the third century, and that this "indicates a certain lack of confidence in the book."[45] J.N.D. Kelly remarks, more trenchantly, that if it "really is the product of Peter's pen, the slowness and reluctance of the Church, especially at Rome, to accord it recognition present a serious problem." He places it among "the luxuriant crop of pseudo-Petrine literature which sprang up around the memory of the Prince of the apostles" and which included the very popular *Apocalypse of Peter* (approximately A.D. 135), the *Preaching of Peter* (early second century), the *Gospel of Peter* and the *Acts of Peter*. He adds that still more writings with Peter's name attached have come to light among those found near Nag Hammadi in Upper Egypt in 1945.[46]

2 Peter, far from being the work of 'Peter', is a reissue of the epistle of Jude, much of which it incorporates. It warns all the faithful—no particular community is addressed—against "false teachers" who will in due course appear, and will duly be consigned to hell (2:1-4). As the writer purports to be the apostle Peter, he here represents their activities as yet to come. But this fiction soon breaks down as he proceeds to complain that—in the blunt English of the NEB—they are greedy for money, follow their abominable lusts ("they have eyes for nothing but women") and are like brute beasts. They were originally within the fold (2:20-21)—note the change to the past tense!—and so they are Christian apostates, not pagans or orthodox Jews. When he specifies what their false doctrines are, the author reverts to the fiction implied by the future tense: they are scoffers who will come in the last days and mock the doctrine of Jesus's second coming as judge of the world, saying that a whole generation has already died with no sign of any such upheaval (3:3-4). From this we may infer that the writer supposed himself to be living in the last times, and that his opponents disputed this on the ground that it had already been said a generation ago and proved false by the fact that everything in the world has continued normally. This in itself shows that the writer was no first generation Christian. What he is combating appears to be an incipient gnosticism: gnostics, as in their own estimation persons already enjoying salvation, were opposed

to apocalyptic doctrines involving a final judgement. Against their "myths", the writer claims to speak with the authentic voice of the original apostles (1:16–17), transmitting the true faith already complete, so that it needs only to be "recalled" (1:12; 3:1–2), not added to or modified.

This emphasis on acceptance of established doctrines reflects a much later situation from that where the 'spirit' could move Christian prophets to make diverse revelations (compare above, p. 31). Käsemann observes: "It is very evident that primitive Christian prophecy was one of the most dangerous instruments, if not indeed the determining factor, in the increasing hold which Gnosticism was gaining on the Church. It was in order to meet this danger that the Church adopted the Jewish institution of the presbyterate, out of which the monarchical episcopate grew. A ministry conferred by ordination is bound to be the natural opponent both of Gnosis and of primitive Christian prophecy" (*Essays*, pp. 187–88). In 2 Peter, only scriptural prophecy is admitted, which, it is said (1:20), no one can interpret by himself. The church is here claiming the exclusive right to its interpretation. There are also other indications of a late date (compare *HEJ*, pp. 185ff).

Commentators do not find this epistle at all edifying. It disposes of the enemy by accusing him of moral depravity, by showering him with offensive proverbs ("the dog returns to his own vomit", 2:22), and by lurid portrayal of his punishment in hell—a classic example, says Käsemann, of tactics which "obviously found ready hearers then as now." What can we say, he asks, about an eschatology "concerned only with the hope of the triumphal entry of believers into the eternal kingdom" (1:10–11), and with the destruction of the ungodly? What can we say of a church which identifies truth with her own traditions, to which assent is demanded? (pp. 191, 195).

It is not surprising that, as the various books of the NT were written over a period spanning some one hundred years, there is some questioning and modification in some of them of the early doctrine of an imminent second coming or 'parousia'. This process is worth brief scrutiny, both because the doctrine is so important to today's conservative Christianity, and because its

development exemplifies two things we have already found characteristic of the NT, namely the way in which a tradition is given
a new twist in its later books, and the importance of utterances of
those who claimed to speak in the name of the risen Lord.

Paul initially believed that the parousia would occur in the
lifetime of his own generation, perhaps even in his own lifetime.
He wrote of "we" (not of "those") "who are alive, who are left
.until the coming of the Lord" (1 Thessalonians 4:15), and
declared that "we shall not all sleep" (not all be deceased) at the
last trumpet (1 Corinthians 15:51). It was because he believed the
parousia to be so near that he recommended sexual abstinence:
"from now on, let those who have wives live as though they had
none", for "the appointed time has grown very short" (1 Corinthians 7:29, RSV). In what are probably later letters, he seems less
confident in this imminence: even if "the earthly tent we live in is
destroyed", we have the prospect of eternal life in the heavens (2
Corinthians 5:1); and his "desire is to depart and be with Christ",
rather than "remain in the flesh" (Philippians 1:23–24).

Revelation, the final book in the canon (although not the latest
to be written) is still confident that the parousia is near, and
begins and ends with assurances that the ghastly visions which
form most of its substance concern "the things which must
shortly come to pass". Jesus will come soon (3:11; 22:20), on the
clouds (1:7) at the final judgement. Mark, the earliest of the four
gospels, makes Jesus give the assurance (at 9:1) that at least
"some" of his auditors will survive "till they see the kingdom of
God come with power" (Matthew changes this to "see the Son of
man coming in his kingdom", 16:28, thus elevating Jesus's status
by assigning the kingdom to him directly, not to God). This was a
loose or floating saying to which Mark has given a specific context; for he introduces it with the words "And he said unto them"
(which detach it from the speech recorded in the previous verses)
and follows it immediately with narrative material. Grässer and
others regard the logion as a reassurance, spoken originally by an
early Christian prophet addressing a community worried because
the parousia had not occurred.[47]

The extended discourse which comprises Mark's chapter 13
reiterates that "this generation shall not pass away until all these

things be accomplished", and 'these things' include "the Son of man coming in clouds with great power and glory" (13:26 and 30). Nevertheless, recourse is made in this chapter to the device, common in Jewish apocalyptic, of alleging that all manner of cataclysmic and other events must precede the end, which therefore is not to be expected quite so soon: there will be false prophets, wars and rumours of wars, but even so, the end will not follow them immediately (13:7). Earthquakes and famines will signal only "the beginning of the travail", for "first the gospel must be preached unto all the nations" (verses 8 and 10). This latter condition surely constitutes a considerable postponement; yet Mark makes Jesus conclude the discourse with injunctions to be continuously watchful so as not to be caught unawares by the Lord's coming (verses 33–37), while at the same time not to be presumptuous by demanding a precise dating of it (verse 32).

I discussed this whole discourse in detail in *HEJ*, chapter 4, where I also showed that Matthew added to it considerably, while Luke rewrote it substantially so as to align it with his own conceptions and his own situation. Throughout his gospel, Luke alternates between the standpoint that the parousia and its attendant circumstances will come soon, and the opposite position, that it will be delayed. On the one hand God will avenge his elect speedily—an assurance given in a context referring to the coming of the Son of man (18:8)—and "this generation shall not pass away until all things be accomplished" (21:32); on the other hand, the belief that "the kingdom of God was immediately to appear" (19:11) is corrected by a parable where Jesus teaches that he must first go far away to receive the kingdom and will be absent for a considerable time. S.G. Wilson has shown that both standpoints are represented in numerous passages in this gospel. We modern readers with our printed texts carefully divided into numbered chapters and verses find it easy to compare different stories in a gospel and to see whether they are consistent. For an evangelist it sufficed to make some point in a given narrative without bothering whether this conflicted with a different point made in another section. Wilson explains the clash in question by pointing to the pastoral situations with which the evangelist was faced. The delay of the parousia had obviously provoked two extremes: on the one hand a fervent renewal of apocalypticism, with false Messiahs coming forward, and, on the other, scepticism as to whether the parousia would ever occur at all. In his gospel, Luke had to combat both these tendencies, but it is noticeable that in Acts he never suggests that the kingdom is imminent: "The time-scheme of Acts allows for a hiatus between the Resurrection and the Parousia in which the Church can exist and grow."[48]

In the fourth gospel the theme of the coming of the kingdom, so characteristic of the other three, has been almost completely dropped: Jesus brushes aside Martha's suggestion that her deceased brother Lazarus will "rise again in the resurrection at the last day." He retorts: "I am the resurrection and the life: he that believeth on me, though he die, yet shall he live: and whosoever liveth and believeth on me shall never die" (Jn. 11:24–26). C.H. Dodd allows that here "the evangelist appears to be explicitly contrasting the popular eschatology of Judaisism and primitive Christianity with the doctrine which he wishes to propound".[49] Earlier in this gospel, Jesus says: "The hour cometh, and now is, when the dead shall hear the voice of the Son of God; and they that hear shall live" (Jn. 5:25). The 'hour' of judgement is future from the standpoint ascribed here to Jesus, the speaker, but present from that of the evangelist. Some commentators hold that it was because not all Christians were satisfied with this revision of the older doctrine that a final editor of the gospel added verses 28–29 in order to reaffirm the older view: "The hour cometh in which all that are in the tombs shall hear his voice, and shall come forth; they that have done good unto the resurrection of life; and they that have done ill unto the resurrection of judgement."[50] Those who deny that these verses were added later hold that, although John "shows a decisive shift away from the future reference", he does not abrogate it altogether (Lindars, *John*, 1990, p. 71).

Today the whole doctrine is what the two Hanson brothers call "an embarrassment to intelligent Christians". They are unimpressed by the reassurance of 2 Peter 3:8–9 that "one day is with the Lord as a thousand years", and that the delay is designed to give sufficient opportunity for repentance; and so they declare that "an event that has been just round the corner for a thousand years is a non-event."[51] Many Christian scholars, says E.P. Sanders (*Historical Jesus*, p. 178) would like to see the relevant passages vanish from the texts.

v. Agreements and Discrepancies between the Synoptic Gospels

In an appendix in his *The Law* (p. 123), Montgomery quotes an apologist who says that, if the accounts in different gospels of the same transactions were in strict verbal conformity with each other, then "the argument against their credibility would be much stronger", for their testimony would then be exposed as collusive. But any synopsis, where parallel passages are set out in adjacent columns, will show that the first three of the four canonical gospels have passages which are identical, down to the same Greek particles. For instance, Matthew's account, in the material it shares with Mark, is abbreviated and Mark's 11,078 words are represented by 8,555; yet of these 4,230 are identical both in form and in sequence. Goulder gives these figures and adds that the enormous number of identical phrases is not to be explained as being due to the community's good memory of Jesus's teaching, as more than half of such phrases are in the narrative, not the words of Jesus.[52] Goulder and others have also found it significant that the individual pericopes occur very largely in the same order in the synoptics. Wenham (*Redating*, p. 7) notes that within the Galilean ministry there are numerous events and teachings which have no obvious logical or chronological sequence, yet are given in the same order in all three synoptics. As a further example he mentions Mk. 6:14–16:8 and Matthew chapters 14 to 28. Here are seventy items, all in order (except for a minor difference in the way the cleansing of the temple and the cursing of the fig tree are related), "and this in spite of various omissions or additions by one or other evangelist." It is difficult to believe that such correspondence could have arisen without a literary connection— without, that is, the one writer drawing on the work of the other or on a common source. Wenham's remarks carry particular weight because he is anxious to *minimize* the literary dependence of one evangelist upon another, and to argue that each one "writes in the way he habitually teaches" (p. xxi). But even he does not feel able to regard the synoptics as independent editions of primitive oral material.

Most scholars, then, agree that the evangelist who wrote second in order of the three made use of the work of the first, and that the third used the work of one or both of his predecessors. The most commonly accepted order puts Mark first, with Matthew and Luke, unknown to each other, taking his gospel as a source. Mason (*Josephus*, pp. 128f) illustrates how probable it is that Matthew depended on Mark by quoting and commenting on the following two passages (I have italicized the words which are different in the two):

Mk. 14:48–54	*Mt. 26:55–58*
Have you come out to arrest me with swords and clubs, as if against a robber? Day after day *I was with you* in the temple teaching, and you did not arrest me! *But* in order that the scriptures might be fulfilled.	Have you come out to arrest me with swords and clubs, as if against a robber? Day after day I *sat* in the temple teaching, and you did not arrest me! *Now all this happened* in order that the scriptures might be fulfilled.
And leaving him, *they* all fled.	*Then* all *the disciples*, leaving him, fled.
And a certain young man was following him, wearing only a linen cloth over his naked body. And they seize him, but, abandoning the linen cloth, he fled naked.	
And they led Jesus off to the high priest, *and all the chief priests and* the elders, *and* the scribes assembled. *And* Peter, from a distance, *followed* him.	*Now those who had seized him* led Jesus off to *Caiaphas* the high priest, *where* the scribes *and* the elders *had gathered*. But Peter *was following* him from a distance.

Mason notes that there is agreement here in sentence structure, vocabulary ('as if against a robber', 'day after day', 'led Jesus off'), word order, and in the weaving together of different plots (Jesus with the high priest, Peter in the courtyard). The differences, he adds, are usually explained as Matthew's improvements: viz. other conjunctions to replace Mark's monotonous 'and'; making

Mark's phrase about the fulfilment of scriptures into a complete sentence; naming the high priest; and omitting the strange and seemingly irrelevant story of the naked young man who is never again mentioned.

Alternative hypotheses (for example that Mark abbreviated the other two synoptics) seem fraught with very serious difficulties, although it must be admitted that the priority of Mark does not dispose of all the relevant problems. Brown is surely right to say that "in all probability the first-century composition of the Gospels was not simple", and that our chances of determining it exactly "are so slim that it is better to adopt a simpler overall approach that solves most of the difficulties and leaves some minor difficulties unsolved." On this basis, he accepts Marcan priority, but with the modification that Matthew and Luke were influenced to some extent also by oral tradition. He also defends the majority view that neither Matthew nor Luke knew the work of the other (*Death*, pp. 42–45). There are some 230 verses common (verbatim or nearly so) to the two that are not found in Mark; they place this shared non-Marcan material in entirely different contexts, and this is one reason why it is unlikely that the one took it from the other and so knew the other. Luke's dependence on Matthew is urged by some scholars, but there are strong reasons against it (such as his failure to reproduce any of the material special to Matthew in his passion narrative). If, then, the common non-Marcan 230 verses were not taken from the one by the other, they must derive from a common non-Marcan Greek source not now extant and known as Q (German Quelle = source). They consist mainly of sayings of Jesus, and so Q is known alternatively as the 'sayings source'. In sum, the majority view is that Matthew and Luke each independently used two sources, Mark and Q (each supplementing them with a certain amount of material that is not shared). Johnson claims, I think justly, that this 'two-document hypothesis' provides a more satisfactory solution of most of the problems than does any alternative.[53] But absolutely decisive evidence is not forthcoming, hence the continuing endless discussion of the whole issue makes arid reading.[54]

What is, however, clear, is that there is a literary relationship between the three synoptics, so that they cannot be called independent accounts, let alone from eyewitnesses. Montgomery cannot deny this literary relationship, but maintains that "eyewitnesses . . . often use supplementary sources by others when they write up what they have seen." But if Matthew and Luke drew on Mark, and additionally on Q, then most of their material, and not mere supplementation, depended on previous written sources; and a major literary relationship between all three synoptics remains even if one eliminates Q by claiming that Luke drew directly from Matthew, or even if one were to suppose that Matthew was the first of the three and was then adapted by Mark and by Luke.

A synopsis not only shows how many passages are closely paralleled sometimes in two of the synoptics, sometimes in all three, but also how often one deliberately modifies or deletes statements in his source so as to make it more acceptable to him. Manipulation of the idea that Jesus's death atoned for our sins and so saved us affords an example. This idea, positively trumpeted out in early epistles,[55] is never explicitly stated by Mark, although at two points he mentions benefits of the death without specifying them; "the Son of man came not to be ministered unto, but to minister and to give his life a ransom for many" (10:45); and "this is my blood of the covenant, which is shed for many" (14:24). Matthew adds to this latter logion "unto remission of sins" (26:28)—words which he has studiously deleted from Mark's account of John the Baptist's activities (Mk. 1:4) so as to insert them here, as appropriate to Jesus's death rather than to the Baptist's preaching (cf. *WWJ*, p. 90). If Matthew thus stressed the atonement, Luke took the opposite course. He seemed unwilling to allow any suggestion that forgiveness of sins depends on the cross, and so the logion of Mk. 10:45 is absent from his version of the incident (Lk. 22:24–27) in which Mark placed it. And Jesus's reference at the Last Supper to his blood being "shed for many" is absent from a sufficient number of ancient manuscripts of Luke's version of the eucharistic words (22:19ff) to justify the conclusion that it was added by a later hand so as to bring Luke here into line with Mark and Matthew (see above, p. 34).

The different ways in which Luke and Matthew write of Peter also betray deliberate manipulation of Marcan material. We saw above (p. 76) that in Mark Peter was unwilling to believe Jesus's plain speaking about his forthcoming death and resurrection, and that Jesus there turned on him and called him "Satan" for this unwillingness. Luke adapts Mk. 8:31–33 so as to omit both this unwillingness and the rebuke earned by it, and—partly by means of other omissions—produces a much more favourable overall portrait of Peter. Matthew achieves the same result by expanding Mark instead of making such cuts. In Matthew, Peter 'confesses' Jesus not only as "the Christ", as in Mark, but also as "the Son of the living God" (16:16). Jesus responds with a solemn blessing ("Blessed art thou, Simon Bar-Jonah: for flesh and blood hath not revealed it unto thee, but my father which is in heaven".) The purpose of both Mark and Matthew with Peter's 'confession' is to convince the reader that the Galilean preacher and the risen Jesus preached by the Christian community are one and the same, that the former already possessed the exalted status of the latter. But Matthew both labours the point and elevates Peter by means of these additions to Mark, which are followed by more added material, namely promises (unknown to the other gospels) that Peter will be the rock of the church and will hold the keys of the kingdom (16:17–19). All this does much to take the sting from the reproachful "get thee behind me, Satan" which follows at verse 23 and which has been allowed to stand from Mark. Nevertheless, by not adopting Luke's method of deleting such negative Marcan references, Matthew has produced what has been called "a somewhat disconcerting inconsistency" in his portrait of Peter.[56] He even shows Peter negatively in one of his expansions, namely of Mk. 6:45–52, where Jesus walks on the water. Matthew makes Peter at first do the same, but then sink down and be chided by Jesus for his want of faith (Mt. 14:28–31, unparalleled). Here the evangelist's motive is not to enhance Peter's status, but to inculcate the power of faith.

The same willingness to adapt source material is apparent in non-Marcan passages common to Matthew and Luke. These, as I have just said, either came from a common source (Q), or were taken by the one evangelist from the other. Did Jesus say "blessed are ye poor" (Lk. 6:20) or "blessed are the poor *in spirit*" (Mt. 5:3); "blessed are ye that hunger" (Lk. 6:21) or "blessed are they that

hunger and thirst *after righteousness*" (Mt. 5:6)? If he said one or
the other, no one can now decide which. The wording in Luke is
what one would expect from a writer one of whose favourite
themes is the reversal of fortunes in the hereafter: those who are
deprived in this life will be compensated in the next. This is the
lesson of his parable of Lazarus and Dives (16:25)—a parable
given only in his gospel. The wording in Matthew is likewise what
one expects from a writer for whom 'righteousness' is a key word,
and who makes Jesus tell his disciples that they will not enter the
kingdom of heaven unless their righteousness exceeds that of the
scribes and Pharisees (5:20, likewise unparalleled). It seems, then,
that the relevant beatitudes give the voices of the evangelists
rather than that of Jesus.

A more striking discrepancy concerns the accounts in the synoptics of Jesus's resurrection appearances to his disciples.
Matthew, following hints by Mark, sites in Galilee the one appearance to them that he records: the risen one has instructed the
women at the empty tomb to tell the disciples to go to Galilee in
order to see him (28:10). They do this, and his appearance to
them there concludes the gospel. In Luke, however, he appears to
them on Easter day in Jerusalem and nearby on the Emmaus
road (eighty miles from Galilee) and tells them to stay in the city
"until ye be clothed with power from on high" (24:49. Acts 2:1–4
represents this as happening at Pentecost, some fifty days later).
They obey, and were "continually in the temple" (24:53). Luke has
very pointedly changed what is said in Mark so as to site these
appearances in the city. (Luke omits Mk. 14:28, "after I am raised
up I will go before you into Galilee"; and he replaces Mk. 16:7,
"he goeth before you into Galilee" with a message which deletes
any such suggestion.)

Montgomery harmonized the accounts by arguing that the
risen Jesus could have moved from Galilee to Jerusalem in a
series of appearances spread, according to Acts 1:3, over forty
days. This hypothesis does not reconcile the movements of the
disciples—immediately to Galilee in Matthew, and not beyond
Jerusalem and its environs in Luke. All the forty-day appearances
of Acts are sited in Jerusalem (1:4). Nor does Montgomery's pro-
posal account for Luke's deliberate alteration of the Marcan mate-

rial, effected so as to bring it into line with a theological principle of great importance to him, namely that Christianity had not broken lightly or readily from its Jewish foundation: it is for this reason that he insists that it was "beginning from Jerusalem" that the Christian mission went forward to "all the nations" (Lk. 24:47), so that the disciples tarried there and did not return to Galilee.

As Luke and Acts are by the same author, one naturally expects them to agree. But they do not always do so: we saw (above, p. 94) how (and why) Acts drops any suggestion that Jesus's second coming is imminent. For the present context it is relevant to note that only Acts, no other canonical book, makes the appearances of the risen Jesus continue for forty days, and that this actually contradicts what is said in Luke, which ends with Jesus leading his disciples on Easter day, after numerous appearances to them, from Jerusalem to the neighbouring locality of Bethany, where he solemnly blesses them with uplifted hands before "he parted from them and was carried up into heaven" (24:51)—on that same day. *The New Bible Commentary Revised* concedes that, if Luke is here taken literally, then "the resurrection and ascension both occurred on Easter Sunday."[57] If one were bent on harmonizing the accounts, one might suppose that the ascension took place twice, that having "parted" from his disciples on Easter day in all solemnity, Jesus returned from heaven, spent forty days with them and then ascended again. It is apropos of exegesis of this kind that James Barr, who was Professor of Hebrew at Oxford, characterized "harmonization through the production of multiple events" as "the most thoroughly laughable of all devices of interpretation. . . . There is no element in the entire fundamentalist approach to the Bible that is more likely to draw upon itself ridicule and derision from without and a deep sense of absurdity from even within the ranks of the faithful."[58] Even the *New Bible Commentary Revised* shrinks from this solution to the discrepancy in question (although, as we shall see, it resorts to it in order to resolve others), and disposes of the problem by taking only Acts' account literally and by regarding Luke's as telescoped and imprecise. As Barr says (p. 60), if harmonization is one tool of conservative apologists, vagueness is another. It is surely more likely that, by the time Acts was written, the author had come to think that, while a brief series of appearances on a single day might be dismissed by sceptics as hallucinations, a sojourn of forty days, during which "many proofs" were presented (1:3), was more substantial. The same verse records that during these forty days Jesus also taught the apostles "the things concerning the kingdom of God"; and a recent study has concluded that this protracted period is needed in Acts "not to allow Jesus enough time to make appearances, but to assure the reader that the disciples are 'fully instructed'."[59]

Even some Catholic commentators are now more liberal than conservative protestants who will not allow that the way a canonical writer represents events is controlled by his theological message. Meier, for instance, concedes that the four gospels are not only "shot through and through with the Easter faith of the early Church", but also "ordered according to various theological programs" (*Marginal*, p. 141). The evidence I have given in this section of this chapter shows that, even when a story has been put into written form in a gospel, it could still subsequently be remodelled; and such changes must surely have been preceded by others, when the tradition was still oral, which were equally drastic, and of which no record survives.

vi. The Fourth Gospel in Relation to the Others

A. OVERALL DIFFERENCES

Whereas the synoptics have long passages in common, no passage of any length in the fourth gospel is verbally identical with anything in them. It has none of their parables, no exorcisms, no suggestion that Jesus associated with 'tax-collectors and sinners', no institution of the eucharist at the Last Supper, very little eschatology (the doctrine of a future judgement is very much played down), different miracles and entirely different discourses comprising whole chapters in which Jesus expatiates on his own importance and his closeness to "the Father". The following is but a brief extract from one of them:

> The Son can do nothing of himself, but what he seeth the Father
> doing: for what things soever he doeth, these the Son also doeth in
> like manner. For the Father loveth the Son and sheweth him all
> things that himself doeth; and greater works than these will he shew
> him, that ye may marvel. For as the Father raiseth the dead and
> quickeneth them, even so the Son also quickeneth whom he will. For
> neither doth the Father judge any man, but he hath given all judge-
> ment unto the Son; that all may honour the Son even as they honour
> the Father. He that honoureth not the Son honoureth not the Father
> which sent him . . . (Jn. 5:19–23)

Not surprisingly, the gospel that has Jesus speak in this fashion
does not record anything that might be understood as depressing
his dignity; hence it has no Temptation of him, no Gethsemane
agony, makes him carry his own cross, and replaces the final cry
of dereliction attributed to him by Mark with a triumphant "It is
accomplished." Surprisingly, however, although very concerned to
demonstrate Jesus's divine glory, this fourth gospel makes no
mention of the Transfiguration (recorded in all three synoptics).
And whereas Mark gives Galilee in the north (plus a few places
even further north and to the east) as the setting of all Jesus's
ministry, except for his journey to Judea in the south in chapter
10 which leads in to his final days in Jerusalem, John locates
most of the ministry in Judea, and makes Jesus active predominantly in the urban setting of Jerusalem, not in the synoptic rural
locations.[60]

Meier justly notes that "the Johannine presentation of Jesus's
ministry is just too massively different to be derived from the
Synoptics", and was dependent on "a stream of tradition similar to, but independent of them" (*Marginal*, p. 44). This can be
seen when John has material that is not unique to him, but is
fashioned very differently from the corresponding synoptic
accounts.[61]

Montgomery's position is that, unless it is possible to point to
actual contradictions between John and the synoptics, they can be
regarded as complementing each other. From this premiss
we should have to suppose that—as E.P. Sanders puts it apropos
of the discrepancies in the teachings—"Jesus spent his short
ministry teaching in two such completely different ways, convey-

ing such different contents, and that there were simply two traditions, each going back to Jesus, one transmitting 50 per cent of
what he said and another one the other 50 per cent, with almost
no overlaps". Hence, he adds, scholars have almost unanimously
concluded that the fourth gospel "represents an advanced theological development, in which meditations on the person and work of
Christ are presented in the first person, as if Jesus said them" (*Historical Jesus*, pp. 70–71). In other words, John makes Jesus preach
a full-blown Christology. It includes such narrow sectarian statements as "I am the way and the truth and the life: no one cometh
unto the Father but by me" (14:6)—for me a recipe for intolerance,
but for Montgomery, who quoted it at the debate, a revelation
which we ignore at our peril. For his part, he finds it "painful" to
hear me "reiterate the old saw" that John's gospel conflicts radically with the others. He refers me to "Theodor Zahn's thorough
discussion of its apostolic authorship early in this century", which
"eventually convinced such contemporary radicals as J.A.T. ('Honest to God') Robinson." It appears, then, that, in spite of the moratorium on the use of theologians, they are allowed to do service if
they reach what are, for Montgomery, the right conclusions. Moreover, the issue raised by me here is not the apostolic authorship of
John but its compatibility with the synoptics. Zahn embraces both
positions, but Robinson affirms the apostolic authorship without
claiming complete compatibility with the synoptics. On the contrary, he thinks that in many instances John had more reliable
information than they. Zahn harmonized all four gospels by making Jesus do at one time what he is said to do in John, and at
another what the synoptics have him do. Additionally, he supposed that John was writing for people familiar with the synoptics, who would be able, in their minds, to supplement his account
with theirs.[62] Robinson does not impute knowledge of the synoptics to John. He takes the events of John's first three chapters,
which take place in Judea, as evidence of an early phase in Jesus's
ministry of which the synoptics know nothing. On this basis he
finds John's placing of the cleansing of the temple during this early
phase "far more convincing" than the synoptics' placing of it at the
end. They, he says, had to put it there because they represent Jesus
as in Jerusalem only at the end of his life, and he quite clearly

implies that they were wrong to do so.[63] He does not suppose, (as does Montgomery) that both are here correct, and that there were two occasions of cleansing.

What Robinson says about the authorship of John is not easy to reconcile with its admitted dependence on tradition. In claiming "priority" for it, he does not mean that it was completed before the synoptics, but that it has greater historical worth. He recognizes that its material "was developed over a period in various stages", so that the gospel is the end product of a process. It is presumably for this reason that its apostolic authorship is not "a hypothesis without any difficulties". Yet he accepts this hypothesis as "the one least open to objection", and so holds that the author "was his own tradition and stood in an internal rather than external relation to it" (pp. 21, 118). Lindars has commented that this conservative conclusion "has not won agreement from the majority of scholars and is unlikely to do so" (*John*, 1990, p. 51).

As for the characterization of Robinson as a "radical" who "eventually" came round to orthodoxy, it is true that his *Honest to God* did purport to take a 'radical' stance, but there is what one might call a certain sleight-of-speech in the way he used the term. As John Bowden has pointed out, "Robinson's 'honesty' in asking radical questions was bound up with another, more hidden, agenda which contained some very conservative items indeed. This was brilliantly disguised by his interpretation of the word 'radical'", which he "always related to its derivation, 'going to the roots', and his roots were thoroughly clerical, Anglican and quite conservatively Biblical" ('Nerve', p. 77). They are clearly visible even in his *Honest to God,* and of course in his *Redating the New Testament,* both of which I have discussed elsewhere.[64] A clerical reviewer of the latter maintained, justly, that it fights "a rearguard action against the change in emphasis of British scholarship which has come about in Robinson's lifetime, which he has never come to terms with, which has left him stranded in the company of the conservative Evangelicals."[65]

B. JESUS AND THE TEMPLE

Montgomery, then, believes that the accounts can be reconciled. He obviously supposes that John could assume that his readers were familiar with the synoptics, and so regarded it as unnecessary to include a good deal of what they record, but set out rather to complement them. Imbert, to whose book he accords the highest praise (see above, p. 70) gives this as the consensus of modern scholarship (p. 26). It may have been until the 1930s, but Lindars (among many others) has noted that it "cannot now be accepted in the face of the considerable evidence that John did not know the Synoptics in the form in which we have them. We can only be sure that he knew such items of the tradition as he actually mentions."[66] If, however, we follow Imbert's 'consensus', then we can argue that, although John records a cleansing of the temple by Jesus at the beginning of his ministry, while the synoptics mention such a cleansing only at the end of it, we are not dealing here with different settings given to a single unique incident: John is recording an event that had passed unnoticed in the synoptics, while deeming it unnecessary to mention a similar event which they placed later in Jesus's career. Jesus in fact—so Montgomery said at the debate—cleansed the temple twice. The cleansing is a major event in his ministry, and the fourth gospel, on which conservatives rely heavily for authentication of his divine status, would be compromised by any admission that it is here at odds with the other three. Hence harmonization, by positing two occasions, is the preferred solution of conservative commentators to the discrepancy[67]—surely, says Lindars, "a counsel of despair" (John, 1990, p. 10). Let us see whether it is feasible.

That a great deal in John is unique to him can be seen at once from Part II of Sparks's synopsis.[68] The pericope of the cleansing is the first to show substantial overlap with traditions underlying the synoptics. The material placed before it is either substantially deviant from what we find in them (John the Baptist's assessment of himself and his relation to Jesus, and the call of the first disciples) or altogether unrepresented in them (the substance of the Prologue, the call to discipleship of Philip and Nathanael—the former figures in the synoptics only in their lists of the twelve, and the latter is not mentioned in them at all—and the marriage feast of Cana, where Jesus turns a vast amount of water into wine). The cleansing is followed in John with more material absent from the synoptics (Jesus's dialogues with Nicodemus, who is unmentioned in them, with a Samaritan woman and with his disciples), so that it stands out as an isolated block of contact with them. All four accounts place the cleansing immediately before a Passover, and represent it as consisting of interference by Jesus (with varying acts and degrees of violence) with what went on in the temple at such a time. Also, in all four Jesus speaks words (not identical but to a certain extent similar in John and the synoptics) which explain and justify his behaviour; and he is finally questioned by opponents as to whether he has the authority to act as he does. This amount of agreement certainly suggests different versions of a single incident.

Mark's version is as follows:

> And he entered into the temple, and began to cast out them that sold and them that bought in the temple, and overthrew the tables of the money-changers and the seats of them that sold the doves; and he would not suffer that any man should carry a vessel through the temple. And he taught and said unto them, Is it not written, My house shall be called a house of prayer for all the nations? but ye have made it a den of robbers. (11:15–17)

I have elsewhere (*DJE*, pp. 163f) noted problems raised by this 'demo': the practices condemned here as robbery were in fact unobjectionable, as is admitted by commentators; the OT allusions on which the condemnation is based are not to the point, while the whole incident could readily have been constructed as 'fulfilment' of OT material; and, finally, Jesus, although single-handed, manages to eject both buyers and sellers and control the whole floor space. (John's account is less implausible in this regard: only sheep and oxen are driven out (2:15), and nothing is said about controlling the floor.) Here I need add only that Mark separates the chief priests' question "By what authority doest thou these things?" (11:28) from the cleansing by noting, immediately after the passage quoted above, that the fig tree (which Jesus had cursed just before this passage) had in the meantime withered, and by then adding sayings from Jesus about the efficacy of faith and forgiveness (11:20–25; some mss. add a further saying

on forgiveness as verse 26). Only then do the chief priests ask
their question, but on a later occasion, when Jesus was again in
Jerusalem and "walking in the temple" (verse 27). This question
must nevertheless constitute a challenge to him to justify the
cleansing (as in John's account, 2:18), not his innocuous walking
about in the temple.

Luke seems not to have liked the violence which, according to
Mark, went with Jesus's behaviour, and eliminates most of it,
passing directly from Mark's "he entered into the temple and
began to cast out them that sold" to Jesus's statement "My house
shall be a house of prayer" (Lk. 19:45–46). Luke also deletes the
incidents of the cursing and withering of the tree, and Jesus's pronouncements on faith and forgiveness prompted by its withering.
Perhaps he felt that Jesus is made ridiculous by cursing it for not
producing fruit when, as Mark had expressly noted, "it was not
the season of figs" (11:13).[69] These deletions mean that, if Luke
were then to return at once to the Marcan sequence, the priests'
question about Jesus's authority would be so close to the cleansing as to seem to have been occasioned by it, as in John and, as
we saw, really also in Mark. Luke avoids this, probably because
he thought that even the residual violence in his version of the
cleansing made this action an inappropriate way for Jesus's
authority to be demonstrated. He avoids the linkage by inserting:
"And he was teaching daily in the temple" (verse 47, unparalleled), so that the priests' question becomes an inquiry as to with
what authority he teaches (20:1–2).

Mark and Luke agree in representing the cleansing and the
teaching accompanying it (Mark) or following it (Luke) as giving
the Jewish authorities their motive for seeking to kill Jesus, so
that the incident preludes the passion narratives. John, however,
has decided to make Jesus's raising of Lazarus from the dead
(unknown to the synoptics) the principal reason for the hostility
to Jesus, and a council of Pharisees and chief priests decides to
kill him immediately after this event (11:47ff). That the Pharisees
are involved in the decisive resolution contrasts with the synoptic
accounts, where the Sanhedrin and its groupings are mentioned
in the passion narratives but not the Pharisees. (It has repeatedly
struck commentators that throughout John the Pharisees appear

more as an official body than as a party.) John's Pharisees are then so worried by the people's interest in Lazarus restored to life that they determine to kill him too (12:10–11). If, then, the raising of Lazarus and not the cleansing of the temple is to be the reason for the plot against Jesus, there is an obvious motive for making the former a prelude to the passion narrative, and for not placing the latter in that position (or removing it from it if that was where John found it in his source material).

John's version of the cleansing has a further feature which, in the synoptics, is associated with their passion narratives, namely a saying about the destruction of the temple (or its innermost sanctuary).[70] In Mark, at Jesus's Sanhedrin trial,

> There stood up certain and bare false witness against him, saying, We heard him say, I will destroy this temple that is made with hands and in three days I will build another, made without hands. And not even so did their witness agree together. (14:57–59).

This is a prophecy about a new temple, different from the old one, in a new Jerusalem. In a section of the Book of Enoch, headed in R.H. Charles's edition 'The New Jerusalem', we read:

> I saw till the Lord of the sheep brought a new house, greater and loftier than that first, and set it up in the place of the first which had been folded up; all its pillars were new, and its ornaments were new and larger than those of the first, the old one which He had taken away, and all the sheep were within it (1 Enoch 90:29).

This Jewish apocalypse obviously had some influence on early Christianity (it is actually quoted in the epistle of Jude), and its ideas were reworked and adapted. Speculation about the New Jerusalem went different ways. According to Revelation 21:22 it would have no temple at all. Paul had said that Christians constitute the temple of God (for example at 2 Corinthians 6:16), and the Dead Sea sectarians thought of their own community as the house which will be built by God's hands at the end of days, into which no ungodly person will enter, and where Yahweh will reign for ever.[71]

Perhaps Mark makes the logion "I will destroy this temple" one that is falsely ascribed to Jesus because, had he really said this, the Jews would have had a valid case against him. Matthew changes the logion from a threat to a claim of power: "This man said, I am able to destroy the temple of God and to build it in three days." This is represented as the witness of "two" (not of "some"), and they are not alleged (as are the "some" in Mark) not to agree that Jesus said what they claim he said. Matthew will have known from Deuteronomy 17:6 that, in capital charges, the consistent testimony of "two or three" (not of one) is acceptable as establishing the true facts. His only reference to false witness is placed in the preceding verses, whereas the "two" produce their unitary testimony "afterward" (26:60–61). By means of these changes, he has made the logion into something that, he maintains, Jesus did actually say, and which expresses what the evangelist himself accepted as true Christology. He has adapted other Marcan passages so as to stress Jesus's power.[72]

Luke tones down the Marcan logion in a different way, reserving all mention of it for Acts 6:14, and even there making it very oblique: false witnesses say that Stephen said that Jesus would "destroy this place."

John's way of making the saying innocuous is to represent it as a prophecy by Jesus of his own resurrection:

> Destroy this temple and in three days I will raise it up. The Jews therefore said, Forty and six years was this temple in building, and wilt thou raise it up in three days? But he spake of the temple of his body. When therefore he was raised from the dead, his disciples remembered that he spake this; and they believed the Scripture and the word which Jesus had said. (2:19–22).

To make Jesus's audience misunderstand his words (by construing them as meaning what they obviously seem to suggest) is what Lindars calls one of John's "favourite tricks" (*John*, 1972, p. 53), not however played in the other gospels. It serves to bring out how completely "the world" fails to understand him.

In sum, we have in John three elements—a cleansing of the temple, a question as to Jesus's authority and a statement about destroying the temple—put together as one early incident in his ministry. In the synoptics, they are not all together, and they are all given in association with the Passion. There are significant differences here between the synoptics themselves, as well as between them and John. It seems reasonable to conclude that what we have here, as so often elsewhere in the NT,[73] are variants and reworkings of similar underlying traditions, not an authentic record of separate historical events.

C. THE DATE OF THE CRUCIFIXION

If simple harmonizing is difficult in this case, it is even harder with the passion narratives. For instance, Jesus cannot have been crucified twice, although the synoptics and John put his crucifixion on different days. In John, the Jews have still to eat the passover meal when they bring Jesus to Pilate (18:28), whereas in the synoptics it has already been eaten before his arrest. All four gospels are anxious, as was Paul (1 Corinthians 5:7), to represent the Jewish Passover as obsolete and as replaced by Jesus's sacrifice. Mark does this by representing Jesus's Last Supper with his disciples as a passover meal (14:12–16) where the words he speaks with reference to the bread and wine give his body and blood ("shed for many", 14:24) the place normally accorded to the passover lamb sacrificed in the temple. For John, however, Jesus's sacrifice replaces the Passover in that he dies at "the preparation for the Passover" (19:14, 31), when the lambs were being slaughtered in the temple. This makes him the true paschal sacrifice, "the lamb of God which taketh away the sin of the world" (1:29); and he dies, as do the paschal lambs, without a bone being broken (19:36; compare Exodus 12:46 and Numbers 9:12). As, then, the passover meal can follow only after his death, his final meal with his disciples is an informal one, whereas in the synoptics it is quite definitely the passover meal, with his arrest, trials before the Sanhedrin and before Pilate still to come before his crucifixion. In sum, "the paschal meal for the Synoptics was on Thursday evening and Jesus died in the daytime after it; for John it was on Friday evening and Jesus died in the daytime before it" (Brown, *Death*, p. 1352). The proceedings at the final meal in John (chapter 13) also differ very substantially from the synoptic representations. Although in all four accounts Jesus prophesies that Judas will betray him, in John there is no "take, eat" formula, indeed no mention of bread or wine; Jesus acts in a way unknown to the synoptics, both by what he does (washing his disciples' feet) and by most of what he says. The Supper discourses, unique to John, extend through the following chapters.

To combine such divergent accounts as records of a single occasion would be implausible enough; but a difference in dates is an actual contradiction. Hence Annie Jaubert's attempt to eliminate it has been widely welcomed in conservative circles (for instance by Imbert, pp. 47–55). She mentions patristic hints that in NT times some quarters reckoned the date of the Passover differently from the official Jerusalem reckoning, and she shows that the Essene sectarians who wrote the Dead Sea Scrolls appear to have followed the calendar of the book of Jubilees, which makes Passover fall on a Wednesday, so that the meal is eaten on Tuesday night. She supposes that Jesus and his disciples used this calendar, so that the Last Supper was, as in the synoptics, a genuine passover meal, but on the Tuesday of passion week, while the death on Friday was, in John's account, the eve of the official Passover. This leaves Wednesday and Thursday for the trial and verdict, so that there is no longer any need to crowd the arrest, Sanhedrin trial, appearance before Pilate and crucifixion into an impossibly short time between a Thursday night supper and Friday. Such haste would, additionally, have been in breach of the requirements of the Mishnaic law—that the Jewish court had to sit in daytime, on two consecutive days, and with the hearing of the witnesses in private—if these stipulations were in fact already in force ca. A.D. 30.[74] Imbert, basing himself on Jaubert's reconstructions, holds that the synoptic gospels were written by A.D. 70, but the fourth gospel some three decades later; that by then only the official calendar survived, and the tradition that Jesus celebrated an earlier Passover had been completely forgotten. Hence in this gospel "all Jesus's activities are presented by John as conforming to the rhythm of the official Jewish feasts, the only ones then in use" (*op. cit.* in note 10 to this chapter, p. 50). Brown, who notes "the amount of learned ingenuity that has gone into the defence of the Essene-calendar hypothesis", asks appositely:

> What evidence is there that Jesus at any other time in his life followed anything other than the official calendar? Calendric adherence was a matter of deep religious identity; no accusation against Jesus

by his enemies accuses him of Essene sympathies or of calendric irregularities. What would prompt Jesus and his disciples to depart so seriously from the official calendar in this instance? Where did they get the lamb for Passover, days before the official time for slaughtering? (*Death*, p. 1368)

Jaubert's thesis has been equally severely criticized by other Catholic scholars.[75] Fitzmyer finds that her harmonization of synoptic and Johannine material "betrays a fundamentalist concern."[76] On the Anglican side, Lindars comments that her theory makes everything fit

> except for one vital factor: John himself is completely ignorant of this scheme. He still has the trials during the night and early morning, and the death of Jesus on the same day. It is difficult to eradicate the impression that the death of Jesus on the eve of the Passover is a purely Johannine invention, dictated by his theological interests, regardless of the traditions which he was actually handling. (*John*, 1972, p. 446)

vii. Discrepancies, Doubts, and Damnation

It will be clear from this whole discussion that the evangelists are quite capable of manipulating their sources. Theologians speak, perhaps a little shamefacedly, of their 'editing' of earlier material. No wonder Montgomery shuns them (or at any rate most of them). The divergence between the gospels is particularly crass in the case of birth and infancy stories of Matthew and Luke and the resurrection narratives of all four. Apropos of the latter Montgomery appealed at the debate to what Frank Morison (a lawyer, of course) has to say in his popular *Who Moved the Stone?* (2nd edition, London, 1953), where much is made of the guard which according to Matthew (and only according to him) was placed on Jesus's tomb by the Jewish authorities. To accommodate this guard, Matthew has to delete Mark's assertion that the women went to the tomb intending to anoint the body, and to represent them as expecting only to visit the tomb, not to enter it (compare p. 60 above). Brown has conceded that the presence of a guard at the sepulchre would make what the other three gospels narrate about the tomb "almost unintelligible."[77] Morison has to admit that there is an intelligible motive for Christians to have invented the guard, namely to make it appear that the body could not have been stolen, and that, if Jesus disappeared from his tomb, he must have done so by supernatural means. In any case, the empty tomb (unguarded) entered Christian tradition only late in the first century, with Mark, and from clearly apologetic motives: mere appearances of the risen one might be dismissed as hallucinations, but an empty tomb was a more objective warrant.

I have discussed Morison's book elsewhere (*JEC*, pp. 320–25), and to what extent his views carry weight can be estimated from his claim that we know Jesus's twelve disciples "better than any other single group of persons in antiquity", when in fact no NT lists of the twelve contain even identical names, and most of the twelve are hardly mentioned at all except in these lists. But if Montgomery can find a non-theologian, preferably a lawyer, who sets out to vindicate the NT, then such work is to be accepted as unbiased and definitive. And if the gospels say the tomb was empty, discussion must proceed from acceptance of this as a true account of the facts. It is obvious that, for him, the admitted necessity of evaluating NT claims about Jesus must not involve calling in question what, in some of its books, is alleged as a factual historical basis for these claims. No secular historian would approach his data in this way; and this is not—as Montgomery and conservative apologists in general suppose—because of Enlightenment prejudices against supernatural phenomena, but because a historian does not rule out in advance the possibility that certain stories in his sources are legendary.

Montgomery concluded his article reporting the debate with the suggestion that, as I am approaching the end of my life, I would do well to avoid any mistake about the question of eternity. Dr. Johnson, whom he mentioned in this connection, was afraid he would go to hell. The implication seems to be that, unless I put my religious house into what Montgomery would regard as proper order, I shall (to put it mildly) face future penalties. From this we see that an apologist of today, while avoiding the blatant crudity of hell-fire sermons, unhesitatingly alludes to judgemental threats in scripture which aimed at cowing the reader into frightened obedience: hell is the place "where the devouring worm never dies and the fire is not quenched" (NEB),[78] and the pain of self-mutilation is as nothing in comparison (Mk. 9:43–48). I would not think much of a god who penalizes honest doubt, and I hope that a majority of Christians find such a god equally repulsive, scripture notwithstanding. As for Dr. Johnson, I think it appropriate to note his maxim that when a man engages in an important controversy—the context shows that apologetics for the faith is what he had in mind—"he is to do all he can to lessen his antagonist, because authority from personal respect has much weight with most people, and often more than reasoning."[79] The maxim is not lost on today's apologists: "Flat-earth theory" is how Montgomery characterized my ideas. Because he refuses to consider the substantial contributions of critical theologians, brushing them aside as he does as victims of arbitrary philosophical and other bias, he does not see the problems posed by scripture, and so remains undisturbed by them. In his book *Crisis* he is fiercely critical of Lutheran colleagues who are driven by evidence that has long since been mounting to concede that the Bible contains errors, but who nevertheless wish to retain in some form the doctrine that it is inspired. He can see that the compromise which results is very unconvincing; and so he remains stuck in the kind of fundamentalism that has led him to Turkey in quest of Noah's Ark (witness his 1972 book on that subject).

5

The Gospel of Mark: History or Dogma?

i. William Wrede's Epoch-Making Book

A. THE ROLE OF THE DISCIPLES

When David Friedrich Strauss showed how much in the gospels is unacceptable as history,[1] his critics tried to discredit him by attacking his belief that Matthew was the oldest of the canonical gospels. Once that position had been assigned to Mark, it was argued that Mark reads like a straightforward and reliable account, and that Strauss's thesis that the gospels are myth-ridden falls to the ground. William Wrede replied to this in 1901 in a book entitled in its English translation *The Messianic Secret*. Räisänen, who covers the same ground in his *The 'Messianic Secret' in Mark* of 1990, to which I am deeply indebted, holds that modern Marcan study begins with Wrede's book, "and no student of the gospels can bypass it" (p. 38).

Wrede begins by noting that, although Mark is admitted to be "just a later narrator's conception of Jesus's life", this "axiom" is all too often forgotten in that, unless we are brought up sharply by such things as contradictions, we are apt to assume that this gospel places us "on firm ground in the life of Jesus itself". All the gospels were written by Christians who could look at this life "only with the eyes of their own time", and who described it on the basis of what was believed in the Christian communities for which they wrote, and with the needs of these communities in

116

mind. Hence before we can begin to inquire what actually happened in Jesus's life, we must first be clear as to "what the narrator in his own time intended to say to his readers." He complains that, instead of clarifying this, commentators go straight to the task of reconstructing the life of Jesus from the texts. But these provide only the barest of frameworks, a good deal of which the commentators themselves find incredible,[2] and so they have to be supplemented with considerable historical and psychological "guesswork", with the result that interpretations to suit every taste proliferate (pp. 5–6). "Each scholar proceeds in such a way as to retain in the transmitted text what can be fitted into his construction of the facts and his view of what is historically possible, but rejects the rest" (pp. 86–87). Things have not changed much since Wrede wrote this in 1901. E.P. Sanders could still say, in 1985: "It is amazing that so many New Testament scholars write books about Jesus in which they discover that he agrees with their own version of Christianity."[3]

Räisänen follows Wrede by illustrating the problems involved in taking Mark's account of the ministry as history. At 4:11–12 the disciples are said to have been given the secret of the kingdom of God, in contrast to outsiders, who are not meant to understand Jesus's teaching and whom he does not want to save (I shall return to this strange passage). But Jesus at once goes on to complain of their incomprehension (4:13), and has to give them additional instruction (4:14–20, 34). Nevertheless, they still lack faith (4:40) and do not understand who he is (4:41). He sends them out to exorcise (6:7), and on their mission they not only do this, but also preach a doctrine of repentance, cure the sick, and teach (6:12–13, 30). When they return, they still do not understand what they can expect of him (6:35–37) and do not understand his feeding of the 5,000 because their hearts were "hardened" (6:52). (Commentators explain that, for the ancients, the heart was the seat of understanding and that the Greek noun πώρωσις [petrifaction] and the corresponding verb [used here] came to mean 'obtuseness', 'intellectual blindness'.) The situation here is that "straightway" after the feeding they are in difficulty, rowing on the lake against a strong wind. He sees their distress, walks on the water towards them, tells them not to be afraid, and enters their boat, whereupon "the wind ceased: and they were sore amazed in themselves; for they understood not concerning the loaves." Wrede commented (p. 104): this can only mean that, in spite of this earlier incident, they still had not noticed that he possessed miraculous powers. Matthew realized that such obtuseness is not to be believed, and so the parallel passage in his gospel makes them acknowledge Jesus as "truly the Son of God" (14:33). Matthew did not notice that this emendation makes Peter's later 'confession' that Jesus is "the Son of the living God" no longer the unexpected stroke of divinely inspired genius that Jesus there declares it to be (Mt. 16:16–18). In this instance as so often, adapting a document so as to dispose of one problem simply creates another.

In Mark's next chapter Jesus declares that "there is nothing from without the man that going into him can defile him." The disciples fail to realize that he is thereby declaring all foods to be clean and are rebuked for their dullness (7:18–19). Then, although they have already been present at the miraculous feeding of the 5,000, they have no idea how he will be able to supply food to another crowd in a desert place (8:4). Even when he then repeats the miracle, they still do not understand him and are accordingly rebuked (8:17, 21). Räisänen asks, appositely: "What on earth did these simpletons preach and teach when Jesus sent them out (chapter 6)?" (*Secret*, p. 18). Wrede's comment is: "Disciples of the kind presented to us here by Mark are not real figures—disciples who never become any wiser about Jesus after all the wonderful things they see about him—confidants who have no confidence in him and who stand over against him fearfully as before an uncanny enigma" (p. 103).

How thoroughly stupid Mark will have the disciples be is illustrated when Jesus tells them, at a time when they are short of bread, to "beware of the leaven of the Pharisees and the leaven of Herod" (8:14–15). They think he is warning them not to fetch leaven for bread from the Pharisees or Herod, for they reply: "We have no bread"! (Compare the parallel passage in Matthew where it is said that it took a little time before they realized that Jesus was not referring to "the leaven of bread", 16:12.) Jesus then interprets their reply as implying that, although they have witnessed the two miraculous feedings, they do not trust him to supply bread. He rebukes them for this, and then catechizes them:

> When I brake the five loaves among the five thousand, how many baskets (κοφινους) full of broken pieces took ye up? They say unto him, Twelve. And when the seven among the four thousand, how many basketfuls (σπυριδων) of broken pieces took ye up? And they say unto him, Seven. And he said unto them, Do ye not yet understand? (8:19–21).

All but the most conservative commentators agree that this conversation could not have taken place. That Mark has earlier recorded two miraculous feedings, with much the same vocabulary and sequence of events in each case, is usually attributed to the existence, before he wrote, of a tradition of one such feeding in slightly different written forms, which he took to refer to different incidents. If so, then Jesus's words here referring to two incidents cannot be authentic. That the words are Marcan composition is obvious from the fact that they presuppose the Marcan written form of both incidents: the baskets were κοφινοι at 6:43 and σπυριδες at 8:8, and the same distinction is made here at 8:19–21. Wrede not only notes this, but is particularly scathing about the whole pericope of which these three verses form the conclusion: in their hardness of heart the disciples have forgotten both miraculous feedings completely, yet they are represented as being able to recall them so as to answer Jesus's questions accurately. And as for their supposing that he is telling them not to fetch leaven from Herod, how is it, Wrede asks, that nobody seems to notice that such nonsense can be read in our oldest gospel? (pp. 104–05).[4] He later answers this his own question by noting the way in which long-standing honoured traditions can dull critical sensitivity: "If Mark's gospel were to come to light for the first time today from some tomb . . . many of the features belonging to it would be recognized without the slightest difficulty" (p. 148). Familiarity with our own traditions makes them seem reasonable, or at any rate inhibits the instant disbelief with which we respond to doctrines not our own.

If we read this Marcan pericope without demurring, Matthew and Luke were more circumspect. Matthew makes Jesus's words about leaven a warning against false teaching, and as Herod had no teaching, the disciples finally understand Jesus to be telling them to "beware of the teaching of the Pharisees and *Sadducees*" (Mt. 16:12). Luke deletes the whole conversation about bread and, in a different context, interprets "the leaven of the Pharisees" as "hypocrisy" (Lk. 12:1).

Returning to Mark, we find that at 8:29 Peter recognizes Jesus as "the Christ". How he achieved this insight after all the previous incomprehension is not explained. Jesus then tells his disciples that "the Son of man must suffer many things and be rejected by the elders and the chief priests and the scribes, and be killed and after three days rise again." In Mark he first used the expression 'the Son of man' of himself at 2:10 and 2:28 when, in front of opponents, he made imperious claims (the right to forgive sins and to be sovereign even over the sabbath). It is never explained what the expression means, and obviously the expectation is that friend and foe alike would understand it. What it actually means has been endlessly discussed, but the way it is used implies that it designates Jesus himself as someone with great power and authority. His teaching that the Son of man must be killed and will rise again is given quite "openly" or "plainly" to the disciples (8:32). Peter, however, does not accept that these events must happen, rebukes Jesus for saying that they must, and is in turn rebuked by him. Jesus repeats his teaching at 9:31, but the disciples "understood not the saying." Wrede finds this very strange (p. 94). They have already heard him say the same thing "openly", and Peter then understood it sufficiently to protest against it. Matthew and Luke sensed the difficulty; for Matthew replaces "they understood not the saying" with "they were exceeding sorry" (Mt. 17:23); and although Luke retains their incomprehension, he attributes it to divine intention: "They understood not the saying and it was concealed from them, that they should not perceive it" (Lk. 9:45).

At Mk. 10:32–34 Jesus foretells his Passion and resurrection for a third time, and in even greater detail:

> And he took again the twelve, and began to tell them the things that were to happen unto him, saying, Behold, we go up to Jerusalem; and the Son of man shall be delivered unto the *chief priests and the scribes: and they shall condemn him to death and shall deliver him*

unto the Gentiles: and they shall mock him, and shall spit upon him, and shall scourge him, and shall kill him; and after three days he shall rise again (The italicized words are omitted in the Lucan parallel, Lk. 18:31–34).

This time Mark does not say that the disciples either protested or failed to understand—for the good reason that the following pericope (where the sons of Zebedee declare themselves able to drink the cup which Jesus will drink, 10:35–45) presupposes that they had understood. Only Luke, who omits this incident with the Zebedees, has a statement about the disciples' incomprehension (18:34) analogous to the previous cases.

Wrede insists that all three of these predictions of the Passion and resurrection are unhistorical. The detail, particularly in the third of them, corresponding so precisely to subsequent events, makes them look like later Christian creations, for which there was an obvious motive: If Jesus died to save us, any idea that he might have been surprised by his death had to be repelled, and so the tradition about his life had to be "corrected" so as to include his foreknowledge of his death, just as it had to be corrected in other ways, for example by making him foretell that the Christian community would be persecuted (pp. 88–89; see below, p. 181f). Luke goes so far as to correct Mark so as to bring this third passion prediction into line with his own account of the Passion, where the Sanhedrin does not condemn Jesus, but sends him on to Pilate without first passing any sentence: so he makes Jesus foretell only that "the Son of man shall be delivered up unto the Gentiles" (18:32), thus omitting Mark's references to the Jewish authorities (italicized in the Marcan passage quoted above).

Wrede (pp. 82ff) finds a further indication that the predictions are unhistorical in the later behaviour of the disciples. They abandon Jesus at his arrest (Mk. 14:50) and (in the appendix to Mark's final chapter) do not believe the women's report of his resurrection (16:11–13). Luke represents two of them as totally unprepared for Jesus's death (24:20–21) and the eleven as incredulous when told of his resurrection (24:11). It really does not look as though he had prepared them by the "plain" speaking ascribed to him at Mk. 8:31 which Peter understood well enough to protest against, nor by the detailed forecast of 10:32–34, which is perfectly clear and where it is not said that they failed to understand. In sum, the predictions present two problems (additionally to ascribing to Jesus detailed foreknowledge in harmony with the different requirements of different passion narratives): first, it is unintelligible that the disciples do not understand such plain language; and second, their failure to understand is not consistently alleged, yet their later behaviour implies that they were completely taken by surprise by what subsequently happened. Three of them (Peter, James, and John) had seen Jesus in heavenly glory conversing with Elijah and Moses at his Transfiguration, and had heard the heavenly voice calling him "my beloved Son" (9:2–7). Yet they were reduced to despair at his arrest and crucifixion.

Wrede insists that Mark was not out to denigrate the disciples (p. 106). In his view, Mark thought it natural for them to behave as they do during Jesus's lifetime, and supposed that it was only his appearances to them after his resurrection that made them aware of his true status. Wrede points out (p. 166) that this cause of their changed attitude is explicit in Luke, where the risen one opens their minds to the meaning of all that is "written in the law of Moses, the prophets and the psalms concerning me" (24:44–45). Wrede also adduces Philippians 2:6ff (Jesus "emptied himself" of divinity when he humbly became a man), Romans 1:4 (he "was declared to be Son of God with power" by his resurrection) and Acts 2:32 and 36 (Peter tells the "men of Israel" that "this Jesus whom ye crucified" God raised up and made "both Lord and Christ"). All three passages, he says (p. 218), are evidence that the oldest Christian belief was that Jesus became Messiah only at his resurrection. His ministry was, then, quite unmessianic; but later Christian reflection could not believe that he had lived inconspicuously, and came to suppose that he had worked impressive miracles and behaved generally in an authoritative way. Such stories were clumsily worked by Mark into some sort of consistency with the older idea by representing the plainest manifestations of his power and authority as not understood, even by his closest associates, until after his resurrection. This failure to understand is thus a "transitional idea" which arose as an "after-effect of the view that the resurrection is the beginning of the messiahship at a time when the life of Jesus was already being filled materially with messianic content" (p. 229).

It is clear that Wrede does not dispute that Jesus lived and died in Palestine at the time of Pontius Pilate, and that after his death his disciples had certain experiences which they interpreted as resurrection appearances of him. Indeed, the argument is that these experiences entirely changed their estimate of him, and Wrede makes a very great deal in his exegesis depend on this one factor. Although, then, his scepticism was not total, his book was far too critical of the gospels to find acceptance at the time. In England, which has so often lagged behind German NT criticism, reaction was particularly negative. William Sanday, although known for introducing German critical scholarship to England, was appalled at the "arrogance" of interpreting such exalted documents as the gospels on the basis of mere "common sense". Having thus stamped Wrede as both conceited and pedestrian, he reinforced the latter point with a little chauvinism: Wrede wrote "in the style of a Prussian official".[5]

We saw that these very disciples who so often understood nothing are nevertheless said at Mk. 4:11–12 to have been given the secret, in contrast to outsiders who are kept in the dark. That chapter begins with Jesus teaching a great multitude many things in parables, and there follows the parable of the sower as an illustration. Then, when he is "alone" with the twelve and a small number of unspecified others, he is asked "about the parables" (verse 10). This could mean about what they signify, or about his purpose in speaking in parables at all. The latter meaning is presupposed by his immediate answer (verses 11–12), but the former by verses 13ff, where he first expresses surprise that they have not understood the parable he has just spoken, and then goes on to explain it to them. Verses 13ff also presuppose that verse 10 was originally worded 'they asked him about the parable' (singular), namely the one parable he had just spoken. This noun was then changed into its plural form so that verses 11–12 could be added, which make verse 10 into a question as to why he speaks in parables at all:

> Unto you is given the mystery of the kingdom of God: but unto them that are without all things are done in parables: that seeing they may see, and not perceive; and hearing they may hear, and not understand; lest haply they should turn again, and it should be forgiven them (4:11–12).

Wrede (p. 58) and others have noted that the Greek rendered here as "unto you is given the mystery" actually has the verb in the perfect tense, implying that the secret 'has been given' to the elite, already and once and for all, not that they gradually grasp what it is all about in the course of their discipleship. Moreover, Jesus here states quite plainly that

1. he speaks to outsiders only in parables, and
2. these are meant to be unintelligible so as to deprive all but the chosen few of any chance of salvation.

For Wrede (p. 62), the procedure here ascribed to him is both cruel and purposeless: to set out to prevent people from being forgiven is cruel; and why bother to address them at all if one deliberately makes what one says unintelligible? He further noted that it is not true that, in the rest of the gospel, Jesus speaks to the multitude only in parables, nor, when he does use them, that they are not clear. To take but one example, the parable of the wicked husbandmen, addressed to his enemies, is perfectly well understood by them (12:12).

The phrases "that seeing they may see and not perceive", and so forth, clearly derive from Isaiah 6:9–10, which is worded differently in the Hebrew text, the Greek translation of it known as the Septuagint or LXX, and the Aramaic version—the Targum read in synagogues as an interpretive translation of the original. Meagher has noted that

> The differences are slight in wording, but powerful in implication. The Hebrew text has God charge Isaiah with the task of taunting the people and making them unresponsive at the same time, so as to prevent their understanding and salvation. The LXX softens this dreadful instruction by changing a taunt to a prediction and assigning the responsibility for their dull rejection of the way of healing to themselves rather than to Isaiah's carrying out of God's orders. The Targum takes the Hebrew original to a still gentler form, in which God seems to be sending Isaiah on an errand of mercy, but with the sad awareness that they have closed themselves off from response and forgiveness. The shift in language is minor; the shift in theological implication is enormous.[6]

The wording may have reached Mark in something like the Targum form, for he has "lest it should be forgiven them", and only the Targum mentions forgiveness: the Hebrew and the Greek have "lest they be healed". Nevertheless, Mark's wording is "not the Targum's gentle exasperation", but is "bent back toward the darker meaning of the original Hebrew", which seems to have been occasioned by desperate anger at the failure of Isaiah's mission. According to Mark, then, "what happens is happening in parables *so that* those who are outside may be left in the dark and excluded from repentance and forgiveness . . . Jesus is teaching in parables as a strategy of deliberate obfuscation in order to prevent the outsiders from seeing, repenting and being forgiven" (*Ibid.*, pp. 120–21).

Matthew and Luke understood very well the cruel predestinarian doctrine Mark here ascribes to Jesus, for each does his best to mitigate it. Mt. 13.13–15 makes the unintelligible parables a punishment for an already existing blindness in the audience, and quotes Isaiah from the LXX accordingly. Luke 8:9–10 omits Mark's "lest they should turn again and be forgiven" but adds words like it to the interpretation of the parable of the sower that follows so as to make not God but the Devil the one who wants those who hear the word to persist in their unbelief:

Mk. 4:15	*Lk. 8:12*
And straitway cometh Satan and taketh away the word which hath been sown in them.	Then cometh the devil, and taketh away the word from their heart, *that they may not believe and be saved.*

Both Matthew and Luke replace Mark's "unto you is given the mystery of the kingdom" with "unto you is given *to know* the mysteries of the kingdom" (cf. note 11 to chapter 1). The added verb and the plural noun make it easier to suppose that the reference is to a series of mysteries which are to be gradually revealed, rather than to a single revelation that has already been imparted (Wrede, p. 58).

As I have already pointed out, it is not in fact the case that Jesus's parables in Mark are unintelligible and are not understood. He speaks to the scribes "in parables" at 3:23, and there is no suggestion that they are perplexed. As we saw, the parable of the wicked husbandmen is well understood, and there are numerous other examples. He teaches the multitudes "as he was wont" (10:1) and "the common people heard him gladly" (12:37). They would hardly have responded in this way to unintelligible riddles. At 7:14 he calls the multitude to hear him "and understand". Meagher (p. 87) says that the overall picture in Mark is that "the crowds see and hear quite well, while the inner circle has difficulties"—nearly the opposite of the policy strangely advanced at 4:10–12.

At 4:33 Jesus "spake the word" to the people with many parables, "as they were able to hear it". This is obviously intended as helpful: he is adapting what he has to say to their capacity to understand him. Moreover, 'speaking the word' is a standard phrase for clear, straightforward imparting of the Christian message, as when Christians in foreign parts "spoke the word" to gentiles (Acts 11:19), or when Jesus himself "spoke the word" in Capernaum (Mk. 2:2). Yet in the very next verse following 4:33 Mark says:

> And without a parable spake he not unto them: but privately to his own disciples he expounded all things.

So 'the word' spoken to the crowds is after all insufficiently clear, and elucidation is vouchsafed only to the disciples. Taking verses 33 and 34 together we have sheer countersense—"missionary preaching which must later be decoded for the chosen inner circle!" (Räisänen, *Secret*, p. 106).

This fourth chapter of Mark's gospel clearly puts together incompatible traditions. Commentators have long been aware that it is in this sense composite. After Jesus has been introduced as the sole speaker for the rest of the chapter with the words "and he said unto them" (verse 11), this formula is quite unnecessarily repeated at verses 13, 21, 24, 26 and 30, indicating that the evangelist has here joined together Jesuine utterances that were originally independent units. Moreover, the setting at the beginning of the chapter is public: Jesus is teaching the crowds from a boat. At verse 10 he is alone with his disciples, but verse 33 suggests that the parables he has been speaking were after all addressed not to them, but to the crowd, and this is confirmed by verse 36. "The private bypath with the closer disciples seems clearly to have been an afterthought, imperfectly carved out of public territory by a somewhat clumsy redactor" (Meagher, pp. 88–89) Eta Linnemann has proposed a complicated but plausible reconstruction of the stages through which the material went.[7]

How did Mark come to write such a muddle? The answer seems to be that he requires the disciples to play more than one role. As Wrede was aware (p. 231), it is they who vouch for Jesus's teaching, and Mark's Christian community has to hold to them as the sole guarantors of it. Räisänen agrees that at 4:11–12 and 34 "the community's own teaching is traced back to a special enlightenment which all outsiders lack" (p. 112). When, contrariwise, the disciples fail to understand Jesus, this is, for Wrede, because Mark has also to hold that their eyes were opened only at the resurrection. Räisänen interprets differently: their incomprehension is meant to "underline the difficulties that Jesus's teaching presents for its hearers" (p. 118), reflecting the experience of Christians of Mark's day that their missionary preaching found little acceptance and that converts were few; when, on the other hand, Jesus preaches successfully to the crowds, as he often does, he is, for Mark, "the great preacher of the gospel, the archetype of the Christian missionary." Hence "the mission experience of Mark's congregation provides the key" to the puzzles of chapter four (pp. 138–39). Both these commentators agree that the confusion arises because "on the one hand Mark is telling a story of what happened when Jesus of Nazareth was active in Galilee and Jerusalem"; and "on the other hand he is projecting the story of his own Christian congregation on to the same screen" (Räisänen, p. 19).

If we now turn from the role of the disciples to that of the outsiders, we find that Jesus's supposed activity in deliberately hardening or blinding them can be explained in the same way. Missionary preachers—Christian and other—have repeatedly found it impossible to get their message across to the obdurate, that however good their sermon, few accept it. Such preachers can console themselves with the thought that God wishes it to be so, that he has determined in advance that an elect will be saved, and has made the rest unreceptive to the truth. The Isaiah passage alluded to at Mk. 4:12 originated as an attempt to explain in this very way the failures of Isaiah's mission. Such predestinarian thinking has repeatedly—in Islam and elsewhere, as well as in Christianity—been inconsistently combined with complaints that outsiders remain outside only because of their own perversity. The two positions are sustained with equal vehemence by Paul when he tries, in Romans, to explain why most Jews refuse to turn Christian: God has actually dulled their faculties (11:7), he "hath mercy on whom he will, and whom he will he hardeneth" (9:18); yet they are to be blamed for abiding by the old covenant, and will be "grafted in" if only they will drop their unbelief (11:23).[8]

B. THE SECRET OF JESUS'S STATUS AS SON OF GOD

At the Transfiguration, a voice out of the cloud designates Jesus as "my beloved Son". When he and his entourage (Peter, James, and John) then descend the mountain, he tells them to tell no one of the whole incident "save when the Son of man should have risen again from the dead" (Mk. 9:9). As usual, they do not understand. They even "question among themselves what the rising again from the dead should mean", although the idea that the dead would rise had been familiar in Judaism since the book of Daniel and is presupposed in the question the Sadducees put to Jesus at 12:18–23 (namely to which of seven husbands whom she survived will a woman be wife in the resurrection?).

The injunction of silence until the resurrection (9:9) is of crucial importance for Wrede's theory that it was the disciples' experiences of that event that changed their attitude to Jesus. According to this theory, the oldest Christian view was that he became Son of God only at his resurrection, but because the church had come to believe that he had been this from the first, it was supposed that he must have kept this his true status a secret, or disclosed it only to his close followers, who failed to understand it (pp. 68, 234).

Wrede writes of the "Messianic secret" rather than the 'Son of God secret', but he uses either 'Messiah' or 'Son of God' to denote Jesus's supernatural status. To avoid circumlocution we can follow him, and speak of Jesus's achieving the status of Messiah at his resurrection, or alternatively of having been Messiah from the first.

Unlike Jesus's human audience, supernatural beings in Mark knew the truth about his status from the first. The "unclean spirits" recognize him as Son of God and address him as such. At 1:23–24 a man with such a spirit cries out: "I know thee who thou art, the Holy One of God." The Gerasene demoniac calls him "Son of the Most High God" (5:7), and "whenever the unclean spirits beheld him, they fell down before him, and cried, saying, Thou art the Son of God" (3:11). This generalization expressly states that it is not the sick persons in whom these spirits lodge, but the spirits themselves who speak in this way. And the Jesus they are addressing is not the merely human Jesus, but the supernatural Son of God. "A direct *rapport* exists between him and them. Spirit comprehends spirit" (Wrede, p. 25).

These stories obviously arose when illness was often ascribed to demonic possession; hence that a story represents words of the sick as utterances of a demon does not make it a legend. Yet why should we go to the other extreme and accept that Jesus did actually converse in this way with supernatural beings? Their recognition of his status is, as Wrede noted (p. 74), simply an element in harmony with the whole Christology of this gospel: the Spirit descends on him at his baptism, a voice from heaven calls him "my beloved Son" (1:11), and the Spirit then drives him into the wilderness for a personal encounter with Satan (1:12). There is, as we have just seen, a further testimony to his sonship at his Transfiguration (9:7). Even his teaching manifests divine power: it operates on the people like something unheard of, and they link it with his control over the unclean spirits as the effluence of one and the same power (1:27). There is really nothing in the substance of his teaching as given in Mark—when it is specified at all instead of being left indefinite—to make such a reaction to it plausible. Wrede hints that, for Mark, this overpowering teaching will have consisted of "the imparting of divine truths such as were for Mark and the community of his day the essential features of the Christian faith" (p. 79): in other words, the doctrine that Jesus died to save us. He adds that, obviously, Mark "could not express this absolutely explicitly in his Gospel"; he could not plausibly represent Jesus as preaching the church's post-resurrection doctrine of salvation (see below, p. 146f). For this reason Mark so often says that Jesus "taught" without saying what he taught. Matthew sensed how unsatisfactory it is to make the audience "astonished at his teaching, for he taught them as having authority and not as the scribes" (Mk. 1:22), when no indication is given of what was taught; so he turned this verse into a comment on the Sermon on the Mount (Mt. 7:28–29), made when Jesus has concluded this discourse which is absent from Mark, but spread over chapters five to seven of Matthew.

In curing the Gerasene demoniac, Jesus does not simply dislodge the "legion" of demons, but allows their request to be transferred to a herd of 2,000 pigs, which promptly rush down into the sea and are drowned. The swineherds then report this to all and sundry "in the city and in the country", so that people come to the scene—Jesus is still there with his cured patient—and, having been told what had happened by eyewitnesses, they "beseech him to depart from their borders" (5:17)—"a commendably restrained response to two thousand drowned pigs" (Meagher, p. 73). We are not told whether the demons also perished. That is of no interest to the narrator. He needs the pigs and their demented behaviour only as visible evidence that the demons have in fact left the man. In the other two examples of encounters with demons, Jesus tells them to be silent (1:25) and not to make him known (3:12). Yet, although there is no suggestion that the demons disobeyed, how can we believe that the secret of his true status was not divulged? His power over them is marvelled at (1:27), and those who marvelled must have witnessed the exorcism and so also his conversation with the demon who cried out the secret. "Mark seems very quickly to forget his own presuppositions" (Wrede, p. 133).

Not only do the demons already know who Jesus is, but also his power to work stupendous miracles would tend to betray his status to all who witnessed them. This problem Mark deals with in the same way—by making him order silence, in these cases about what he has done, sometimes even when such an order is quite senseless, as the miracle has already become public. Thus he restores Jairus's daughter to life in the presence only of Peter, James and John, and "charged them much (RSV "strictly") that no man should know it" (5:43), even though the house where he has done this was already full of mourners who knew that the girl was dead (Wrede, pp. 50–51). The prohibition could not possibly be implemented, but "Mark does not notice this" and has "only a limited capacity for transposing himself into the historical situation with which he is dealing" (p. 133). Likewise, Jesus repeatedly commands sick people—the reference is not here to cases of demonic possession—to keep the fact of their healing secret, yet performs the cures in the full glare of publicity. It will not do to say that public healings begin only after injunctions to silence cease; for already at 2:1ff there is a cure before everyone's eyes, while miracles that are to be kept secret occur much later (p. 17). He even tells the cured Gerasene demoniac to tell his friends "how great things the Lord hath done for thee". The man complied, published the whole matter in the Decapolis, "and all men did marvel" (5:19–20). Thus the instruction to be silent is sometimes senseless, and sometimes entirely lacking, and sometimes the precise opposite is actually enjoined.

Miracles apart, there is much in Jesus's behaviour and in people's reactions to him that is incompatible with the idea that his status went unrecognized: "At the entry into Jerusalem he permits himself to be fêted as Messiah, the blind man of Jericho calls him 'Son of David' (10:47), and before the High Priest he acknowledges in plain terms that he is Son of God (14:62)" (p. 70). Wrede finds such contradiction of the idea of secrecy inevitable, in that, if Mark's Jesus had really kept himself and his powers strictly concealed, then his life would hardly have been worth relating. To demonstrate that he was God's son, he had to be shown as acting with appropriate powers (pp. 125–26).

Wrede's conclusion is that "Mark no longer has a real view of the historical life of Jesus" (p. 129), whose person he conceives "dogmatically" as the bearer of supernatural dignity. Mark did not, in Wrede's view (p. 145), originate the idea that Jesus kept his status secret during his ministry. He thinks that the clumsiness and inconsistency with which this motif is handled in Mark excludes this. It was, in his view, taken from pre-Marcan tradition, and arose as an attempt to reconcile the earliest view of Jesus's ministry (as having been unmessianic) with later stories which credited him with pre-resurrection behaviour displaying supernatural powers. If we allow that the old idea is more likely to represent the truth than the later stories, it would follow that the historical Jesus did not in fact give himself out as Messiah, and that "Mark is very far removed from the actual life of Jesus and is dominated by views of a dogmatic kind" (p. 145). His Jesus acts with divine power and knows the future. His actions are not humanly motivated but derive from divine decree. "In this sense the Gospel of Mark belongs to the history of dogma" (p. 131), and so is a good deal closer to the fourth gospel than is commonly supposed (p. 145). One can see what it was in Wrede that provoked Sanday's intemperate comments.

Finally, Wrede shows how Matthew did his best to avoid some of Mark's absurdities. "Prohibitions to the demons are lacking. . . . The story of Jairus's daughter contains neither the prohibition nor the feature of the three confidants. On the contrary, in the concluding verse (Mt. 9:26) we read: 'And the report of this went through all that district'" (pp. 152–53). After the second prophecy of the Passion it is not said that the disciples did not understand (see above, p. 120). Clearly, Matthew found Mark's picture of them "no longer tolerable" (p. 160). He made them much more consistently "the guarantors and representatives of Jesus's teaching and of the true understanding of his person" (p. 163), thus reflecting "the general view that the church has of them" (p. 164). Luke remains closer to Mark, and can retain their incomprehension because he so much stresses that their eyes were opened only after the resurrection (p. 179; see above, p. 122).

Wrede is quite unimpressed by what he calls the "much-lauded concreteness" of Mark, so often taken as an indication of its historical accuracy. He quotes, as a particularly characteristic passage, 7:24f:

> And from thence he arose and went away into the borders of Tyre and Sidon. And he entered into a house, and would have no man know it: yet he could not be hid. But straightway a woman whose little daughter had an unclean spirit, having heard of him, came and fell down at his feet. . . .

He comments that one might in the same fairy-tale manner tell of a disguised Spanish prince journeying into French territory, where he went into a house because he did not wish to be recognized, but a poor woman heard of it and sought him out (p. 142).

Precisely in the passages he has adduced in his book, there is "a strong lack of concreteness", and merely "a brief hasty word of Jesus's or someone else's and a short remark on the impression it made." Throughout the gospel the scene changes rapidly, and does so even within individual incidents; and who is being addressed or dealt with fluctuates likewise, with "the people or the disciples now appearing and now withdrawing". Moreover, the "psychological and other motivations which would be the precondition for giving palpable shape to the events are lacking . . . because they were not thought of at all." In any case, concreteness would not mean authenticity: "A document can have a strongly secondary and indeed even quite apocryphal character and yet display a great deal of concreteness" (p. 143).

Although Wrede writes clearly, his book is not easy to read, as the abundant detail is confusing. Räisänen (*Secret*) gives a very lucid summary, and a comprehensive account of alternative proposals that have been made to explain the data. He himself agrees that the secrecy motif is one of several in Mark, and that others are inconsistent with it (p. 24). Jesus is killed because of his christological claims (14:61), so there can be no secrecy here. Hence although the disciples so often grasp so little, his opponents *must* understand what his claims are: "An apparently absurd story world therefore results: while those close to Jesus understand nothing, those vehemently opposed to him grasp everything that matters!" (p. 229), and do so well before the passion narrative (2:7; 12:12, etc.). Again, the disciples are not always uncomprehending, as they have to function as teachers of others (6:7ff) and also as reliable mediators of Christian truth for the future. And Jesus himself at times "acts as the proto-missionary, proclaiming the gospel and teaching the word" quite openly and publicly (pp. 213, 247).

ii. Mark and Community Tradition: K.L. Schmidt and Form-Criticism

In 1919 K.L. Schmidt gave Marcan studies a new direction with his book on the 'Framework' of the story of Jesus,[9] where he raised the question of the stages through which traditions about Jesus had passed before their inclusion in the gospels. He showed that Mark's account of the Galilean ministry is merely a series of separate, short single stories (pericopes); and he argued that each of these had been transmitted, originally orally, in the preaching and teaching of early Christian communities. Each story was designed to represent a point of doctrinal interest to these early Christians, the miracle stories, for instance, showing how great Jesus's powers were. The stories seldom indicated where or when he spoke or acted as he did, as that was not doctrinally important. He adds that, as Christianity originated as a cult, these stories must be understood in the light of their setting within the cult, in the practices of public worship (p. vi). In other words, the main purpose of the anecdotes was not to preserve the history of Jesus, but to strengthen the life of the church. Nineham, who is greatly indebted to Schmidt and his successors, explains more fully what was involved. The people passing on the stories were "preachers and teachers, speaking at meetings for public worship or address-ing groups of catechumens and the like". They would tailor what they said to the particular needs of a given audience: if a lesson in good-neighbourliness was required, the parable of the good Samaritan could be recited; if there was some doubt whether to pay taxes to the Romans, what we now have at Mk. 12:13–17 would be suitable. "Consequently, the order in which the inci-dents were recounted would vary from church to church, in accordance with local needs; and there would be no compelling motive for preserving, or even remembering, the order in which they actually occurred during Our Lord's lifetime" (*Mark*, p. 22).

Schmidt (pp. 63ff) takes the story of the healing of the leper as typical of a Marcan pericope: "And there cometh to him a leper, beseeching him" (1:40). There is no indication of time or place. Of the cured leper, it is said that he "went out" (verse 45)—from what (a synagogue or a house?) is not indicated. The story is quite independent of the anecdotes that precede and follow it. My quotation of its initial words shows that it is linked to what pre-cedes it only by the simplest of all links—the word 'and', quite often the only linkage between Marcan pericopes. Links else-where are almost as simple; for example 'and' combined with 'again' ("and he went forth again"; "and he entered again into the synagogue"; "and again he began to teach"); or "immediately", rendered "straightway" in the RV ("and straightway he entered into the synagogue . . . And straightway there was in the synagogue a man with an unclean spirit"). The feeding of the 4,000 is introduced with the quite unspecific "in those days" (8:1).

Schmidt shows that Matthew and Luke obviously felt that this was not good enough and so introduced references to time or place so as to bind individual pericopes together. Thus Matthew makes the leper come to Jesus as he came down from the mountain after the Sermon on the Mount (Mt. 8:1–2). Luke does not indicate the time but provides a place: "And it came to pass, while he was in one of the cities, a man full of leprosy . . . " (Lk. 5:12). Variations between different manuscripts of Mark also show a tendency to localize the stories. There was a conflict of interests here: on the one hand a certain antiquarian desire to be assured of the where and the when; on the other the cultic practice which fastened only on a story in itself, apart from any context (p. 77).

As Mark's material paid so little regard to chronology or topography, he could not arrange it so as to give a true itinery in truly chronological sequence. There is no historical reason why, for instance, the section about the cleansing of a leper—those six verses in chapter 1 are independent of the context on either side—should occur at this point in the narrative rather than at any other (p. 76). And the same is true of many other pericopes. Schmidt is referring here only to the account of the ministry. He does not dispute that Mark's passion narrative is continuous and replete with indications of time and place: "The passion narrative will have been read out in public worship as a continuous lection. Only as a whole could it give the answer to a question that repeatedly surfaced in the missionary period of the church, namely: how could Jesus be brought to the cross by the people graced with his signs and wonders?" (p. 305).

Sometimes the very nature of a story requires some indication of locality. A tale involving a boat must have a sea or sea-shore setting. A heathen person is essential to Mk. 7:24–30, so this story must be sited in heathen territory: "And from thence he arose and went away into the borders of Tyre and Sidon" (verse 24). But there is nothing precise: Jesus would fain remain concealed in "a house", but a heathen woman extracts a miracle from him. That is all (pp. 198–99). The link with the preceding story is also tenuous: the 'from thence' in "from thence he arose" seems to mean from "the house" of verse 17, which is as vague as many another Marcan setting—"the mountain" or hill-country, "the shore" (of the lake of Galilee), a "lonely place" or "the synagogue".

Some stories require a reference to time. The call of the disciples naturally comes early in the ministry. Synagogue preaching and sabbath-breaking behaviour must take place on the sabbath. The setting in the cornfields on the sabbath (Mk. 2:23) is necessitated by the story thus introduced, and provides the basis on which the Pharisees take Jesus to task because his disciples do what they say is forbidden on the sabbath (plucking ears of corn). But, as usual, precise details are lacking. We are not told on what sabbath or in what neighbourhood. Such questions, says Schmidt (p. 89) must not be asked of an individual anecdote which is not linked to the preceding or following one chronologically, but only thematically, in that it is one of a series which portray Jesus responding to hostile criticism. As Mark's material did not give him any true chronology of Jesus's deeds, he (or a predecessor on whose writing he drew) was reduced to grouping them in this way, that is, by their themes—a series of parables in chapter 4 and of miracles in chapter 5. Mk. 2:1 to 3:6, which includes the cornfield episode, comprises five stories where Jesus, in conflict with opponents, says something of importance for the gospel message; e.g. "the Son of man hath power on earth to forgive sins" (2:10); "I came not to call the righteous, but sinners" (2:17).

Returning to the cornfield episode, we see that it must be set at harvest-time (April to mid-June). Schmidt observes that only here, in this pericope, is a season specified, apart from the setting of the Passion at a roughly similar season (Passover). It has often been supposed that this entitles us to infer that, for Mark, the whole ministry lasted but a single year. For Schmidt no such inference is justified. Mark has put individual anecdotes into a series, giving no indication of in what year or years the different events of the ministry occurred. It is pure chance that one of the anecdotes required a spring setting. Others may equally well have occurred at some other springtime or at another time in some other year. Schmidt begins his book (pp. 1–17) with an amusing account of the often heated attempts to come to terms with the contradiction between the supposed one-year ministry of the synoptics and the Johannine chronology of apparently three years (indicated by John's references to three Passovers). Catholic commentators had struggled to harmonize the two, as any admission of contradiction would militate against the reliability of the gospels. Protestants, on the other hand, were willing to give up the fourth gospel as historically worthless, but clung all the more to the synoptic outline of Jesus's life as a historically accurate sequence. Schmidt holds (p. 91) that there is in fact no synoptic chronology of the ministry with which the Johannine narrative can conflict, and that Mark in fact gives no indication of how long the ministry lasted. When, for instance, he groups together in successive narratives the stilling of the storm, the cure of the Gerasene demoniac, the raising of Jairus's daughter and the cure of the woman with the issue of blood (4:35–5:43), he does so because they all tell of acts of divine power and all require or happen to have had a setting on or near the sea (pp. 150–51). There is no reason to suppose that they really occurred in succession or even in the same year.

Schmidt also notes (p. 92) that in the cornfield episode nothing is said that motivates the appearance of Jesus's opponents, the Pharisees, at 2:24. Nineham takes up this point, saying: "It is idle to ask what the Pharisees were doing in the middle of a cornfield on a sabbath day; the process of oral tradition has formalized the stories." Hence there is "a considerable element of truth" in the judgement that "Scribes or Pharisees appear and disappear just as the compiler requires them", as "part of the stage-property and scenery, like 'the house' and 'the mountain'" (*Mark*, p. 107). In the same way Jesus is repeatedly able to 'call the people' to be his audience. Those responsible for the anecdotes collected by Mark had no difficulty in supposing that there was a multitude at hand, ready to be summoned when Jesus wants to make some public statement. Thus, although in the context he has been addressing only his disciples, he summons the multitude to hear his views on the costs and rewards of discipleship (8:34). Schmidt notes

(p. 221) that Mt. 16:24 wisely makes him here address only the disciples.

Because Mark had no knowledge of the real order in which the events of Jesus's ministry occurred, he sometimes puts disparate sayings together simply because a word or phrase is common to them, although their meanings are not at all cognate. Schmidt instances (p. 233ff) Mk. 9:36–50:

> Whosoever shall receive one of such little children in my name. . .

> We saw one casting out devils in thy name.. . .

> Whoever gives you a cup of water in (the) name, because ye are of Christ. . . .

These sayings about the 'name' are followed by two about 'fire': in hell "the fire is not quenched. For everyone shall be salted with fire." This mention of salt leads to the addition of two further sayings where it functions as the connecting catchword: "Salt is good, but if the salt have lost its savour, wherewith will ye season it? Have salt in yourselves and be at peace with one another."

Schmidt called his book 'The Framework of the Story of Jesus', and he holds that this framework consists of short generalizing summaries of Jesus's behaviour which he calls "Sammelberichte" (summary statements), frames in which the individual anecdotes are placed. They are quite general in their wording and so they do not allow, any more than do the anecdotes, any chronological inferences (p. 13). Some ease the transition to the next pericope (p. 33), others bear no relation to what follows. Examples from Mark are:

> And he went into their synagogues throughout all Galilee, preaching and casting out devils. (1:39)

> And he went forth again by the seaside; and all the multitude resorted unto him. (2:13, followed by the call of Levi with which it has no connection)

A somewhat longer summary is given at 3:7–12, emphasizing Jesus's very extensive success (p. 106): he withdrew to "the sea" but is followed by a great multitude from Galilee, Judea, Jerusalem, Idumea and elsewhere, who were "hearing what great things he did", for "he had healed many".

Schmidt regards these summaries as in the main Mark's own compositions (p. 160)—younger therefore than the individual anecdotes. These latter cannot be traced back to any precise point of origin (p. 105), but will have been repeated again and again in the oral tradition; whereas the summaries are artificial constructions of a particular writer. C.H. Dodd, who criticized Schmidt in an influential article in 1932, nevertheless allowed that "the main stuff of the gospel is reducible to short narrative units and the framework is superimposed on these units." He also allowed that the Marcan order of the ministry's events "is in large measure . . . the result of the Evangelist's own work, rather than directly traditional."[10]

R.H. Lightfoot did much to introduce the work of Wrede, Schmidt, and their successors into Britain. In his Bampton lectures of 1934 he showed that Westcott's statement of 1851—"St. Mark is essentially a transcript from life"—is quite unacceptable, and he called Sanday's condemnation of Wrede "regrettable".[11] He found it no longer possible to maintain the patristic view that Mark was put together from statements by Peter: we now see it as "a compilation of materials of different date, origin, character and purpose, many of which may have had a considerable history—whether oral or literary or both—before they were finally inserted into this gospel, at least a large part of the book being formed from anonymous traditions which had long been current in the church" (p. 25). In a later book, he outlines Schmidt's arguments concerning the topographical and chronological vagueness of Mark, and he follows him in stressing that the little stories served the interests and reflected the concerns of the early church. In them, "the Lord Himself is always central, either in word or act, or in both: frequently enemies seek to oppose or provoke Him; if the disciples are present, they are seldom more than lay-figures." What is emphasized is "the immense impression made by the Lord. . . . We read again and again of the astonishment, bewilderment and fear produced by the mighty works and by the teaching." And in all the stories of conflict with opponents "the sympathy of the reader with the Lord's position is assumed."[12]

Lightfoot is here making the point that each of the individual stories in Mark has its "Sitz im Leben", its 'setting in the life' of the church, in that it expresses interests that are related to faith; and it is to these interests, not to historical concerns, that it owes its formulation and preservation.

The attempt to trace gospel pericopes to one or other of the literary forms to which preachers would naturally resort (such as miracle stories, conflict stories, or stories inculcating some moral point) has become known as 'form-criticism', and I give a brief appraisal of it in *DJE* (pp. 70–74). Nineham, who follows Lightfoot, stresses that

> If the form-critics have shown anything, they have shown the essential importance of the factor they call *Sitz-im-Leben* in the preservation of the material included in our gospels: that is to say, no such material is likely to have survived for long unless it was relevant to *something* in the life, worship, beliefs and interests of the earliest communities.[13]

For instance, Christians and their Jewish opponents will have argued about whether it was necessary to keep the sabbath. For this reason the Christians will have narrated stories in which Jesus defends, against Jewish critics, the practice of the later church of not keeping it (Mk. 2:27–28). In his book Schmidt does not often raise the question whether such stories are historically accurate accounts of Jesus's words and deeds—in a later essay he gives, as we shall see, a surprisingly conservative answer to it. But many of his followers have held that the relevant behaviour was simply ascribed to Jesus in order to justify the church's practice. Käsemann, for instance, says that, as it was religious, not historical interests that the individual sayings and stories served, the overwhelming mass of the tradition "cannot be accepted as authentic." The "preaching about Jesus" came almost entirely to supplant his own preaching, "as can be seen most clearly of all in the completely unhistorical Gospel of John" (*Essays*, p. 59).

In their recent study of the synoptic gospels, Sanders and Davies offer some criticisms of the form critics, but agree that they were right to say that "in the gospels one can see individual and originally independent units. The pericopes do not flow along smoothly in chronological order." There is a 'rounding off', in that each one has a marked beginning and end, and "one does not run on to the next as would be the case if they originated as part of a coherent and consecutive narrative." It follows that "the individual pericopes can and in fact must be studied apart from their present settings if one is to get behind the gospels as we have them to earlier situations"—whether these are to be found in the actual life of Jesus or, as the more sceptical hold, only in the early church.[14] The artificiality of some of the present settings is evident from comparison of the gospels: "The parable of the Lost Sheep in Matthew is addressed to the disciples, as admonition, but in Luke to the Pharisees, as rebuke" (p. 339). That the various parts of the synoptics are self enclosed can be illustrated from the way in which Jesus's opponents vary early and late in the narrative: the synoptics "make no connection between the Pharisees, who are depicted as opposing Jesus in Galilee, and the chief priests, who were instrumental in his trial and execution in Judea" (p. 135). At Mk. 3:6 the Herodians and the Pharisees plot to have him killed, and Mark reintroduces them at 12:13 where they try to trap him with a question. But "when it comes to the arrest and the trial, neither Pharisee nor Herodian appears" (p. 149), nor in the equivalent narratives in the other two synoptics. After the point in the narrative represented by Mk. 12:13, the Pharisees actually appear again only in a narrative unique to Matthew where, with the chief priests, they ask Pilate, after the execution, for a guard to the tomb (Mt. 27:62).

Schmidt emphasized that it follows from his investigation that no biography of Jesus can be constructed from the synoptics (p. 317). So many commentators have allowed that Mark leaves gaps in his record of Jesus's life, but have assumed that what he does narrate is given in proper temporal sequence. In fact, says Schmidt, there is not even this relative coherence, and the whole collapses into individual stories. Mark's outline is not a row of pearls, arranged at a distance from each other but nevertheless in a chronological line, so that one could interpolate, now here and now there, other pearls—further incidents—as Matthew and Luke do, with no impairing of true chronology. Rather is it a heap of pearls with no linear arrangement, even if now and then a few of them do belong chronologically together (p. 281).

It has by now become customary to say that 'the gospels are not biographies', but Nineham wonders how often the full implications of the statement have been faced. A 'life of Jesus', he says, could be written "only if the writer has exact information about the order in which the various episodes in the subject's career occurred and a sufficiently detailed knowledge of them to be able to show for what reasons he felt and acted and developed as he did" (*Explorations*, p. 22). Such information is simply not forthcoming. Yet biographies continue to appear. People have had a long time to fill in the gaps left by the gospel records and, as E.P. Sanders notes (*Historical Jesus*, p. 76), "an apparently endless amount of energy and inventiveness to use in the endeavour".

In an essay of 1923 Schmidt designated the gospels as unpretentious writings for ordinary folk, not "Hochliteratur" (cultured literature) but popular "Kleinliteratur", and not biography but "cultic legend" emanating from the life of a religious community.[15] He compared the synoptics, particularly Mark, with collections of the German tales of Faust and Eulenspiegel, in that the earliest compilers did not, as did the later ones, obtrude their own ideas and manipulate the material to make it exemplify some overall interpretation, but put the individual items together almost higgledy-piggledy (p. 92). We are apt to assume that a biography written by an individual author is more reliable than a collection of anecdotes about the person in question; and Schmidt grants that this is true if we are comparing what a modern historian writes about someone to a collection of tales about him. But he holds that in antiquity there was no sharp distinction between historiography and rhetoric: the historian or biographer was something of a poet who aimed at literary effectiveness, whereas the collector of popular tales—then as now—intruded his own thinking far less (pp. 80–81). Schmidt thus suggests that a collection based on community tradition has a certain reliability which may be lacking in more pretentious literary performances: "That the people as community became the vehicle and creator of the tradition makes its content secure" (p. 124), i.e. gives it a firm and, it is implied, reliable foundation. He allows that an early Christian community will have felt edified and strengthened as a group by its stories of Jesus, just as the legends of the saints owe their origin to the cult of the saints and in turn promote this cult (p. 100). A certain tendentiousness and lack of detachment towards the material is, then, undeniably present. But he holds that it is less distortive than when the collection is reworked and given the stamp of an individual mind—as when Mark's collection was reworked by Matthew and by Luke. The "fidelty to the material which characterizes all popular tradition" (p. 131) is thereby lost, whereas in the oldest layers of the gospels "the smell of Palestinian earth" is still distinct (p. 128).

This whole idea that folk-traditions are reliable because free from individual, self-conscious shaping is not sustainable. The idea has a certain superficial plausibility mainly because it is seldom known where given oral traditions, ancient or modern, originated, and precisely who invented them. But such stories, circulating by word of mouth, although generally anonymous vary constantly in particular details from one telling to another; and such variations are good evidence against credibility. In a number of books (such as *The Vanishing Hitchhiker*, 1981, and *The Mexican Pet*, 1986, both published by Norton in New York and London), the folklorist Professor J.H. Brunvand has collected and commented on numerous supposedly recent and believable happenings—"urban legends" told repeatedly even in today's highly technological world. He distinguishes two kinds of variations: adaptations to make a given story fit local conditions (such as circumstantial details of name, place, time, and situation) and introduction of new elements (new characters or additions to the plot) which aim at explaining the story or making it in other respects more plausible. There is also normally an appeal to source authorities—it all is said to have happened to, for instance, a friend of a friend of the storyteller. Such stories, says Brunvand, can survive if they possess a strong basic story-appeal, a foundation in actual belief (in that such things are acceptable as possible occurrences), and a meaningful message or moral—often something appropriate to the desires and anxieties of the society in which the stories circulate. To find acceptance they need not be true, but merely believable: "The truth never stands in the way of a good story." It is not possible to retain much faith in the truth of community tradition once one has read Brunvand's books.

Recent studies of Mark, while endorsing Schmidt's estimate of its non-literary quality, are more reluctant to adduce this as evi-

dence of reliability. Reiser finds Mark's syntax and style comparable to that of Hellenistic folk-literature, below the level of literary
forms of the 'koine' (the 'common' [universal] Greek of the
Graeco-Roman world of the time). This lowly type of writing,
Reiser adds, was regarded by the educated with a contempt comparable to what cultured Germans have felt for the German
'chapbooks' (pamphlets of tales and tracts hawked by pedlars).[16]
Bryan observes that students with just about enough knowledge
of Greek to cope with the gospels will find, say, Plutarch or Philo
hard going, but will have little difficulty with the type of contemporary narrative prose designed for popular consumption, such
as Chariton's *Callirhoe* (a romantic novel probably from the mid-
first century A.D.). Bryan includes a selection from such popular
material in the original Greek at the end of his book so that his
readers can ascertain this for themselves. He concludes that Mark
wrote in "a genuine popular literary style", and notes that Origen
and other Christian apologists found themselves obliged to
defend such simplicity against criticism.[17]

All this is of interest in view of attempts that have been made—
because Mark does not hold up as history—to interpret its details
as forming subtle and ingenious literary patterns with symbolic
significance, as mysterious signals with hidden meanings for the
reader to decipher. The kind of 'training' purveyed in the literature
departments of our universities has produced a climate in which
scholars delight in the necessary display of ingenuity. Meagher
has countered all such make-believe by giving a detailed demonstration that Mark is "the product of a rather ordinarily clumsy
writer, probably working on materials that had come to him in
ordinarily clumsy form" (p. 58). Räisänen too insists that Mark is
not an example of the kind of sophisticated literature where (if
indeed anywhere!) one might be entitled to assume subtle verbal
links and associations, or recondite connections between distant
passages. He adds that, if it is hard to imagine a theologian who
would hide a sophisticated network of associations in such lowly
garb, it is "harder still to imagine a *readership* in Mark's time and
culture that would have understood such a message". Moreover,
"even such relatively well-educated readers as Matthew and Luke
obviously missed the alleged symbolic contents, interpreting Mark

in a straightforward way as an historical account of the words and deeds of the Lord. Nor were they blamed for this until modern critics entered the stage" (pp. 22–23).

iii. The Trial of Jesus and Persecution of Christians

The problems militating against accepting Mark's account of Jesus's trial before the Sanhedrin as historically accurate have been endlessly discussed. Brown calls his own detailed account of the various attempts to overcome them "just the tip of the iceberg" (*Death*, p. 553). Even if they could all be resolved, it is surely quite likely that what Mark wrote was influenced by the relation between Christians and Jews that obtained at his time of writing. His account is a Christian picture of attitudes held by adversaries, and "rarely in such a conflict does one side do justice to all the nuances of the other." Furthermore, it is not a picture painted at the time of the events portrayed, but considerably later, "in a period when the issues separating those who believed in Jesus from those (Jews) who did not had become more clearly and hostilely articulated". Admittedly, it will have been based on earlier material, but a pre-Marcan passion narrative, if there was one, cannot be reconstructed, and even that would not necessarily be historically accurate (*Ibid*, pp. 54–55, 545, 556).

At Mk. 14:61 the high priest asks Jesus: "Art thou the Christ, the Son of the Blessed?" and receives the answer "I am", which he immediately designates "blasphemy"; whereupon the whole assembly condemned Jesus "to be worthy of death". Clearly, he is here condemned for being what, in Christian eyes, he is. Already Wrede (*Secret*, p. 75) saw that Mark is here putting into the high priest's mouth the status Jesus had for the evangelist's own Christian faith; and the court's judgement ("blasphemy") likewise represents what Christians had experienced as the standard Jewish reaction to this claim. "In this way," says Anderson, "Mark makes clear the major issues dividing the normative Jewish and Christian teachings and attitudes."[18] At 2:7 he has already used the term 'blasphemy' to designate orthodox Jewish reaction to Jesus's claims.

Anderson holds further that Mark's trial narrative was influenced by the fact that when he wrote it, Christians were expecting that they might themselves have to face persecution and trial and that stories of Jesus on trial made their appearance at this particular stage in the development of early Christianity; for Paul knows nothing of any such stories, nor of the charges mentioned in either the Jewish or the Roman trials in any of the gospels (p. 119). That Mark's account was itself not regarded as authoritative is evidenced by the substantially different accounts of Luke and John. Thus, "even by the time of composition of all four canonical gospels, there was no authoritative account of a Jewish trial of Jesus" (p. 125). Indeed, he adds, these gospels show that it was not even agreed that there had been such a trial, for it is attenuated in Luke and practically eliminated in John (cf. *WWJ*, pp. 135f). So the question must be asked: why was the church not content to follow the path taken by Paul in concentrating on preaching the crucified and resurrected Messiah? Anderson finds the answer to lie in the subsequent fear of persecution.

In Mark there are references of a general kind to persecution and resultant apostasy. Jesus is made to interpret his parable of the sower as meaning that what is sown is "the word", the Christian message, and that some accept it for a while, but stumble "when tribulation or persecution ariseth because of the word" (4:14, 17). Mark must have in mind here the situation of Christian preachers and their auditors well after the time of Jesus, for Christians were not at that time persecuted. Then, at 10:29–30, Jesus says that those who have sacrificed everything ("houses, or brethren, or sisters, or mother or father or children or lands") "for the gospel's sake" will receive ample compensation "now in this time" (presumably in the fellowship of the Christian community), albeit "with persecutions". We saw (above, p. 79) that, in the NT the word 'gospel' does not mean a written document, but 'good tidings' about the salvation of the world by the coming of Christ. Here again, the reference is to the church's post-resurrection proclamation of Jesus who died for the sins of the world; and since it would be an anachronism to make him himself preach this 'gospel' before he suffered and died (see above, pp. 129f) Mark very often does not specify the precise content of his preaching. He is said to have "taught" (1:21) and "preached" (1:39) in such a way as to have "astonished" his audience (1:22) with an authoritative, but unspecified "new teaching" (1:27). When at 1:15 he urges repentance because "the kingdom of God is at hand", this is not new, and does not go beyond what John the Baptist has just been represented as saying. Thus he urges belief in "the gospel" (1:15) without saying what this gospel is. The followers of the Marcan Jesus must be prepared to lay down their lives for this unspecified "gospel" (8:35). Mark was obviously not bold enough to make his Jesus preach a full-blown Christology, as does the fourth gospel.[19]

Even more significant than the generalized references to persecution are passages where Mark indicates that Christians will be brought into court because of their beliefs, and urged to abjure them so as to escape capital punishment:

> And he called unto him the multitude with his disciples and said unto them, If any man would come after me, let him deny himself, and take up his cross and follow me. For whosoever would save his life shall lose it, and whosoever shall lose his life for my sake and the gospel's shall save it . . . For whosoever shall be ashamed of me and of my words in this adulterous and sinful generation, the Son of man also shall be ashamed of him, when he cometh in the glory of his Father with the holy angels. (8:34–38)

> They shall deliver you up to councils; and in synagogues shall ye be beaten; and before governors and kings shall ye stand for my sake. . . . And when they lead you to judgement, and deliver you up, be not anxious beforehand what ye shall speak; but whatsoever shall be given you in that hour, that speak ye; for it is not ye that speak, but the Holy Ghost. And brother shall deliver up brother to death, and the father his child; and children shall rise up against parents and cause them to be put to death. And ye shall be hated of all men for my name's sake. (13:9–13)

The second of these two passages states that one member of a family will denounce another to the authorities for the capital offence of being a Christian: the phrase "cause them to be put to death", in this context of "delivering them up to death", makes sense only if professing the "name" for which they will be hated is a capital crime.[20]

Pliny, writing from Bithynia to Trajan in A.D. 112, asked whether merely professing the "name" of Christian was a criminal offence, or whether only the "crimes" associated with the name were punishable. That he asked this question implies that there was no general edict proscribing Christians at that time, and Trajan's reply shows that he did not intend to pronounce one. Nevertheless, as Frend notes, "Christianity was not a *religio licita* and if it drew attention to itself then its members were liable to punishment. . . . Open profession of Christianity had been and continued to be an offence."[21] Pliny in fact had Christians who refused to renounce their faith executed. How long such a danger had already existed for them in the empire is not clear. Nero's persecution, following the fire which destroyed a large part of Rome in 64 (for which he blamed Christians), was an isolated incident, confined to Rome (compare *HEJ*, p. 81). The evidence of the so-called Christian Apologists of the second century exculpates Vespasian (Emperor from 69 to 79). It has often been suggested (mainly on patristic evidence) that general intolerance commenced in the latter part of Domitian's reign, from ca. 86, but some recent writers find that there is no substantial evidence that he behaved worse to Christians than did his predecessors.[22] Sherwin-White has pointed to "the extreme insignificance of the Christian communities in the vast framework of the empire", so that "there arises a general improbability either that the Christians seemed important enough to the government of Nero and Domitian to require a measure of universal suppression, or that any action was more than local and temporary." He adds that Christians were nevertheless liable to execution because they refused token homage to the gods of the empire, the *di nostri*, and that this was counted as *contumacia* (obstinate disobedience to a judicial order).[23]

It is plain from Pliny's letter that the persons he dealt with were accused simply because they were Christians; and it is plain from Mark that much in his gospel is a tract for the times—times of formal persecution of Christians as Christians. We cannot name the Roman city or emperor concerned, but Norman Perrin is surely right to say that "preparation of his readers for the possibility of persecution is a very real part of the Marcan purpose."[24] This certainly suggests a date later than Vespasian for the composition of Mark. And the date must be late enough for Christianity to have become recognizably distinct—from the standpoint of pagan observers—from its Jewish parent. This may well point to ca. A.D. 90.

But what bearing does this question of persecution have on Mark's narrative of Jesus's trial? Anderson's suggestion is that Mark makes him behave, at his trial, as a Christian, indicted for the offence of being a Christian, should behave. He envisages that, when Mark wrote, orthodox Jews were trying to frustrate Christian missionizing by stirring up public hostility against them and on this basis denouncing them to the Romans. This "pattern of accusers plus public hostility is well known from accounts of later Roman persecutions of Christians" (p. 121), and no more than this is portrayed in Mark's passion narrative, where "Pilate does not find Jesus guilty of a political or any other crime." The sole factors in his decision against Jesus are "the influence of his accusers and the public hostility which they have stirred up (15:15)". Jesus's unequivocal "I am" in reply to the high priest's question "can only be understood as a Christian confession", in that we are to see in the whole scene not only Jesus, but also the Christian of Mark's own day, as the defendant; the scene "surely reflects Mark's conception of events prophesied at 13:9 ('they shall deliver you up to councils', etc.) and fulfilled in his own time." Jesus, like the persecuted Christian of a later generation, is put in a position where he must openly declare allegiance to the prime article of Christian faith:

> Other charges do not require an answer, and in fulfilment of Isaiah 53:7 and Psalm 38:13–16 the accused is silent. . . . But he cannot remain unresponsive to the question 'Do you believe that Jesus is the Christ, the Son of God?' There is no way out; the accused must either deny the confession as Peter explicitly does (14: 68–72), making himself vulnerable to the Son of Man's denial of himself at the final judgement (8:38), or he must 'hold fast the confession' (Hebrews 4:14), risking his life now but saving it for eternity. Naturally, in Mark's narrative Jesus makes 'the good confession' (1 Timothy 6:12–13). (p. 120)

Mark's Jewish trial "serves positively to identify the individual as a Christian", and is followed by a Roman one to secure a condemnation by the authorities before whom Christians in Mark's day were haled. In sum:

> Jesus has to play two different roles in Mark's gospel: one as the redeemer and Lord of the community and another as its model of discipleship. Jesus represents both the one who 'gives his life as a ransom for many' (10:45) and those who stand before governors and kings and are brought to trial (13:9). (p. 122)

If Anderson is right, the hostility of the Jewish crowd to Jesus in Mark's passion narrative reflects the hostility of orthodox Jews to Christians in the evangelist's own day, and their readiness to indict Christians. It could, of course, also be historically accurate, in that the crowd was hostile to Jesus in passion week. But this is unlikely in view of the way the crowd has been up to that point portrayed in Mark. The first hint of its hostility comes at 14:43, when, sent by the priests, it effects Jesus's arrest. Earlier, the priests did not dare to arrest him in public for fear of the crowd (12:12), nor even to express an opinion about John the Baptist contrary to that of the crowd (11:32). They feared a tumult if Jesus were openly arrested, let alone killed, during the feast (14:2). "They feared him, for all the multitude was astonished at his teaching" (11:18). Yet at 15:11 they are able to incite the crowd against him. Räisänen, noting these discrepancies, comments that Mark *believed* that Jesus, in his ministry, had attracted crowds—hence the acclamation accorded him in earlier chapters, for instance at 7:37, "he hath done all things well"—but *experienced* that Christian preachers in his own day failed to do so (*Secret*, pp. 135–36).

In sum, we are faced with the question whether Mark's passion narrative is not so much an account of the trial of Jesus ca. A.D. 30, but a record of Christian reactions to Jews and Romans at the time when this gospel was written. Many would agree that this second stage has at any rate to some extent influenced the evangelist's portrayal of the first.

iv. Recent Defence of Mark's Reliability

Although one may quarrel with some details of the work of Wrede, Schmidt, and their followers, they have made it hard for subsequent scholars to read Mark as a straightforward transcription of historical events. Nevertheless, conservative evangelical commentators still regard this gospel as directly based on Peter's recollections, and will not allow that its author adapted earlier traditions about Jesus, still less that what he wrote was in considerable measure a response to issues of concern to his own Christian community. Blaiklock typifies this standpoint, saying: "The marks of an eyewitness are apparent on every page of Mark's swift narrative. In his language we seem to catch the accents of Peter's voice."[25]

Gundry's recent massive commentary shows no embarrassment at the way the Marcan Jesus restricts salvation to a few. He does not deny that Mk. 4:11–12 represents Jesus as deliberately unintelligible to "outsiders" in order to keep them from conversion and forgiveness. His purpose, says Gundry, was to "desensitize" them with his unintelligible parables so as to "separate out his true family" from them.[26] If it then be asked why he bothered to speak to them at all, why he did not "spare himself the trouble of having to obscure the truth in parables and then having to clarify it to his disciples in private", we may answer that he was "only following the example of Isaiah, not in respect of obscuring the truth, but in respect of speaking to people who he knows ahead of time will be lost" (p. 201).

Gundry's comments on some of the other Marcan passages I have mentioned in this chapter are similarly feeble. Jesus's absurd command that his raising of Jairus's daughter be kept secret when it is bound to become public is explained as his wish for secrecy to be maintained only long enough for him to make "a getaway" from the crowd (p. 276). There is no suggestion of any such motive in the text, and in the incident leading up to the raising he has shown no anxiety to be rid of the crowd. The disciples' repeated failure to understand his predictions of his Passion is, for Gundry, simply a foil that makes his foreknowledge stand out all the more (pp. 11, 504). He is quite rapturous about Jesus's wonderful foresight here and elsewhere in Mark. Commentators have long been aware that this gospel falls into two contrasting halves, portraying Jesus first as a worker of stupendous miracles and an authoritarian personality in Galilee, and then as resigned and even helpless in the hands of his opponents at Jerusalem, where his supernatural powers are manifest not from miracles (with the exception of the fig tree which withers when he curses it) but from numerous predictions of events, most of which either come true in the course of the narrative or had come true by Mark's time of writing. In chapter 14 he predicts how the room will be found in which he will eat the Passover with his disciples; also his betrayal by one of the twelve, the flight of the disciples, Peter's denial and his own resurrection, after which he will go before the disciples into Galilee; and finally the coming of the Son of man with the clouds of heaven. In the previous chapter he had foretold the destruction of the temple, persecutions, the advent of false Messiahs, and various cosmic catastrophies of the end times. Gundry is very impressed, particularly by his ability to predict small events as well as large ones, for instance where the colt will be found for his triumphal ride into Jerusalem: "The disciples will find it as soon as they enter a village. It will be male, tied, previously unsat upon. Someone may ask why they are untying it (11:1–6). Delicious detail" (pp. 10–11).

Other examples of the disciples' incomprehension—other, that is, than their failure to understand the passion and resurrection predictions—are also not satisfactorily accounted for by Gundry. We saw that, although they had already (at 6:35–44) witnessed Jesus's feeding of 5,000, they are a little later represented as having no idea that he will be able to feed a multitude: "Whence shall one be able to fill these men with bread here in this desert place?" (8:4). Gundry supposes that they had not forgotten the earlier feeding, but had failed to recognize that it was a miracle (p. 400)—this even though the text has emphasized that they had been well aware that with only five loaves and two fishes they had sated the hunger of 5,000 and then collected twelve baskets of left-overs. Their question at 8:4, which I have just quoted, leads to a second miraculous feeding of a multitude and, as noted above (p. 119), most commentators allow that Mark drew on two variant written versions of a single feeding, but supposed them to refer to different events because some details are not identical. Gundry sees that the two accounts are not only very similar, but are both followed by a sea crossing and by a discussion about bread (p. 395). This whole pattern is repeated in Jn. 6:1–58, and many commentators have inferred that both evangelists here drew on an early tradition of a miraculous feeding and of events following it. But convinced as he is that Mark's informant was Peter, Gundry will not countenance "stages of traditioning between Jesus and Mark" (p. 18). He accounts for the admittedly "close and obvious similarities" between the two Marcan feeding stories by pointing to "a tendency to assimilate traditions to each other, even to amalgamate them with each other". And he thinks that more than one miraculous feeding is just as historically acceptable as "more than one exorcism, more than one healing of the blind, etc." (pp. 399–400). Supposed dependence on Peter is also invoked to explain why Mark begins his gospel with the adult Jesus being baptized, and—unlike Matthew and Luke—has nothing to say about the circumstances of his birth and early life: "Peter's association with Jesus did not start till their adulthood; so Peter's preaching probably omitted Jesus's earlier life. Thus also Mark omits it" (p. 29).

Conservative scholars continue to make something (in some cases much) of what has become known as 'the Qumran Mark'. In an article in *Biblica* 53 (1972) the Jesuit papyrologist Fr. J. O'Callaghan claimed that a fragment from cave 7 at Qumran, which had been sealed in A.D. 68, recorded part of Mk. 6:52–53, so that Mark must have been available in Palestine at an earlier date and, as it was certainly not written there, composed even earlier, perhaps ca. A.D. 40. Wenham thinks that O'Callaghan's arguments "must be taken seriously", although he is aware that they have "sharp critics" (*Redating*, pp. 178, 288 n.17). How implausible they are was pointed out immediately after their publication by Vermes in a letter to the *Times* (1 April 1972), where he commented: the papyrus fragment in question is at its maximum 1 inches long and 1 inch wide. On it arranged in five lines are: nine perfect letters, three of which form the only complete word, καὶ, 'and'; two imperfect letters which it is possible to reconstruct with a fair degree of probability; six defective letters, the reading of which is problematic; and two quite illegible traces. To see Mk. 6:52–53 in this "flimsy material", O'Callaghan

1. "positively identifies the imperfect, the defective and the illegible letters, and accords to them the same degree of reliability as to the nine perfect ones";
2. assumes that his fragment has lines of 20–23 letters, simply because "two other better preserved but totally unconnected papyri found in the same cave contain 16–23 letters per line". This assumption enables him to "make good the gaps to either side of the extant and partially extant lettering so that the whole will match the Gospel passage".

Vermes goes on to say that, even so, O'Callaghan's reconstruction "leaves no room for three Greek words solidly attested in Mark by all the major codices." There is indeed a parallel omission in a second-century Coptic manuscript, but this variant is "so unimportant that most New Testament editors ignore it". Furthermore, "to fit the Marcan text, Fr. O'Callaghan has to sacrifice one of the nine perfect letters, a plainly visible *tau*, and to read instead a *delta*", and justifies this by saying that "in the popular Greek pronunciation in Egypt and Asia Minor, the two letters were interchangeable."

In the *Times* of 7 April 1972, C.H. Roberts added further objections:

> Of one line, only the trace of one letter survives: in each of the other four lines the last surviving letter is incomplete. In three out of the four Professor O'Callaghan proposes to read letters which are not listed by the original editors as possible alternatives, but which are essential for his identification. Only rarely can it be said with confidence what such incomplete letters are; much more frequently it can be said what they are not.

O'Callaghan claimed to have identified a further verse from Mark on another fragment, and in later publications two more verses of it in two further fragments and also, on yet others (all from the same cave), verses of Acts, Romans, 1 Timothy, James, and 2 Peter. He admitted that some of these identifications are tentative. Aland, who has written a very thorough refutation of these findings, notes that they were all made, at any rate in the first instance, from photographic reproductions and differed, in some cases substantially, from what the editors of the originals had found. He notes also that in most of O'Callaghan's reconstructions, letters of decisive importance are undecipherable, or not clear enough to be deciphered with certainty, and that, in the one case where his reconstruction is acceptable, it consists of six letters on three lines, each line having one, two or three letters, which can be made to yield (as O'Callaghan claims) James 1:23–24 only if one of the Greek words of these two verses (ἑαυτον) is omitted, whereas none of more than 500 manuscripts consulted omits it.[27] Roberts has shown that the six letters, as arranged on the fragment, could quite well be interpreted—if one is determined not to leave them anonymous as their original editors did—as fitting any one of numerous passages in the Greek OT, the Septuagint, and he offers six such possibilities straight away. He adds that it would not be difficult to 'prove' equally well that the lines came from a passage in Plato or Demosthenes: "Identifications on this scale are an exercise not in scholarship but in fantasy."[28] Aland declares (p. 16) that the whole "naive" assumption that a sequence of letters, even if they are only few, can yield only one specific text is "over and done with". The Leeds textual critic J.K. Elliott comments that this and other relevant articles by Aland ought finally to have buried the Qumran Mark.[29] Elliott calls Carsten Thiede's recent attempt to resurrect it "a publication cashing in on human gullibility".[30]

Wenham, we saw, takes O'Callaghan seriously and himself holds (on other evidence) that all three synoptics "are probably to be dated before 55"—Mark quite probably "in the mid-40s". One reason why he takes this view is that the author of Acts, who knew that Paul would "stand before Caesar" (27:24), does not report the outcome of his trial in Rome and—so Wenham infers—therefore wrote before the case was decided; Luke is earlier than Acts, and Mark in turn earlier than Luke (*Redating*, pp. xxii–xxiii). But there are reasons for thinking that the author of Acts knew that Paul had been condemned and executed. Its final verse states that Paul lived in Rome in relative freedom in lodgings at his own expense "for two whole years" (28:30). Haenchen is surely right to say that whoever wrote this knew that after these two years a change occurred, and what it was that had happened.[31] The

author has earlier made Paul say repeatedly (20:25 and 38) not
only that imprisonment and affliction await him, but that he will
never subsequently return to the areas where he has laboured as a
missionary. This implies that the author knew that Paul was never
released from prison. Acts is certainly anxious to show that the
Roman authorities were not hostile to Christianity, and this plea
would have been compromised had its story concluded with a
Roman execution of its principal character (see *HEJ*, pp. 150ff).

By accepting patristic statements about the gospels quite
uncritically, and also by assuming that all mentions of 'Mark' in
the NT refer to the same person (p. 176), Wenham is able to
regard Mark's gospel as "substantially the teaching of Peter . . . ,
probably written before the apostle's death, quite possibly shortly
after a stay in Rome by Peter from 42 to 44" (p. 182). Rome is
alleged by Irenaeus (late second century) and later Fathers to be
the place where Mark was written. This view evidently arose from
combining Papias's claim that Mark was dependent on Peter (discussed above, pp. 75ff) with traditions (current from the late second century, cf. *JEC*, pp. 216–17) linking Peter with Rome. That
he was there in 42 was the view of Jerome (fourth century). Wenham admits that the evidence for this is late and contradictory,
and has been rejected as worthless even by numerous "fairly conservative scholars" (p. 147).

Wenham's uncritical attitude to traditions of the Roman
church is matched by a similar acceptance of those of the church
of Alexandria: in the fourth century it claimed Mark as its
founder. Eusebius records at that time: "They say that Mark set
out for Egypt and was the first to preach there the gospel which
he had composed" (*Ecclesiastical History*, ii, 16). There is evidence
of a church in Egypt before 150; and according to Wenham "there
is a whole decade in the 50s when Mark could have been evange-
lising in Egypt" (pp. 175, 177). In actual fact, Mark's gospel is
poorly represented, in comparison with others, among the Egyptian papyri, and this argues strongly against the claim that it was
early and authoritatively used there.

Wenham dates Matthew even earlier than Mark, at ca. 40
(p. xxv): "Peter knew Matthew's gospel (either in a Semitic or
Greek form) and it is Peter's teaching that Mark records" (p. 198). He

admits, however, to some element of speculation here, "with small measure of checking our guesses" (p. 199). As for Luke's gospel, it was "apparently well-known in the mid-50s" (p. 243), for Paul mentions a "brother whose fame is throughout the churches" (2 Corinthians 8:18); this man "is evidently Luke, and his fame derives from his gospel-book" (p. 223), hence this gospel pre-dates Paul's epistle. I have tried to indicate (above, p. 79) how baseless this interpretation of 2 Corinthians is. Wenham, however, finds it "strongly supported" by references in "the early great fathers" (pp. 230–31). The earliest he mentions is Origen (third century).

Wenham realizes that he must answer the question: "if the gospels were written very early, why are they not referred to in the rest of the New Testament?" (p. 217). As we have just seen, he supposes that Paul does allude to the gospel of Luke; and he finds "echoes of the sayings of Jesus" constantly creeping into Paul's words (p. 218). He is obviously assuming that a Pauline saying which has some resemblance to a saying of the gospel Jesus derives, even if indirectly, from Jesus; whereas in fact the influence may well have gone the other way: e.g. ethical and other principles valued by Paul came in time to be ascribed to Jesus and thereby stamped with his authority. Paul himself, as we saw, does not so ascribe them.

Wenham claims that "the thinness of appeal to the Jesus-tradition" continues in later writers—he instances the Apostolic Fathers—even though they wrote when the existence of the gospels is no longer debatable but "virtually undeniable" (p. 219). This is simply not true. Whether the gospels were known to the Apostolic Fathers is very questionable. What they did know was a fair amount of the 'Jesus tradition'. Wenham himself allows that one of their number, Ignatius of Antioch, knew "many details about Jesus" (p. 296 n.8). He did indeed; he mentions the virgin birth, he names the mother of Jesus and says Jesus was baptized by John and persecuted by Pilate. There is nothing comparable to this in Paul. "The fallacy of the argument from silence", says Wenham, "is seen most clearly in the case of Luke. He knew all the Jesus-material of his gospel, yet when he came to write Acts he did not repeat it there" (p. 219). Did he not? The following details are mentioned in Acts:

1. Jesus was "of Nazareth", performed many miracles and signs (2:22) and went about doing good and healing all oppressed of the Devil. (10:38)
2. God anointed him "with the Holy Ghost and with power" (10:38); and Jesus himself said: "John indeed baptized with water, but ye shall be baptized with the Holy Ghost". (11:16)
3. He prophesied the destruction of the temple (6:14), had twelve disciples and was betrayed by one of them, Judas, who acted as a guide to those who arrested him. (1:16)
4. He was committed for trial by the Jews and repudiated by them in Pilate's court. Pilate wished to release him, but they insisted that he release a murderer instead (3:13–15). Jesus was also tried by Herod and the trial took place in Jerusalem (4:27).

It is no surprise that Wenham regards his book as giving "much for which to be thankful". If the synoptics are to be dated within 15–25 years of the death of Jesus, when many were still alive who could confirm or contradict what was written in them, then they are to be accepted as reliable; and "the right of the Christian church to maintain its traditional stance with regard to the foundation documents of the faith without impairing its integrity" is confirmed (p. 244).

Any defence of Mark must come to terms with its profusion of miracles. They are much more prominent than in the other two synoptics, since Mark has so little of their sayings material. There is no suggestion in any of the early canonical epistles that Jesus worked miracles, nor even in the writings of the earliest (the 'Apostolic') Fathers (Clement of Rome, Ignatius of Antioch, and Polycarp of Smyrna). Moreover, it is well-known that the gospel miracle stories are paralleled in Greek and Roman literature. R.M. Grant infers from his detailed investigation of such parallels that "a thoroughgoing distinction between Christian and non-Christian miracle stories cannot be made."[32] Yet such a distinction continues to be affirmed. The classical philologist Wolfgang Schadewaldt, who died in 1974, held that "Jesus did miracles, but not like other miracle workers. He always refused to make his miracles his credentials."[33] We have only to read as far as Mark's second chapter to find that this is not true. Jesus there authenticates his claim to be able to forgive sins—for his opponents a claim so outrageous as to be blasphemous (2:7)—by performing a miraculous healing:

> But that ye may know that the Son of man hath power on earth to forgive sins (he saith to the sick of the palsy), I say unto thee Arise, take up thy bed . . . And he arose, and straightway took up the bed, and went forth before them all: insomuch that they were all amazed. (2:10–12)

Hengel includes Schadewaldt's essay in his own book where, although he pleads for Mark's reliability, he is less than enthusiastic about the miracle stories. He is anxious that this profusion of what has been called "pious legend" should not lead us to think that Mark was too remote from Jesus to be devoid of "authentic reminiscence"; for there are, he says, numerous examples, both pagan and Christian, of eyewitnesses (or those near to them) crediting historical personages with miracles. A life of the fourth-century St. Martin of Tours written by his friend Sulpicius Severus is "bursting with them"[34]

It is not hard to see why in time Jesus came to be credited with miracles. Paul was opposed by Christian teachers who stressed their own miraculous powers. These rivals of Paul will naturally have supposed that the Jesus from whom they derived such powers had himself worked miracles and lived conspicuously, not, as Paul supposed, obscurely (see *DJE*, pp. 97ff). There was also anxiety to show that God was truly at work through Jesus. Hence in Acts Peter is made to tell the men of Israel that "Jesus of Nazareth" was "a man approved by God . . . by mighty works and wonders and signs which God did by him in the midst of you" (2:22). His exorcisms, showing his power over even supernatural beings, were for Mark an important way of indicating that he was the authentic son of God not only in his risen state, but also during his life on earth. Even so, Mark has to admit that "false Christs and false prophets" can work miracles (13:22), as presumably his own community was exposed to their blandishments. Another relevant factor is that Christians expected immortality: 1 Thessalonians 4:13–14 exhorts them not to sorrow over the dead as do the rest of mankind who are without hope. This expectation was founded on Jesus's own power over death, and it was natural not to limit this to his resurrection but to extend it by stories that he raised the dead during his ministry. Such restorations were not totally unfamiliar: at 2 Kings 13:21 a dead man is restored to life on touching the bones of Elisha; and Herod Antipas supposed that the miracle-working Jesus was "John the Baptist risen from the dead" (Mk. 6:14). All these factors contributed to make Jesus into a miracle worker.[35]

6

The 'Sayings Gospel' Q

Mark's first nine chapters portray Jesus as active in Galilee and even further to the north, after which he moves south to Judea, spending the final days of his life in Jerusalem. It is possible to regard Mark's story of the Jerusalem Passion as a historicizing of the indeterminate Pauline view of Jesus's crucifixion—particularly as it is constructed so extensively from OT material: "Take the scriptural references away, and the story of the death has vanished."[1] Paul and other early Christian writers had set Jesus within history, but not in a specific historical context; and I have summarized (above, pp. xxviiff) what I have said elsewhere as to how in time it could come to have been supposed that the Jesus of the Pauline and other early letters had died at Pilate's behest ca. A.D. 30. However, it is hardly feasible to account for the Galilean ministry in the same way. Miracles and teachings could well have accrued to Jesus in the course of developing tradition, but why Galilee? And why was he represented as a wandering preacher who confined his preaching to the villages and hamlets (not the cities) of Galilee and its environs? Galilee had long been exposed to hellenistic influences when the Maccabees annexed it, only as late as 100 B.C.; and Roman rule began little more than a generation later, with Pompey's capture of Jerusalem in 63 B.C.

Galileans became indifferent to both Jewish and Roman regimes; they had "no reason to be loyal either to the Romans or to the Herodians, or to the temple establishment in Jerusalem" (Mack, *Lost Gospel*, p. 62). Mark's gospel is the first surviving document to credit Jesus with a ministry in Galilee, and the basis for doing so needs to be explained.

Recent work on Q has proved helpful here. I have hitherto spoken of Q as the source of non-Marcan material that Matthew and Luke have in common. There are scholars (notably M.D. Goulder) who explain the overlap without positing Q at all, by supposing that Luke took the relevant material from Matthew. But the majority accept that these two wrote independently of each other, both drawing on Q as one of their sources.[2]

There is strong evidence that Q existed in written form, not merely as oral tradition. First, about half of it is verbally identical in Matthew and in Luke, and differences in the other half can be explained as due to one or the other evangelist—sometimes both—adapting the source so as to improve it stylistically or theologically. In these cases a primitive text has to be reconstructed that may not be absolutely identical with what now stands in either gospel. That Matthew has adapted Q (as well as he has Mark) in order to serve his own distinctive ends is betrayed by the fact that words and phrases that appear in his reworking of his Marcan source, as well as in material found only in him, are also found in his version of the Q material; for example, repeated references to 'righteousness'.[3] Luke seems on the whole to have done less editing of Q, and so scholars cite Q texts by their Lucan position: thus Q 10:12 = either Lk. 10:12 as it now stands, or this verse from which a primitive text must be reconstructed.[4]

Further reasons for supposing that Q existed in written form are given by Kloppenborg: 1. It contains a number of unusual and peculiar phrases; in oral transmission these would surely have been replaced by more common expressions in at least one of the synoptic versions. 2. There is considerable agreement between Matthew and Luke in the sequence of the units when there is no logical reason for them to occur in that particular order.[5] 3. There is doubling of some Marcan and Q material: an incident in Mark may be included by Matthew or Luke (or both) both in the Marcan sequence and in what appears to be its relative position in Q.[6] If Q traditions had been oral, they could easily have been conflated with the single Marcan version. Finally, 4., Q is without the mnemonic devices—important in Homer and in rabbinic traditions—which would be required as an oral basis for verbatim or near-verbatim agreements, and there is no evidence for mnemonic practice in the Christianity of the time.[7]

The original language of Q was Greek. There is no evidence that any NT books are written in a Greek that was translated from Aramaic.[8]

Q includes two miracle stories (a healing and an exorcism) and a general statement concerning Jesus's miraculous powers: the blind receive their sight, etc. (Q 7:21–22). It also includes a dialogue with the Devil, who challenges him to authenticate himself as "the son of God" in the story of his Temptation. But most of Q comprises Jesus's sayings, and when it was first isolated from its setting in Matthew and Luke it was hailed as a record of his authentic voice, proclaiming an unselfish ethic and largely, if not completely, free from the miracle and myth encumbering him in the canonical gospels. The contrast between Q and Mark, which has one miracle after another during the Galilean ministry and few teachings there, is particularly striking.

It was felt to be important to take the Q sayings as compiled without significant editorial interference, which would have given the voice or voices of editors rather than that of the historical Jesus. Further study, however, has identified considerable editorial work. The sayings are not simply strung together, but grouped into clusters each one of which is coherent: there is a grouping of four beatitudes and another of seven woes; and some clusters have a unifying theme, such as prayer. The whole collection has characteristics familiar from other antique sayings collections, and so may be regarded as a representative of a known genre. Jewish and other 'wisdom' literature expatiates on the principles of virtuous living: 'wisdom' collections of maxims, proverbs and injunctions were common, and several blocks of material in Q take the form of such sapiental instruction. There is also, as we saw in chapter 2 above, a mythological figure of Wisdom in Jewish tradition, a supernatural personage who can lead man into the path of truth. In Q the authority of Jesus is greatly enhanced by associating him with this mythological personage. If he was a sage, and his instructions wise, it was not a big step to regard him as an envoy of this Wisdom figure, as—with John the Baptist, who is mentioned in Q—one of Wisdom's children (Q 7:34–35).

What makes Q so very distinctive in early Christian literature as compared with the Pauline and other early epistles is not only the extensive teaching it ascribes to Jesus, but also its setting of his life in an identifiable time and place. By associating him with John the Baptist it places him unambiguously in first-century Palestine. (Josephus had mentioned John as alive then, but had not linked him with Jesus.) As to place, Q specifies the locality of Jesus's ministry by representing him as cursing Galilean localities that would not accept his message (Q 10:12–15). Mark, although very different from Q, has its own version of some of the traditions represented in Q, and one instance of this is that both speak of John the Baptist. But whereas in Q he appears as a prophet in his own right, Mark has adapted the tradition to the Marcan Christology and subordinated him to Jesus.[9]

What Q does not affirm about Jesus is as instructive as what it does. Admittedly, it may have been more extensive than the non-Marcan passages common to Matthew and Luke, as they have a certain amount of further similar material that they do not share. We know that they both omitted material from their Marcan source, and they could have done the same in their use of Q, so that some Q passages may be preserved by only one of them. Nevertheless, Q as it can be reconstructed from these two evangelists is a substantial document; and the Jesus of this Q is not the Messiah (the word 'Christ' does not occur), and is not accompanied by a select group of disciples: none are named in Q, and those who 'follow' him are not even termed 'disciples'. More significant still is that there is no mention of Pilate, nor of Jesus's Passion, crucifixion, or resurrection. The silence of a few sayings or narratives on these matters would not be significant, but the size of Q is—in the words of one of its cautious students—"sufficient to make the absence of reference to the death of Jesus as explicitly vicarious or saving . . . a significant silence".[10] Q adopts the 'deuteronomistic' portrait of Israel's history as having consisted of persistent disobedience to Yahweh, accompanied by persecution of his messengers, the prophets. The community represented in Q saw itself in this tradition, as followers of a Jesus who called Israel to repentance and who as such are persecuted. Hence the Jesus of Q is made to say: "Blessed are ye when men shall hate you . . . for the Son of man's sake . . . , for in the same manner did their fathers unto the prophets" (Q 6:22–23). Wisdom traditions are invoked for the same purpose. Proverbs 1:20–33 represents Wisdom as warning against the doom consequent on rejecting her message; and in Q (11:49) Wisdom figures as the agent who sends out prophets who are persecuted. Thus Jesus suffers the usual fate of Wisdom's envoys—rejection and perhaps worse. This is not spelled out, and is the nearest Q comes to hinting that he may have died a martyr's death. It has been held to explain why there is no passion narrative in Q. In the deuteronomistic tradition that Israel always persecuted its prophets, his death would be understood not as salvific, but as evidence of Israel's continuing impenitence.[11] It is not simply a matter of Q's being silent about salvific implications, but of a different explanation of suffering—as being the normal lot of the envoys of God or of Wisdom.[12]

It used to be said that, as a document consisting mainly of sayings with no mention of the Passion or resurrection, Q cannot be regarded as a gospel. But in 1945 the Coptic Gospel of Thomas was discovered, consisting of 114 of Jesus's sayings—about one third of them have parallels in Q—with no indication of where or under what circumstances he spoke them. It has no narrative framework, no birth or childhood stories and no account of a public ministry. There is criticism of the Pharisees and one mention of John the Baptist, but no suggestion of contact between him and Jesus. There are no healings or exorcisms, and nothing about a trial or about Jesus's death and resurrection. Many now date the Greek original underlying this Coptic text in the final quarter of the first century.[13]

One sign of editorial work in Q is that much of it has been organized into a literary unity by the motif of announcement of imminent judgement and polemic against 'this generation' which refused this message. Some commentators hold that this theme sits uneasily with the Q theme of a Jesus who teaches a humane ethic (for example 'love your enemies'), and that such 'wisdom' material was formed without knowledge of the theme of judgement, which was added at a later stage in the development of Q. However, not all accept that there are such chronologically distinct layers in it, and those who posit a layering are not in full agreement as to which material belongs to which stratum, nor as to whether all the supposed successive redactions were completed before A.D. 70.

By far the most readable account of the whole history of work on Q is Mack's *The Lost Gospel* (his term for Q), which is also a spirited championing of the argument for its chronological layering. He distinguishes an earliest layer in which Jesus advocates liberation from traditional social constraints: one should sell one's possessions (Q 12:33–34), break with family ties (Q 9:57–62), beg unashamedly (Q 11:9–13) and not worry about what to eat or wear (Q 12:22–31). Mack believes that this is the nearest to the historical Jesus that we can get (p. 203) and that the life-style here advocated is close to the behaviour of Cynics in the hellenistic traditions of popular philosophy.[14] They criticized conventional values and were known for fearless, carefree attitudes. This Cynic analogy has been challenged by (among others) Tuckett, who holds that the missionaries of Q gave up all their security not, as did the Cynics, in order to live a life of austerity as a means of achieving lasting contentment, but in order to proclaim their urgent message that the kingdom of God is at hand: "It is this theme of eschatology which dominates all forms of asceticism in Q and which alone provides the purpose of the (possibly) ascetic injunctions."[15] As the judgemental theme is so important for the organization of the Q material, Tuckett and others hold that it was present from the first, so that from the first Q represented Jesus as a prophet.

Mack, however, offers an account of how the judgement theme could have been introduced into Q only later. The message of Q's earliest layer, he says, is that customary pretensions are hollow. What is advocated instead is not a theological system, but a simple, 'natural' life-style: Solomon in all his splendour was less magnificent than the lilies of the field (Q 12:27). The natural order is here imagined as a realm of divine rule—as 'the kingdom of God'—by contrast with the prevailing social order: the poor are fortunate because they have God's kingdom (Q 6:20). Mack believes that, while the people who followed these Cynic-style precepts of Jesus presumably included some Jews, there is nothing characteristically Jewish, nor even religious about the precepts; and that Galilee, with its ethnic and cultural mix, is an understandable location for them. He supposes that in time loyalty to this Jesus movement involved a clash with Jewish propriety, particularly as represented by the Pharisees, and that the Jesus people then responded by confronting them with OT traditions which seemed to vindicate their own unconventional life-style against that of the Pharisees. In this way, the issue of loyalty to the Jesus movement came to be phrased as a Jewish question that was answered in Jewish terms: the Jesus people had now become a distinct group that was willing to see itself reflected in the traditions of Israel (*Lost Gospel*, p. 142). Threats of an apocalyptic judgement were introduced into Q at this stage, in the 50s or 60s of the first century, and they represent an example of the way the Q people invaded the territory of their Jewish detractors and used its idioms against them (p. 146). Only at this second stage in the development of Q does the kingdom of God begin to be spoken of as a realm to be realized by a final judgement at the end of time. It would follow from this view of Q's growth that the traditional view that Christianity emerged as a reformation of the religion of Judaism is erroneous. The appeal in Q to the OT, to what Mack calls "the epic of Israel", was "an ad hoc strategy that was not integral to the primary motivations of the Jesus movement" (p. 213).

For Mack, then, Jesus has been upgraded in importance as Q developed, and has been upgraded even more in what he calls "the fantastic portrayal" of him in the canonical gospels—a portrayal which constitutes "the result of a layered history of imaginative embellishments of a founder figure" (p. 247). He concludes that "Christian mythology can now be placed among the many mythologies and ideologies of the religions and cultures of the world" and "the Christian myth can be studied as any other myth is studied" (p. 254). Mack is Professor of New Testament studies at the Claremont School of Theology in California.

However radical and speculative we may find some or all of this, it is difficult to regard Q as all of a piece. Admittedly, some of its incompatibilities are normal in religious writings and so do not constitute evidence that earlier and later traditions have been there combined. For instance, Jesus's charge to his followers urgently to proclaim that "the kingdom of God is come nigh" (Q 10:9) culminates consistently enough in his cursing numerous places which have already refused his message. ("Capernaum . . . , thou shalt be brought down unto Hades.") But this bitter denunciation is then followed by an astonishingly abrupt change of mood where he breaks into thanksgiving to the Father for hiding "these things from the wise and understanding" and revealing them only "unto babes". Whereas, then, that portion of Israel which rejected the messengers has just been denounced and consigned to hell, we are now told that God intended the mission to fail to convince all but a few: he has deliberately withheld the light from all but the little fellowship of babes. We saw above (p. 128) how often such oscillation between assigning unbelief alternately to human perversity and to divine predestination is met with in religious apologetics. Better evidence that Q combines originally independent layers is the injunction "leave the dead to bury their own dead" (Q 9:60)—said in answer to someone who requests leave to bury his father before following Jesus. This is outrageously unjewish, violating not only filial piety, but also the command to honour father and mother. It is incompatible with the meticulous observance of every tittle of the law enjoined at Q 16:17. Again, the passage where Jesus speaks of himself in the manner of a gnostic redeemer is quite out of character with the rest of Q:

> All things have been delivered unto me of my father; and no one knoweth who the Son is, save the Father; and who the Father is, save the Son, and he to whomsoever the Son willeth to reveal him. (Q 10:22)

Not surprisingly, commentators have found that this reads more like the fourth gospel than anything in the synoptics. Hence Jacobson says: if a parallel is to be sought, then there is "the way in which the alienation of the Johannine community from their fellow Jews gave rise to, or was at least accompanied by, claims to be the exclusive recipients of divine revelation". This "encourages one to seek in the Q community a development parallel to that in the Johannine community."[16]

Mack believes that Jesus was upgraded in this way only in a third and final redaction of the Q material, and that the Temptation story (Q 4:1–13) was introduced into it at this stage, where Jesus figures as "Son of God" in a mythical confrontation with the Devil. The use of this name (ὁ διάβολος) for the evil one is unique in Q ('Satan' is the term for him at Q 11:18). The setting—first the wilderness, then a mountain top from which "all the kingdoms of the world" can be seen "in a moment of time", and finally the pinnacle of the Jerusalem temple—is obviously mythical; and narrative form is unusual in this sayings gospel. Jesus here repulses the Devil with OT quotations—the only explicit quotations in the whole of Q—in a way which makes him very beholden to the Jewish scriptures. According to Mack, it is only at this late stage in the development of Q that these are accepted as ethical guide lines: "It is easier for heaven and earth to pass away than for one tittle of the law to fall" (Q 16:17). Mack sees in this "the earliest evidence for an accommodation of the Jewish law within the Jesus movement, an accommodation that, when we meet it again in the Gospel of Matthew, can be called Jewish-Christianity" (p. 176).

Attridge observes that numerous students of Q, whether they regard Jesus with Mack as basically a sort of Diogenes or alternatively as a prophet, all tend to be struck by its silence on his death and resurrection, and by the relative paucity of explicit christological titulation on it. They agree that "Q was produced by 'non-kerygmatic' Christians", that is by "people who would not have summarized their stance as followers of Jesus with credal formulae like Paul's in 1 Corinthians 15:1–5" (Christ died for our sins and rose again).[17] When Q was first isolated from Matthew and Luke, many regarded it as 'catechetical support' or 'parenetic' (morally exhortative) supplementation of this 'Easter kerygma'. As long as this latter was considered to be the essential element of any Christian preaching, it was hardly possible to regard Q otherwise. But many of its pericopes display no catechetical or parenetic interests at all, and its message is organized along its own distinctive lines, independent of any 'Easter' proclamation.

The position, then, is that, while the manifold sayings of Jesus represented in Q are absent from the Pauline and other early epistles, the saving significance of his death and resurrection is absent from Q. The lesson seems to be that Christian origins are multiple, and that the Pauline churches formed only one of the relevant strands. We saw in Chapter 2 how much Paul is indebted to wisdom traditions; and ideas about wisdom—not quite the same ideas—constitute a link between his theology and that of Q.

Mack is justly critical of the almost universal view that Christianity can be explained only by taking the 'Easter' events, particularly the appearances of the risen one, however interpreted, as the indisputable point of origin, even if everything alleged to have been subsequent to them is treated more sceptically.[18] He is equally critical of the associated view—reached by combining Paul's references to an early Jerusalem church with the account of Christianity's development in Luke-Acts—that everything leading to later developments began in Jerusalem.[19]

We have, then, on the one hand the essentially supernatural Pauline Jesus who lived on Earth (if Paul was right in supposing this) well before Paul's time, and on the other the much more tangible teacher and prophet of Q, active at a time and place at no great remove from Q itself. Mack believes that, in spite of all the differences, the ideas of Jesus in the Pauline communities were derived from the ideas of Jesus entertained by the Q people (*Lost Gospel*, p. 216). He supposes that, because the Pauline communities were a mixture of Jews and gentiles, they found it expedient not to be specific about who killed Jesus, nor when, as any answer specifying Jews or Romans would have offended one or other section of the mixed worshippers. But mixture does not seem to have operated in this way in the case of the communities for which the gospels were written. He also supposes that the focus on the death and resurrection of Jesus as the Christ, characteristic of the Pauline congregations, made it no longer necessary to cultivate memories of Jesus as a teacher (p. 219). But Paul needed to press certain teachings (compare above, p. 13), would surely have been glad to cite Jesus in support of them, and would have been able to do so had he derived his Jesus from people who thought of him as a teacher. It is surely better to regard the two Jesuses as independent until they were brought together by Mark (as Mack agrees they were) and to see the common factor of wisdom traditions as facilitating the fusion. That there was a drastic remodelling in the process need cause no surprise. As Mack himself notes (p. 210), the same has happened often enough again in the succeeding centuries, so that today we have even a feminine Christ.

7

Are the Gospels
Anti-Semitic?

i. Matthew and the Pharisees:

Chapter 23 and its Lucan Parallels

The scurrilous language used about Jews in the NT has been designated "a source of shame (finally) to Christians and a well-
grounded source of fear to Jews".[1] A classic example is Mt. 23
where Jesus calls scribes and Pharisees hypocrites, blind guides,
white-washed sepulchres, serpents, murderers, and a brood of
vipers who will be sentenced to hell. There is not much of the so-
called Christian spirit in these fulminations against whole classes
of men, many of whom may well have been as respectable and as
well-meaning as our bishops and clergy today. When Paul says
that before he became a Christian he was "a Pharisee as to the
law" (Philippians 3:5), he is not confessing to former hypocrisy,
but using the name as a title of honor, and "claiming the highest
degree of faithfulness and sincerity in the fulfilment of his duty to
God as prescribed by the divinely-given Torah".[2] Paul can be scurrilous enough when it suits his purpose, and in the same chapter
refers to those who advocate circumcision of (presumably gentile) Christians as "dogs" and "evil workers". To abuse opponents
was the near universal practice of antiquity,[3] well exemplified in
the Qumran sectarians, who wrote of 'the man of lies', 'the
spouter of lies', 'the man of scorn', 'the wicked priest', 'the lion of

wrath', and 'the seekers after smooth things'. Much of their invective is directed against other Jews who did not match their own ideas of purity. Hatred is apt to be strongest between groups which are closest together, particularly if, as is usually the case, they are competing for support from the same persons. Rank outsiders might be excused for not knowing 'the truth', but 'heretics' can be charged with wilfully rejecting it. Thus the Pharisees had enemies within Judaism who accused them of hypocrisy and ostentation;[4] and in the NT the brief epistle of Jude consists almost entirely of vilification of rival Christians, who are said to follow their lusts, to commit shameful deeds, defile the body, flout authority, insult celestial beings, pour abuse on things they do not understand, and to be grumblers and malcontents, eating and drinking without reverence at Christian love-feasts. If they really were such a wild lot, they could hardly have "wormed their way" (verse 4) unobtrusively into the church and needed Jude's denunciations to expose them. It seems, then, that he is simply employing traditional rhetoric in order to discredit Christians whose views differed from his own. To take it at face value would be like judging Catholics of the Reformation period from Protestant comments. Marxist condemnation of whole classes is equally arbitrary.[5]

Jesus's attack on his own neighbours in Mt. 23 is also quite incongruous, placed as it is immediately after his endorsement of the OT command "Thou shalt love thy neighbour as thyself" (Mt. 22:39) and in a gospel where he states that he has come "not to call the righteous but sinners" (9:13) and where he even enjoins love of enemies (5:44). The whole of chapter 23 is an expansion of Mark's brief denunciations (12:38–40) of the ostentation, greed and hypocrisy of "the scribes", as its position betrays. (In both gospels the relevant material occurs between Jesus's question in the temple, as to whether the Christ is the son of David, and his prophecy that the temple will be destroyed.) Matthew makes Mark's three verses into a sustained and much more ferocious attack on scribes *and Pharisees* by supplementing Mark here with material from Q. Luke also reproduces Mark's words, likewise at the same point in his narrative (20:45–47), and supplements them with the Q material. But he places this latter earlier in his gospel (11:37–52), in an entirely different context—representing Jesus as a (very ungracious) guest to dinner in a Pharisee's house in Galilee.

Matthew's supplementation goes beyond both Mark and Q, for some of it has no equivalent elsewhere, so that the evangelist either drew it from some source or sources (not extant) or composed it himself. The latter is probably the case when scribes and Pharisees are addressed as "ye offspring of vipers" (23:33), for he seems to have had some liking for this appellation of them: at 3:7 he had made John the Baptist address Pharisees and Sadducees (not, as in the Lucan parallel, "the multitudes") with these words, with which he again designates the Pharisees at 12:34 ("Ye offspring of vipers, how can ye, being evil, speak good things?") in a sentence absent from the Lucan parallel. He is clearly intensifying and expanding the criticism of the Pharisees already visible in Q.

This hostility is explicable from the fact that Matthew was writing near the end of the century when Pharisees had probably become prominent among the post–A.D. 70 rabbis. They were admittedly not exclusively in control of rabbinic Judaism, so that we cannot draw a direct line of descent from pre–A.D. 70 Pharisaism to rabbinism (nor from the former to the later Diaspora leaders);[6] but to associate the two would come readily both to Matthew and to his readers. In this way, a Jesus placed in the third decade of the century was made into a critic of the Pharisees, when in fact they can hardly have been prominent as opponents of Christianity in the whole of the first half of the century; for, as Burton Mack has noted, "in the Pauline corpus, rife with ideological controversy pertaining to 'Judaizers', the law and cultic codes, there is no mention of Pharisees other than the single self-reference to Paul's own former way of life" (*Myth*, p. 42). We saw that he believes that criticism of the Pharisees was introduced only secondarily into Q, ca. A.D. 50 or 60.

A series of seven specific 'woes' spoken to scribes and Pharisees begins at 23:13. Six of them are introduced with the vocative "hypocrites", absent from the Lucan parallels, and this again suggests Matthew's own hand, as a certain fondness for such vocatives is evidenced in the way he inserts them into Marcan material.[7] In some contexts, 'woe' (οὐαι in the Greek) can mean merely 'alas for you', expressing sorrowful pity, without imprecation: the οὐαι of Mt. 24:19 does not curse pregnant women who have to flee, but sympathizes with them. But οὐαι is sometimes threatening and judgemental, as in the following Q passage which expresses resentment, characteristic of Q, at the failure of the Christian mission: miracles performed in Galilean localities had met with no response, and so these places will fare worse at the judgement than notoriously sinful cities:

> Woe unto thee, Chorazin! Woe unto thee, Bethsaida! for if the mighty works had been done in Tyre and Sidon which were done in you, they would have repented long ago in sackcloth and ashes. Howbeit I say unto you, it shall be more tolerable for Tyre and Sidon in the day of judgement than for you. And thou, Capernaum, . . . shalt go down unto Hades: for if the mighty works had been done in Sodom which were done in thee, . . . (Mt. 11:21–23 = Lk. 10:13–15).

Such threats are characteristic of Matthew's Jesus, who refers repeatedly to those who are to be cast into outer darkness where there is "weeping and gnashing of teeth" (8:12; 22:13; 25:30). As the whole context of Mt. 23 is likewise condemnatory, it looks as though the 'woes' there are judgemental, particularly as they are formulated in the same way as in the Q passage just quoted.[8] Furthermore, 'woe unto them who do so and so' is well attested in the OT as an imprecatory formula.[9]

The first 'woe' in Mt. 23 calls scribes and Pharisees hypocrites because they "shut the kingdom of heaven against men", and neither enter in themselves, nor allow those who would enter to do so (verse 13). 'The kingdom of heaven' stands for the Christian community: eventual entry into the former comes from membership of the latter,[10] which the Jewish authorities are preventing. The Lucan parallel makes Jesus use the past tense and thus look back at the failure of the mission to Jews; the scribes (Luke prefers the term 'lawyers' for these legal experts later known as 'rabbis') have squandered their chance of salvation:

> for ye took away the key of knowledge: ye entered not in yourselves, and them that were entering in ye hindered. (Lk. 11:52)

This formulation surely distorts whatever the Q original was: 'entering in' applies to the kingdom, which Luke does not mention, but not to 'the key of knowledge', which he does.

It hardly needs pointing out that scribal and Pharisaic failure to turn Christian and their hindering their kind from doing so may have been offensive to Christians, but would deserve to be called hypocrisy only if its practitioners did not themselves believe in the faith they were promulgating. The same criticism must be made of stigmatizing as hypocrisy their missionary zeal: they "traverse sea and land to make a single proselyte" and then "make him twice as much a child of hell" as themselves (Mt. 23:15, without synoptic parallel). If this is so, their teaching can hardly be as sound as—surprisingly—verses 2–3 claimed.[11] What we have in this second woe of verse 15 is surely no more than the familiar experience that converts are apt to be even more zealous than those who convert them. Beare notes, on this verse 15, that "Catholics often find that converts from Protestantism are bent on showing themselves 'more Catholic than the Pope'." (*Matthew*, p. 454).

As the Pharisaic misdemeanours specified in these first two woes do not constitute hypocrisy, attempts have been made to show that here Matthew is using the term in some unusual sense. But what he understands by it is perfectly clear from his address to scribes and Pharisees in 15:7–8:

> Ye hypocrites! Well did Isaiah prophesy of you saying 'This people honoureth me with their lips, but their heart is far from me.'

The third woe, on the breaking of oaths (23:16–22), occurs only in Matthew and seems to be based on his misunderstanding of rabbinic discussions. Haenchen notes in this connection that, in Israel, the name of God was too holy to be mentioned, and was replaced in oaths by such terms as heaven, temple, altar, and so forth. Oaths formulated in this way might then be broken if it was subsequently claimed that, by, for instance, 'heaven', only the sky and not God had been invoked. Many rabbis simply refused to accept such evasion; others sought alternative formulations which excluded it, saying that if the oath is sworn by the gold of the temple or by the sacrifice on the altar, then there is unambiguous reference to the property of God and hence to God himself. Matthew misunderstood this and supposed that the rabbis were happy to allow oaths sworn by the temple or the altar to be null and void, while they insisted that those sworn by the gold of the temple or the gift on the altar be kept.[12]

The fourth woe returns to Q material and this time scribes and Pharisees are called hypocrites because they are meticulous over tithing but fail to implement "the weightier matters of the law", namely "judgement" (condemnation of evil), mercy and "faith" (fidelity), to which they should also have attended (23:23). Here, then, although their neglect of essentials is denounced, their scrupulosity is condoned. That they were in fact meticulous observers of (at any rate some of) the law's stipulations is strongly suggested in both Christian and Jewish traditions; and so smugness rather than hypocrisy would be a more likely criticism of them. This is what Luke's parable of the Pharisee and the publican (18:9–14, without synoptic parallel) ascribes to them, although it is itself a caricature of Pharisaism.[13]

The last of the woes is built on the legend that all the prophets died for their testimony. Their murder, says Garland (p. 179) "had become almost an article of faith in heterodox Judaism despite the fact that none of the three major canonical prophets nor any of the twelve minor prophets suffered a violent death at the hands of the people." One reason why the contrary was believed was the conviction that Israel must have been guilty to have been so severely punished by God in repeated humiliations of defeat and conquest.[14] Jesus here says that scribes and Pharisees build the sepulchres of the prophets they admit their fathers killed, and claim, hypocritically, that had they lived then, they would not have been "partakers with them" in this blood (23:29–31). The Lucan equivalent states that, in building these tombs, they are "witnesses and consent unto the works of their fathers" (Lk. 11:47–48). As commentators have observed, this is like saying: the people of Geneva built a monument to Servetus, killed there at Calvin's instigation; therefore they are as wicked as his killers.

In the sequel, the charge even against the present generation becomes murder:

Mt. 23:34	*Lk. 11:49*
Therefore, behold, I send unto you prophets and wise men and scribes: some of them shall ye kill and crucify: and some of them shall ye scourge in your synagogues and persecute from city to city.	Therefore also said the wisdom of God, I will send unto them prophets and apostles; and some of them they shall kill and persecute.

Matthew here makes Jesus speak about an act he is performing in the present (sending prophets and others to be scourged and killed). But in Luke he is not referring to himself (even though elsewhere, such as 1 Corinthians 1:24, the term 'the wisdom of God' is used as a title of the pre-existent Christ); for the verb 'said' is in the third person and the past tense, and the initial 'also' (και) indicates that 'the wisdom of God' is being introduced as a new speaker (whereas the previous verses had given Jesus's own words). Whereas, then, in Matthew, Jesus is sending prophets in the present, in Luke 'wisdom' spoke in the past of who *will* be sent "unto them" (not "unto you", as in Matthew, for a present audience was not being addressed). It is surely clear that the saying must originally have been a Wisdom saying, from a Jewish Wisdom book (or an oral tradition about Wisdom) otherwise unknown. We cannot suppose that Luke ascribed to Wisdom a saying which, in his source, was given as a saying of Jesus. It is much more plausible that Matthew, understanding Jesus himself as the Wisdom of God, put a Wisdom saying into his mouth and into the present tense.

Luke's version places the logion very clearly in a Christian milieu by saying that "prophets and apostles" will be sent. He may well have been thinking of the persecution of apostles and leaders which he describes in Acts. Matthew's version, in which Jesus is sending scribes who will be persecuted, shows that there were Christian scribes when he wrote, successors of the Jewish ones, as is also implied at 13:52, where there is mention of "scribes made disciples to the kingdom of heaven". These are presumably to be understood as 'our scribes' (those belonging to the Matthean community), in contrast to 'their scribes' (orthodox Jewish ones) of 7:29. Again, Matthew refers here at 23:34, to "your synagogues" in an address to Jews, but elsewhere to "their (αὐτῶν) synagogues" when Christians are addressed (10:17). His Jesus never uses the term 'our synagogues', but speaks as though Christianity had already broken with the synagogue—a break which in fact occurred later than the 20s and 30s. In numerous references to synagogues Matthew adds the word 'their' whenever the context in itself fails to indicate that the synagogue is an institution belonging to the 'hypocrites'.[15] Przybylski points out that Matthew's desire to portray the synagogue solely as a place of corruption is further indicated by his deletion of the Marcan reference to it (preserved in Luke) in the story of the man who came to Jesus and "worshipped him".[16]

Matthew is also the only canonical evangelist who makes Jesus speak of a Christian "church". "My church" of 16:18 is in obvious contrast to the phrase 'their synagogues' of other passages; and at 18:15–17, also without synoptic parallel, the 'church' is twice mentioned as if it already existed as a regulative body. It is thus not surprising that the later church placed Matthew at the very head of its canonical collection of twenty-seven books, quite apart from the fact that it was valued because it includes so many sayings of Jesus that are lacking in Mark, the older gospel.

After Jesus's reference to Jewish persecution of Christians, Matthew makes him add that "all the righteous blood shed on the earth" from "the blood of Abel" onwards shall come upon "this generation" (23:35–36). We may query why contemporaries of Jesus should be blamed for such pre-historic crimes as the murder of Abel, but that one generation is punished for the sins of its predecessors was a not uncommon view in antiquity, which was more concerned with the community than with the individual. Guilt was thus regarded as collective, accumulating like water in a dam, which overflows disastrously once it reaches a certain height. Murders in former times, bad as they were, did not bring the measure of guilt to such fullness: God bides his time (see Genesis 15:16, "the iniquity of the Amorite is not yet full"), but once sin has reached certain proportions, his longanimity will be exhausted. In the present context, the Pharisees will "fill up the measure" of their fathers (verse 32).

By the suffering of "this generation", Matthew surely had in mind those Jews who experienced the destruction of their country in the war with Rome from A.D. 66. His community was also faced with the failure of the Christian mission to Jews: the supreme messenger to Israel, the Son of God who was to be the final judge had been rejected. As Garland (p. 89) and others have observed, to attribute both these factors to the wickedness of the Jewish leaders was a source of comfort, even though it proved an embarrassment to later Christianity. Most commentators today, far from trying to separate out some of Mt. 23 as authentic utterances of a historical Jesus, are glad to be shot of it all. Beare declares in his commentary that "a Christian expositor is under no obligation to defend such a mass of vituperation" (*Matthew*, p. 461). From a Jewish standpoint, Sandmel is "puzzled that Christians can read this chapter and still speak of Jesus as a kindly man" (*We Jews*, p. 125).

ii. Matthew's Relation to Jews and Gentiles

Turning now to Matthew's passion narrative, we find that he introduces small additions to Mark's account so as to make the Jewish forces ranged against Jesus more culpable. It is only in Matthew that they are said to pass Jesus on to Pilate with the express purpose of having him "put to death" (27:1–2). All the people (27:22) demand Jesus's crucifixion—the 'all' is a significant addition to Mk. 15:13–and in a verse without synoptic parallel "all the people" answer Pilate's plea for clemency with: "His blood be on us and on our children" (27:25). The persons here gathered before Pilate have hitherto been termed a 'crowd' (ὄχλος), but here it is "all the nation" (λαός) that shouts for Jesus's blood.

It is unfortunate that such passages are often read as a historically accurate record of what actually happened, when in fact they are but amendments to an earlier narrative, and—like other amendments in Matthew's passion narrative—are quite unconvincing as history. For instance at Mt. 27:43 (unparalleled) the chief priests' mockery of the dying Jesus includes a sentence very close to the wording of Psalm 22:8, and obviously drawn from there, namely: "He trusteth on God; let him deliver him now if he desireth him." In the Psalm these words are not spoken to a criminal, but by non-believers to the righteous one of God, who suffers innocently at their hands. It may be a fine piece of irony on the part of Matthew to cast the Jewish establishment in this rôle, but, as Buck observes, "this whole situation is just too incongruous" to be historically plausible.[17] He also notes that, correlatively, the gentiles are placed in an improved light. Only in Matthew does Pilate's wife urge her husband not to proceed against "that righteous man" (27:19) and Pilate dissociate himself from Jesus's Jewish accusers by taking water and washing his hands in innocence (27:24). Moreover, the centurion who, at Mark 15:39, declares Jesus to be "the Son of God" is made into one of a whole chorus of companions who make the same positive declaration (27:54). This was surely no first-hand reporting, but deliberate manipulation of existing tradition from a particular Christian perspective.[18]

Surprisingly, there is, as I showed in *DJE* (pp. 106–09) pro- as well as anti-Jewish material in Matthew: he at times adapts Mark's version of Jesus's arguments with Jewish authorities so as to bring him closer to an orthodox Jewish standpoint. What we see in Matthew is a Jewish Christianity, cognisant of gentile Christianity and not wishing to exclude it, but insisting on its own interpretation of the Torah and on Jesus's status as Messiah of Israel against mainstream Judaism represented by the Pharisees. Matthew's church may have included some gentiles, but it was predominantly Jewish Christian, existing in an orthodox Jewish environment and concerned to define itself in opposition to that environment. Hare is surely right to say that Matthew's hostility to orthodox Judaism is "far too intense to be a matter of literary convention", and that "some kind of unhappy contact with Pharisaism" is required to explain his attitude. Persecution of Christian missionaries seems to have been what was involved. This is suggested by the references to killings and scourgings at 23:34, and by the logion "blessed are ye when men shall reproach you and persecute you" (5:11—the Lucan equivalent makes no mention of persecution). Jesus's charge to his disciples when he sends them out as missionaries is of interest here. Hare (pp. 98ff) notes that Matthew begins it at 10:5–14 by including its Marcan

equivalent—Mk. 6:7–11, where there is no suggestion of persecution–but he then continues it (10:16ff) by transferring to this earlier context the substance of Mk. 13:9–13, which there refers to
the tribulation which will characterize the world's final days.
Mark has:

> They shall deliver you up to councils; and in synagogues shall ye be
> beaten; and before governors and kings shall ye stand for my sake
> and for a testimony unto them (13:9).

By placing this and the following Marcan verses in a context
where Jesus, early in his ministry, is telling his disciples how they
will be received when they missionize, Matthew indicates that
persecution is the normal reaction to Christian missionary activity, and is not confined to the end-time, although when he comes
later to speak of that, he agrees with Mark that it will also occur
then (Mt. 24:9).

iii. Similarities and Differences between the Gospels Concerning the Jews

If Matthew does indeed represent a predominantly Jewish fac-
tion's critique of mainstream Judaism, then his anti-Jewish
remarks were not intended as an *en bloc* condemnation of all
Jews, but only of those who had not turned Christian—although
he had to allow that this was the position of the vast majority.[19]
But once Christianity became an essentially gentile religion, his
harsh words were naturally taken as anti-Semitic pure and simple. The same is true of the fourth gospel. There, 'the Jews' is a
term of opprobrium for Jesus's opponents, even though he himself and his supporters are also Jews. This term 'the Jews' distinguishes him from his own people in a way that is not found in the
synoptics, and is not credible in the life of a Jewish Jesus of
ca. A.D. 30. It is intelligible as a Christian way of designating
unbelieving (non-Christian) Jews at a time when the two faiths
had become separate entities. That this situation obtained when
the fourth gospel was written is indicated when the author not
merely makes Jesus predict that his followers will be "put out of

the synagogue" (16:2), but in two passages (9:22 and 12:42) even commits the anachronism of implying that the expulsion had already occurred at the time of his ministry. The separateness of the two faiths is also indicated at 9:28 where "the Jews" are made to distinguish themselves, disciples of Moses, from the disciples of Jesus—who for their part claim Moses as their own, so that Jesus can say (to "the Jews"): "If ye believed Moses, ye would believe me; for he wrote of me" (5:46). Although, then, the term 'the Jews' in this gospel means only those who have rejected Christianity, they are described in the harshest terms: their father is the devil, a liar and a murderer, and their will is to do this murderer's desires (8:44). It is, then, not surprising that later Christian readers of such passages should have become violently anti-Jewish.

Paul had clung to the hope that, once Jews see many gentiles converted to Christianity, they will be stimulated to claim their own rightful place within the true Israel of the church (Romans 11:2 and 25–26). But he wrote before the destruction of Jerusalem, regarded by rabbis as punishment for Israel's sins, and by Christians as God's final rejection of Israel. Most later Christian writers were no longer capable of allowing his assessment that non-Christian Jews had a genuine "zeal for God", even though it is "not enlightened" (Romans 10:2).

Luke is the most ambiguous of the evangelists in his attitude to the Jews, as emerges from what he says about Jesus's relation to Pharisees. We saw that at 11:37–44 he makes him the guest of a Pharisee when denouncing Pharisees in terms familiar from other gospels; and he chooses the same setting for two other passages where they are denounced (7:36–47; 14:1ff)—a setting which has been interpreted as an attempt to modify his inherited anti-Pharisaic tradition (see *WWJ*, pp. 121–22).

In Acts, also by Luke, the Pharisees even appear as the allies of the apostles, especially of Paul. Wilson has pointed out that the author was particularly anxious to depict Paul as at all times a faithful and law-abiding Jew and as deferring to Jewish scruples (for example 16:1–3; 21:17–27), however much such deference "strains the reader's credulity, not to mention that of the historian who knows Paul's letters". Luke's purpose here was, he says, to defend Paul against the charge that he encouraged *Jews* to desert Jewish practices; and what better witnesses could there be of the untruth of such a charge than the support of the predecessors of the leading Jews of Luke's day?[20] Nevertheless, as Wilson is well aware, Acts somewhat incongruously combines this with repeated references to 'the Jews' as the enemies of the church, in a manner found elsewhere within the canon only in the fourth gospel. Thus in Acts the Romans oppose neither Jesus nor the apostles except under pressure from 'the Jews', and Paul is made on three solemn occasions to repudiate them for their rejection of the gospel and to announce his turning to the gentiles (13:46; 18:6; 28:28), thus indicating that the Jewish mission was at an end. Wilson concludes: "The positive aspects of Judaism and its crucial contribution to Christianity are, from Luke's point of view, largely a thing of the past. The present reality for Luke and his readers was that the Jews belonged to a separate and hostile entity, the synagogue" (p. 116).

After Jesus's frequently hostile exchanges with the Pharisees during his public ministry, it is surprising how little they are represented in the gospels' passion narratives (see above, p. 141). In the synoptics he predicts his own Passion on three occasions, saying that elders, chief priests and scribes will be involved, but makes no mention of Pharisees. They are also not involved in the plotting with Judas. Matthew has to amend Mark in order to introduce them at 21:45, and at 27:62 he gives them a part in his story (unique to him) of the posting of a guard at the tomb. Even in John, where the Pharisees seek in chapter 11 to have Jesus arrested, they are mentioned only once (at 18:3) in the passion narrative.[21] It really looks as though there was no firm Christian memory that the Pharisees as such played a role in the crucifixion. Brown mentions this (*Death*, p. 1432) as a possible conclusion to be drawn from the evidence.

My quotations have shown that many gospel passages could be taken as unreservedly anti-Jewish if both the context in which they are placed and the social and religious context in which their authors were operating are ignored. For Matthew the cry raised at 27:25 ("his blood be on us and on our children") will have meant that the children of the speakers paid for their parents' guilt when Jerusalem was destroyed some forty years later. This Christian commonplace was ethically bad enough (compare above, p. 51); but the verse was later taken to mean that Jews are to be punished for all time for their role in Jesus's death. Brown quotes Origen, who commented to this effect on this verse, as "an early voice in a series of patristic statements that would grow in intensity", and which were authoritatively and publicly repudiated only a generation ago at the Second Vatican Council, in the declaration that what happened at Christ's Passion cannot be blamed upon all the Jews then living, nor upon the Jews of today. Brown adds that, if this seems merely to affirm the obvious, it nevertheless constitutes a repudiation by a very traditional church of attitudes towards the Jews uttered by some of its most venerated Fathers and Doctors. He refers to E.H. Flannery's *The Anguish of the Jews* (second edition, New York: Paulist, 1985) where, he says, "some of the greatest names in Christian history (Augustine, Chrysostom, Aquinas, Luther, etc.) are quoted . . . as advocating with frightening ferocity the right and even the duty of Christians to dislike, hate and punish the Jews" (*Death*, pp. 384–85). That this has not been an exclusively Catholic attitude within Christianity is shown by Luther's infamous 1543 tract 'On the Jews and their Lies', where he gives Christians the following "sincere advice" concerning Jews: confiscate their literature, burn their synagogues and schools, raze their houses and herd them into communal, supervised settlements, put them to manual labour and abolish safe conduct for them on the highways.[22]

In any case, Christian doctrine has it that the death of Jesus was the working out of a divine plan for man's salvation. Why, then, blame the human agents who caused this benefit? Even Judas is a mere agent in this divine schedule. Jesus is represented as acknowledging this and as yet condemning him: "The Son of man goeth as it is written of him; but woe unto that man through whom the Son of man is betrayed" (Mk. 14:21; cf. 9:12).

8

Ethics and Religious Belief

i. The Sermon on the Mount

Matthew's Sermon on the Mount is mainly non-Marcan material, comprising chapters 5 to 7. Some of it is not represented at all in other gospels, and some is Q material, as inexact parallels in Luke reveal, many of them scattered over six chapters there instead of forming a single discourse.

In this Sermon, Matthew's Jesus declares: "Till heaven and earth pass away, one jot or one tittle shall in no way pass away from the law" (5:18). This endorsement of "the law" and "the prophets" (verse 17) validates the whole religious constitution of the OT: for 'the law' was the Jewish term for its first five books, and 'the prophets' meant the books from Joshua to 2 Kings and from Isaiah to Malachi. There is some irony in the fact that the gentile church has given this gospel such a prominent position in its canon while rejecting its allegiance to Torah.

Jesus introduces his endorsement of the Jewish law by telling his audience not to suppose that he has come in order to destroy it (5:17). Betz argues that this is directed against those who did think on precisely such lines, and may have been aimed at Pauline-type gentile Christians who did not hold to the provisions of the law and who, as we know from Galatians, were severely criticized by Jewish-Christians for this latitude. The condemna-

186

tion of those who break even minor stipulations of the law and who teach others to do the same (verse 19) is certainly irreconcilable with Paul's missionary practice. Betz finds it very strange that "such conflicting interpretations of the teaching of Jesus could arise so soon"; the fact that they nevertheless did constitutes for him "the profound dilemma of the Sermon on the Mount in relation to the historical Jesus".[1] The dilemma exists only for those who accept that the Jesus whom Paul worshipped gave such teachings in the opening decades of the first century.

The Sermon makes it clear that Jesus's requirements concerning righteousness are more stringent than what was deemed necessary by the scribes and Pharisees (5:20). And so we are not surprised to find that he supplements the law: the law forbad murder, but he prohibits even anger (verse 22). This was felt to be excessive, hence numerous manuscripts have changed the prohibition to 'anger without cause'. The same verse stipulates that even to call someone a fool makes one "liable to the hell of fire". This is ridiculously severe, and leaves one asking why Jesus himself set such a bad example in this regard (whoever does not follow his teaching behaves like "a foolish man", 7:26; cf. 23:17, "ye fools and blind") and whether Paul has been sent to hell ("claiming to be wise, they became fools", Romans 1:22). Again, the law forbad adultery, but Jesus declares that the mere desire is as reprehensible as the act: "Everyone that looketh on a woman to lust after her hath committed adultery with her already in his heart" (5:28). There follow references to being "cast into hell" (5:29 and 30), and in a later chapter Jesus tells that, at the final judgement, mankind will be divided into two groups—just two—one of which will be saved and the other consigned to "eternal fire" (25:41, unparalleled). It is not surprising to find a commentary declaring that "Matthew has given us a grim book" and that "the Christ he presents is on the whole a terrifying figure" (Beare, *Matthew*, pp. viii, 43).

The Sermon continues with a prohibition of divorce, except on the ground of the wife's "unchastity" (5:32). This issue surfaces again in one of Jesus's confrontations with the Pharisees (see below, p 193). In the OT the right of the husband to 'put away' his wife is taken for granted, but the grounds on which he might do so are not precisely defined (Deuteronomy 24:1) and were open to differing interpretation, so that in restricting them, Jesus is not in conflict with the Mosaic law. The parallel passage of Lk. 16:18 prohibits the husband without qualification from divorcing his wife and then remarrying. Commentators claim that this does not conflict with the law, which permits but does not command divorce, so that to refrain from taking advantage of its permission would not be to act illegally. The same is often said to apply to his prohibition two verses later in the Sermon of the swearing of oaths (Mt. 5:34), where he rules that any supplementing of a plain "yes" or "no" is "of the evil one" (verse 37). Whether to prohibit and even to vilify what is expressly provided for in the law is really compatible with unequivocal acceptance of its every detail is a moot question.

Jesus goes on actually to repudiate one of the law's commands, namely "thou shalt give life for life, eye for eye, tooth for tooth" (Exodus 21:23–24, repeated at Leviticus 24:20 and Deuteronomy 19:21). Expressly against this, he urges "do not resist one who is evil" (Mt.5:38–39). Does this mean that we should allow any kind of crime to go unpunished? Should we allow not only ourselves but also our family and our neighbours to be wronged, and make no resistance to the wrongdoers?

Matthew himself probably regarded none of the rulings in the Sermon as conflicting with the Mosaic law. He will have thought all of them to be no more than radicalizations, consistent with Jesus's statement at 5:17 that he came to "fulfill" the law—a vague expression which implies that he achieved its true intentions, and which allows him considerable latitude in interpreting it. Although Matthew makes him seek table-fellowship with "publicans and sinners", and to justify such behaviour in the face of criticism from those zealous of the law (Mt.9:10–13, reproducing the substance of Mk.2:15–17), the evangelist also takes some care not to represent his teaching as unreservedly innovatory; for in adapting Mk. 1:22ff so as to make it a commentary on the Sermon on the Mount (compare above, p. 193), Matthew omits the Marcan statement that Jesus astonished his audience with what they declared to be a "new" teaching (Mk. 1:27; Mt. 7:28 has simply "they were astonished at his teaching").[2] Matthew equally significantly drops Mark's statement (7:19) that Jesus declared all foods clean.

Later in Matthew's Sermon comes an apology for divine providence which was presumably meant to reassure worried doubters: they are not to be exercised about obtaining food or clothing, as their heavenly Father will feed them, as he does the birds of the air (6:25–26). Regrettably, this doctrine has saved neither man nor bird from starvation—in spite of Jesus's assurance that, if we first seek God's "kingdom and his righteousness", adequate food, drink and clothing will be ours (verses 31–33).

The next chapter assures the auditors that their Father in heaven will "give good things to them that ask him" (7:11). Luke avoids any materialistic implication, and has it that the Father "will give the Holy Spirit to them that ask" (11:13). Matthew then adds the 'Golden Rule'—do as you would be done by—familiar, as Beare notes (*Matthew*, p. 192) not only in Judaism, but also "in the literatures of Buddhism, and of Islam", and in "the wisdom of Greece and Rome (Herodotus, Seneca)". In its negative form ('what is hateful to yourself, do not do to your neighbour'), the rule is ascribed to the Jewish sage Hillel, who died ca. A.D. 10. But all traditions tend to attach highly-regarded sayings to the names of highly-regarded teachers. Neusner observes that this particular saying "went from country to country and from culture to culture, always being attributed to the leading sage or wise man of the place. It is a virtually universal teaching of wisdom, and its attribution to Hillel tells us that he was regarded as the supreme authority within the Pharisaic movement." He adds that the name of Hillel "could always be added to make stories more impressive", and that the one thing clear about "the rather odd and alien materials" about him is that they were "made up or constructed for some purpose other than to preserve the very words Hillel had spoken, the very deeds he had done. The interest in Hillel always was to find in him a model for the time of the story-teller."[3] I have dwelt on this matter because of the obvious parallel with traditions about Jesus. Neusner himself calls the figure of Hillel "a counterpart to the problem of the historical Jesus", and finds them both equally elusive.

Much in the Sermon on the Mount was, in Renan's well-known phrase, "the current money of the synagogue". As an example, the first two petitions of the Lord's Prayer ("Thy name be sanctified, thy kingdom come", Mt. 6:9–10 = Lk. 11:2) are paralleled in the ancient Yiddish prayer from the temple period which Strecker translates as follows:

> Glorified and hallowed be his great name in the world,
> which he created according to his will.
> May he let his dominion reign
> during your lives and in your days and in the lifetimes of
> the whole house of Israel
> in haste and in imminent time.
> Praised is his great name for ever and ever.[4]

Beare notes that, in the four petitions which make up the second part of the Lord's Prayer, "there is not a single clause that is without parallels in Jewish prayers known to us" (*Matthew*, p. 175). Some phrases in the Prayer were expanded before they were placed in Matthew as words of Jesus. Matthew has "our father, which art in heaven", instead of Luke's simple "father". Matthew's "thy will be done, as in heaven so on earth" is absent from Luke, as is also "but deliver us from the evil one". These are generally agreed to be liturgical expansions, as is also the 'doxology' ("for thine is the kingdom" and so on). Although widely spoken in Christian services as the conclusion of the Prayer, it is absent from both Matthew and Luke. It occurs in the mid-second century work known as the *Didache*, but "is not found in any Greek manuscript of Matthew earlier than the fifth century", nor in the Latin Vulgate (Beare, p. 171). In sum, the main body of the Prayer is no more than a compilation of phrases already in Judaic use, while the Matthean additions and the doxology show how readily 'words of Jesus' could be manufactured. It is difficult to avoid the conclusion that we are faced here not with speeches reported by those who heard them, but with community tradition that has passed through stages of reworking.[5]

The burden of much of the Sermon is that the goods of this world are nothing in comparison with those offered by God in heaven to his faithful. Divine rewards are worth much more than human ones, so that the sensible man works for the former. The

Christian who is aiming at everlasting life must expect to wait for his reward (5:11–12). He must forego ostentation, but if he gives alms, fasts and prays unobtrusively, he will be duly rewarded (6:1–18). Luke even suggests that, the more he suffers in this world, the more substantial will be his recompense in the other (6:24–25; 16:25).

Jesus concludes the Sermon by insisting that it is necessary not only to hear but also to do "these words of mine"; so we must keep all the minutiae of the Jewish law, avoid anger completely, shun divorce (unless our wife is unchaste), swear no oaths, turn the other cheek to anyone who strikes us (5:39), let him who would take our coat have our cloak as well (5:40), and be perfectly confident that God will provide us with adequate food and clothing. It is not surprising that Betz, one of the closest recent students of this Sermon, calls it "the New Testament text most remote from modern men and women" (p. ix). Yet it has so often been represented as the perfect ethical guide—a position sometimes defended by saying that we are not to take all of its precepts literally, just as, so we are told, we do not really need to "hate" our own father, mother, wife, children, brethren, sisters, and even our own life, as Luke's Jesus (at 14:26) would have us believe.[6] But it is difficult to see how we are to know when to take Jesus literally unless we have some independent criterion of what is really right and wrong; and if we do have such a criterion, if we know independently of him what is right, then we do not need him as an ethical guide. Furthermore, it is not reasonable to take his words literally when we approve of them, and non-literally when we don't, and then pretend that his teaching constitutes the ethical ideal. Canon Harvey concedes that it "cannot be totally and generally 'obeyed' by any community of people living real lives in the real world." Jesus, he says, "proclaimed what may fairly be called a state of emergency", in that he declared that the kingdom of God is at hand. Whether or not he was mistaken in this—Harvey does not wish to reopen this "old debate"—his alarm call underlies "much of the most distinctive moral teaching in the gospels". Harvey thinks that he did not intend to provide his followers with a set of moral rules, but "rather to challenge us to live 'as if' the kingdom were already a reality". I do not find this distinction altogether clear. In any case, Harvey allows that truly Christian behaviour today might not, in any particular case, be "the apparently reckless and irresponsible surrender recommended by Jesus, but the more prudent course that follows from attending carefully to moral principles that are generally assented to outside as well as inside the Christian community" (*Commands*, pp. 22, 160–61, 192, 194, 210).

Some of the unappealing precepts in the NT cease to appear so repulsive if they are understood as intelligible responses to situations facing the early church. Families will have been split over whether to accept the new faith, particularly from the time when the rupture with Judaism had gone beyond healing. In such circumstances a Christian may well have found himself hating other members of his family as the cost of his discipleship. Hence the logion of Lk. 14:26–27. Again, many early Christians were poor and could find consolation in supposing that poverty was not only virtuous but also religiously enjoined. Hence the logia where Jesus is made to praise it and to repudiate wealth. Embarrassment arises when the modern reader, ignorant of the circumstances in which such logia originated, takes them as timeless principles calling for his unqualified assent. If he does not then reject them, he may be tempted to argue that they do not really mean what they say. R.J. Hoffman puts this whole matter well in an informative article which he concludes with the words:

> Such ethical teaching as the New Testament contains is of an occasional variety and reflects situations within the embryonic church of the first and second centuries. . . . Those situations, we need to remind ourselves, are largely unfamiliar to modern readers and the solutions proposed by the gospel writers for dealing with them are as distant from us—and hence potentially as irrelevant for us—as the situations which called them into being. ('The Moral Rhetoric of the Gospels', in *Biblical v. Secular Ethics. The Conflict*, edited by R.J. Hoffmann and G.A. Larue, Buffalo: Prometheus, 1988, p. 68)

ii. Marriage and Divorce

Genesis 2:22–23 states that, since woman originated from Adam's rib, he calls her "bone of my bones and flesh of my flesh"; and because mankind was thus created in two sexes ("male and female he created them", 1:27), a man shall "leave his father and his mother and shall cleave unto his wife; and they shall be one flesh" (2:24). At Mk.10:6–8 Jesus quotes these passages as prohibiting divorce, but gives Genesis 2:24 not from the Hebrew ("they shall be one flesh"), but from the Septuagint ("the twain shall become one flesh"). The original was not advocating monogamy—the OT has many examples of polygamy—but the Septuagint, which is probably as late as the second century B.C., may be seeking here to defend monogamy. Neither of the Genesis passages was understood in Judaism as making marriage indissoluble, but Jesus uses them as an argument for the indissolubility of monogamous marriage, for he continues:

> What therefore God hath joined together, let not man put asunder. . . . Whosoever shall put away his wife and marry another committeth adultery against her; and if she herself shall put away her husband and marry another, she committeth adultery (Mk. 10:9–12).

I have above (p. 30) given two reasons why it is unlikely that the whole exchange (10:2–12) between Jesus and the Pharisees is the record of an authentic dialogue: in particular, the final verse of it, quoted above, urges the wife not to seek a divorce when in the Jewish law of the time she was not entitled to one. Meier thinks that the earliest form of Jesus's prohibition of divorce may have looked something like the Q form behind Mt. 5:32/Lk.16:18:

Mt. 5:32
Every one that putteth away his wife, saving for the cause of fornication, maketh her an adulteress, and whosoever shall marry her when she is put away committeth adultery.

Lk. 16:18
Every one that putteth away his wife and marrieth another, committeth adultery: and he that marrieth one that is put away from a husband committeth adultery.

Here divorce is viewed as something only the husband could effect. Mark, however, "working in a Greco-Roman legal setting, where women could divorce their husbands, expanded the tradition he received to make the prohibition apply to women as well as men." Matthew, in assimilating this Marcan material at 19:9,

reflected the Jewish-Christian background of his church by drop-
ping its final verse which allows the wife the legal possibility of
divorce (Meier, *Marginal,* p. 132).

There are variant readings in the mss. of all these passages.
Logia which raised contentious issues or laid down rules which
were felt to be unreasonable were particularly prone to change:
Mk.10:24 on the iniquity of riches is an example,[7] as is also the
total prohibition of anger at Mt. 5:22 (compare above, p. 187).
The Birmingham theologian David Parker has recently pointed
out that, in the case of sayings of Jesus on marriage and divorce,
the manuscript variations in all three synoptics are considerable,
and that "what we have is a collection of interpretive rewritings of
a tradition."[8] He justly complains that many recent church
reports offering ethical guidance have presupposed that each saying exists only in one text form, and that if the authors of these
reports had looked at the bottom of the relevant pages of their
printed Greek texts and read the *apparatus criticus,* "they would
have discovered that they were grasping at shadows." "Textual
criticism", he adds, "is often seen as the most recondite of pur-
suits", but "the study of these passages shows it to be indispens-
able if we are to deal in realities rather than in pious fictions"
(pp. 381–82).

In this connection it is of interest that what Paul says on
divorce is, by his own account, not completely in line with
what he supposed Jesus to have ruled; for having explicitly
quoted "the Lord" to the effect that partners in marriage
are to stay together, he nevertheless goes on to allow on his own
authority an exception to this dominical ruling: a couple may
separate if one of them is an unbeliever and wishes the separa-
tion (1 Corinthians 7:15). This is comparable to the way in
which Matthew softens the total prohibition of divorce ascribed
to Jesus in Mark by allowing a man to put away his wife
in the case of her "fornication" (Mt. 19:3ff, compared with
Mk. 10:2ff). Canon Harvey comments that these examples
betray that "those who saw in Jesus's words the formulation
of a clear and absolute rule for the behaviour of church members were obliged to allow for exceptions right from the start."[9]
Now that its attitude to divorce and divorcees has come to make

the church unpopular, theologians are more ready to point out that inflexibility on the matter is not unambiguously scriptural after all.

iii. General Considerations

Much of what today's religious apologists write is inspired by understandable concern over ethical standards. Montgomery, for instance, is convinced that what he calls the "biblical higher law" provides "an explicit non-question-begging standard of absolute justice" (*The Law*, p. 46), and that practically all our troubles have resulted from abandoning it. He does not see that some of the maxims put into Jesus's mouth are quite unacceptable; and he bases some of the principles he advocates on indefensible exegesis—declaring, for instance, that all persons are to receive equal protection under the law because "God almighty has declared . . . that 'there is neither Jew nor Greek'" (*Ibid.*). In fact, the speaker here, at Galatians 3:28, is not God but Paul, and if his directives are to be accepted as binding, those who have wives must "live as though they had none". His ethic in this latter passage (as elsewhere) sprang from his conviction that the final judgement was at hand, was thus situational rather than absolute, and the situation envisaged was a delusion. Furthermore, what he says at Galatians 3:28 is not that all persons, but that all who accept his version of Christianity, have equal status: "You are all one in Christ Jesus." Christians who accept doctrinal niceties other than those of which he approves are, in chapter 1 of the same epistle, roundly cursed. There is certainly no offer of equality to those altogether outside the faith, and Christian churches have been slow to extend such an offer, as, for instance, Jews who experienced Luther (to mention but one offender) were well aware.

This verse of Galatians to which Montgomery appeals annuls discrimination not only between Jew and Greek "in Christ", but also between male and female. This does not prevent Paul from denying Corinthian women the right to speak in the public services of the church, instead of which they are to "ask their husbands at home if they would learn anything" (1 Corinthians 14:34–35). He even represents the silence he enjoins as "a commandment of the Lord" (verse 37). Paul characteristically speaks as a campaigner, saying what will cope with the problems raised by the particular situation facing him. The contradictions are particularly crass in what he says about the Jewish law—as on the one hand holy, just and good, but on the other as outworn, obsolete, and even provocative to sin.[10] To take such a person as an ethical guide would be absurd.

To trace our woes to the critical scholarship of the eighteenth century and later (*The Law*, p. 55) is to ignore the fact that the record of the church from Constantine to the Reformation is in many respects a deeply shameful one; and John Kent has justly deplored the failure to recognize that the outcome of the Reformation and Counter-Reformation "was outburst after outburst of iconoclasm, civil and national war, and the torture and execution of religious opponents on the ground that their opinions were dangerous to society." The conflict between Catholic and Protestant "developed a ferocity out of any proportion to the apparent religious differences involved"; "this ferocity revealed a mutual heartlessness within the religious emotion itself, and this lack, an inner religious failure, generated a corresponding indifference to religion in others."[11] Brown, having occasion to give details of violent internal strife within Judaism between 200 B.C. and A.D. 200, is well aware that "Christians, motivated by the 'love' of God and the defense of 'truth', have matched or surpassed in intensity such religious hostility during two millennia of hating and killing fellow Christians" (*Death*, p. 395). People who are convinced that their own doctrinal commitments represent the will of God, and who set about implementing them, have been and still are responsible for any number of God-inspired atrocities. James Barr observes that "the situation in the present-day Middle East sufficiently demonstrates the result that follows when ancient ideologies of war, people and land are allowed to survive and grow without adequate ethical evaluation", and are given this allowance because of "the simple confidence that, if God has commanded something, that fact must override and blanket out all other ethical considerations".[12]

The impulse of hatred, which may be quite devoid of rational basis, is the origin of countless actions, individual and collective.

Although it often originates from clashes of interest, it may persist even when interests have ceased to conflict. The impulse of sympathy or attraction may also lack rational basis. By rationalism I here mean no more than the endeavour to adapt means to ends. Because in such endeavours we often misjudge, we are not irrational. Irrational behaviour is that which a normal person would not expect to be effective. Rational people are capable of being deluded, and there are always individuals willing to exploit this weakness. The latter are least of all to be called irrational and are often the cleverest.

The way hatred can remain efficacious after its original exciting causes have vanished is well illustrated by tribalism and nationalism. These presumably originated from competition for limited resources. Just as the individual is not strong enough to prosper except in the strength of his group, so he regards other members of it as his supporters in his quest for land and resources claimed at the same time by another group. But tribal hatreds may persist even when such competition is no longer a significant factor. Hatred of Jews in Europe—not in the Middle East, where rivalry for the same territory is operative—is a particularly crass example. Demagogues can of course persuade a group that it is being disadvantaged by another: the fundamental tendency of loyalty to one's own group is there and, like any other tendency, can be inflated out of all proportion by those anxious to exploit it.

I have discussed the basis of morality in the chapter of my *Religious Postures* entitled 'Morality, Religion, and Reason'. Here I will note only that basing ethics on divine precepts is often defended by the argument that 'you can't get an *ought* from an *is*', so that ethical precepts necessarily transcend empirical fact. But this is to misunderstand the relation between precept and fact. You cannot tell someone what he should do unless you know what he is aiming at, or what you want him to aim at. If you do not know this, you can tell him only the consequences of different possible actions. Such factual information informs us impartially how actions and events are related; precept follows only when we know what event is desired. If we want protection from injury or exploitation, we see that there must be certain general rules of behaviour within our community, and that if they are to be adhered to, every individual must respect them, and therefore we ourselves must respect them. No theistic commitment is involved here.

It is not hard to see why the doctrine that these rules must be absolutely inflexible has a certain appeal. Approval of one's fellows and fear of censure are among society's chief integrating forces. But if they are to be effective, there must exist a climate of opinion, a common attitude of approval and disapproval towards certain forms of behaviour. If this attitude is not universal or nearly so, its influence on the individual is much diminished. In a community where it is permissible to put everything into question, the climate of opinion becomes unsettled, certain acts are no longer universally approved or disapproved, so that the ordinary person's main motive for social behaviour is very much weakened. In modern democracies this has become an increasingly serious problem. Fundamentalists—Islamic as well as Christian—think it can be solved by the tyranny of their sacred books. In fact they have to be very selective in what they choose as true and as binding from these books.

Such selectiveness is very apparent in religious apologetics— for instance in the little manuals published by the Bible Society, such as Derek Tidball's *Using the Bible in Evangelism* (revised edition, 1993). "The Good News", he says (p. 6) is that "God 'did not send his son into the world to be its judge, but to be its saviour'" (Jn. 3:17). He refrains from quoting the next verse, where the evangelist explains why no judging is necessary, namely because believers are to be saved anyway, and non-believers are condemned already. On a later page, Tidball finds it necessary to admit that scripture includes "harsh passages regarding judgement", because he is there concerned to urge caution in their use for purposes of evangelism (p. 68). His Christianity, like Montgomery's, is of a familiar, narrow kind: "Jesus is the only way to God" (p. 31, supported with appropriate quotation from the NT). It is a short step from this to Jerry Falwell's Moral Majority manifesto of 1979: "If a person is not a Christian, he is inherently a failure."[13] And this, in turn, has its basis in scripture, for Paul argues (Romans 7:14–25) that, if man is apart from Christ, all his moral efforts end in total failure.[14]

Tidball recommends his trainees in evangelism to meet objec-
tors by "putting the onus on them" to say what they think is "the
central message of the Bible"—as if the thirty-nine books of the
OT and the twenty-seven of the NT, representing material compiled by many writers over hundreds of years, can be expected to
have a uniform message. The late Dr. David Oppenheimer once
remarked to me that one might perhaps make a rough and ready
distinction between the OT and the NT by noting that in the latter
there are no more heavenly commands to massacre one's van-
quished enemies, such as were issued via Moses in Deuteronomy
(7:2; 20:17) and via the prophet Samuel in relation to the
Amalekites; that this no doubt was because the Christians of the
first century did not have the power to carry out such commands;
and that, as if in compensation, the NT includes a deal of pious
gloating over the eternal sufferings in an after-life of the enemies
of Jesus.

James Barr has summarized what Deuteronomy 20 teaches.
Its central law "provides three categories: 1. if a city outside the
land (given by God as an inheritance to Israel) accepts an offer of
peace, it is to become subject to forced labour; 2. if a city outside
the land resists attack, all males are to be killed, but women,
small children, cattle and all other goods are to be taken and
enjoyed as sport; 3. if it is a city that is within the land of the
inheritance, including Hittites, Amorites, Canaanites, and so on,
nothing that breathes is to be left alive" (pp. 217–18). Montgomery has unabashedly defended such tribal barbarism on the
ground that it "served a special purpose in preparation for the
coming of the Messiah" (*The Law*, p. 77). This from someone who
expresses concern at present-day decline in standards.

Since the period recorded in the books of Samuel and Kings,
Judaism has had relatively few opportunities for committing
spectacular God-inspired atrocities. This is not true of its younger
rivals, Christianity and Islam. Some non-semitic religions have a
somewhat better record. The Olympian cults of Periclean Athens
appear to have provided much enjoyment and fun with very little
shedding of human blood. Lucretius, four centuries later, seems
to have been unable to reinforce his attack on religion with anything more shocking than an old myth about the sacrificial killing

of Iphigenia. Nevertheless, it is difficult to avoid Kent's generalization that, today as of yore, "the spread of piety is as closely
linked to intolerance, cruelty and warfare as it is to any growth of
charity." He adds that "it is no answer to this objection to talk
about the evils of Stalinism: Marxist humanism is as rare as
Christian charity; it is the shortage of both that is the major problem of the late twentieth century" (pp. 6–7).

Epilogue: the Scholar and the Preacher

Clergy who are not willing simply to reject or ignore scholarly criticism of the NT are faced with a serious problem. They cannot with good conscience preach traditional Christian doctrines and are also aware that some of the negative results of scholarly criticism are now too well-known to be altogether ignored. Yet they can hardly tell their congregations that what has been proclaimed as Christian truth for nearly 2,000 years is little better than moonshine. Eric Franklin's *How the Critics can Help* (London: SCM, 1982; reissued 1994 by Xpress Reprints) aims at helping them over this dilemma.

Franklin is himself both a scholar and a parish minister. His scholarship is evidenced in his *Christ the Lord* (London: SPCK, 1975), which is a serious blow to those who would take Luke-Acts as sources of accurate information about the historical Jesus and the early church. Luke's gospel has often been found more acceptable than the other three in the canon because it serves as an easier basis for liberal-humanitarian interpretations of Jesus which seem plausible even to the uncommitted; and many have argued that Acts shows such accurate knowledge of details of Roman administration (distinguishing, for instance, correctly between senatorial and imperial provinces) that it must be accepted as a

well-informed account from a meticulous historian. But as
Franklin points out (pp. 176, 216f), from the fact that the author
knew some history, it does not in the least follow that he would be
unwilling to manipulate his material when to do so suited his theological ends. And Franklin shows that what this canonical
author has given us is in fact an adaptation of earlier material
about Jesus—a reinterpretation guided by his desire to reassure
Christians of his own day who were perplexed because Jesus's
second coming had not occurred and because the Jews had
become fiercely hostile to Christian claims. Franklin's case can
naturally be argued most cogently apropos of Luke's gospel, for
here (as is not so with Acts) the prime source (the gospel of Mark)
is extant, and his use of it "shows that he was no slave to his
sources" (p. 34).

Franklin stresses the significance of Jesus's ascension for
Luke's Christology. This was not taken from an earlier gospel, for
it is unmentioned in Mark (and also in Matthew), and the brief
reference to it in the appendix to Mark was clearly written by
someone familiar with Luke. Luke may, of course, have drawn it
from some tradition or other, but as Franklin says, it is likely that
"he himself was responsible for understanding it as an actual
event in time and space" (p. 192). Luke relates the event twice—
once at the end of his gospel and once at the beginning of Acts;
and as we saw (above, pp. 101f) the two narratives serve somewhat different purposes and are for that reason to some extent in
contradiction. Their implications are also not completely to be
harmonized with those of other—more traditional—christological
statements in Luke-Acts. "All this", says Franklin, "points to the
conclusion that Luke's scheme is an artificial one and is most
likely to have been of his own making" (p. 33). At his ascension
Jesus rises to the right hand of God, that is, he shares in his sov-
ereignty, and receives from him the Spirit, which is then (at the
first Whitsuntide) imparted to the disciples. The point of such
narrative is to convince the reader that "Jesus was no hero of the
past, but the Lord of the present" (p. 174) whose second coming
can confidently be expected in spite of its delay.

Franklin reverts to these matters in his *How the Critics can
Help*, from which my further quotations from him derive. In this

book, however, he tries not to go too far in stating objections to the reliability of the NT. He does indeed reiterate that "Luke's Ascension narrative is there because it is the ideal vehicle of his theology", so that "it is just not possible to say what 'hard' history it embraces" (p. 67). But this falls short of saying that there is nothing historical at all about what Franklin himself has shown to be a legendary story. In the same way he writes of "the seeming inconsistencies" in the gospel resurrection narratives (p. 62), even though he has just shown that these inconsistencies are more than apparent and arise in part from Luke's "deliberate alteration" of Marcan material (p. 60). He holds that we can continue to have confidence in the canonical gospels because they are not as uniformly positive about Jesus as the apocryphal ones —they have not tried to hide his "ambiguity"—and because what they assert poses so many "formidable difficulties" for them that it cannot be sheer invention (p. 69). Both these factors refer primarily to Jesus's crucifixion which "upended all expectations and seemingly reversed any possible 'proofs' of his true status" (p. 68). For Christians to claim that "the cross . . . was in fact God's answer to the needs of the world" was a "seeming absurdity" (p. 77). But it is not seemingly but really absurd to suggest that implausibility of a religious claim argues for its truth. Hermes was widely worshipped as a supposed Arcadian cattle-thief, Osiris as a supposed chopped-up Egyptian. There is as much 'ambiguity' here as with Jesus.

On Jesus's second coming Franklin is, however, straightforwardly negative: the gospels' depiction of it and "even their expectations of it are no less mythological than the Old Testament's accounts of creation" (p. 90). We are not to pretend that, when Jesus spoke of an early end to the world and a final judgement, he was using "symbolic language", or was really alluding only to his Transfiguration or resurrection, or to the fall of Jerusalem in A.D. 70 and the subsequent emergence of the universal Christian mission (pp. 113–14). The early church certainly understood his proclamation of the end quite literally (as is clear from 1 Thessalonians 4 and 1 Corinthians 15), and so to interpret what he said differently would involve "the church in a great misunderstanding which totally undermines the effectiveness of Jesus as it leaves

him wholly out of touch with their thinking" (p. 115). The reason
why he proclaimed such an erroneous doctrine was that apocalyptic ideas belonged to his intellectual environment, and he was
fully human and "a genuine man of his age" (p. 116).

If the NT sometimes records Jesus's delusions, shared by its
authors, at other times it does not mean what it quite plainly
says; for Franklin does not believe in angels (p. 5), nor in "a personal devil" (p. 21), and as he wants preachers to be able to draw
on the gospel stories of Jesus's Temptation, he has to hold that
this incident, represented in them as a historical event and understood as such for the best part of 2,000 years, was not meant to be
taken in that way at all. "At this point . . . the biblical narrative
was speaking pictorially rather than literally and factually"
(p. 22). Angels and demons represent merely one particular form
of an underlying idea. It is possible to regard belief in angels as
"expressing the conviction that the final reality within and beyond
the world is personal rather than impersonal" (p. 91). One can
only comment that this makes belief in angels a very misleading
way of expressing a highly questionable idea.

The clergyman cannot avoid the miracle stories, although
preaching on them "is perhaps the most difficult task of all"
(p. 154). Scepticism about them sometimes springs not from
unwillingness to believe in the supernatural, but from a sense of
their "near irrelevance" or even "absurdity". What, for instance, is
the point of Jesus's walking on the water? "What was he trying to
do or to prove" (p. 124). The preacher is advised to take this particular story as "arising out of the creative response of the early
church to their overwhelming apprehension that Jesus was their
Lord" (p. 162). But the stories of exorcisms and healings are to be
accepted as based on something that Jesus actually did. Behind
them "would seem to stand real recollections of his authority and
power." He "confronted men with the full reality of God's presence and in him therefore they were grasped by the wholeness of
God's life." "Only with difficulty" can it be denied that this wholeness "should at least in some cases have permeated out so as to
embrace the physical" (pp. 163f). This is to regard Jesus on the
model of an electrically charged wire or magnet with power that
overflows into what is brought into contact with it. It is a model

we find in the gospels: "All the multitude sought to touch him: for power came forth from him and healed them all" (Lk. 6:19). Mark's story of the woman with an issue of blood suggests that faith in his power is a proviso: "She said, If I touch but his garments, I shall be made whole." When she touched them, Jesus "perceived in himself that the power from him had gone forth" (Mk. 5:28–30). Some of the older commentators were embarrassed by this model of an electrically charged Jesus, but not so Franklin.[1]

The miracle of the virgin birth can hardly pass unmentioned at Christmas. Belief in it "does not rest upon either Matthew's or Luke's accounts which cannot really be harmonized and which cannot of themselves bear the weight of rigorous historical enquiry, but upon the tradition to which they bear witness and from which they spring." And what validates this tradition? "Its own strength, its conformity to the whole life of Jesus, its continuing ability to inform, its appropriateness to Christian truth, and the inner assent both of the community and its individual member" (p. 73). Many a myth could be validated in the same way. That Wilhelm Tell founded the Swiss Confederation in the face of foreign oppression is a strong tradition, conformable to the (supposed) whole life of the sturdy independent Tell, and appropriate both to national truth and to the assent of the Swiss people.

Yet Franklin is aware that it will not do to find the truth of a story in its "ability to appeal to its hearers and ultimately to move them" (p. 80). "Enthusiasm of belief is no guarantee of the truth of that which is believed. Fanaticism has its successes, and wishful thinking is not necessarily transitory" (p. 56). Nevertheless, he claims not only that the evangelists' response to Jesus was "rooted in an historical event", but also that "the enthusiasm of the response itself witnesses to the greatness of that event" (p. 70). He even suggests that the early Christians' 'response' to the resurrection validates the gospel record of Jesus's pre-resurrection life. For "the resurrection did not occur in a vacuum." "The resurrection presence needed the life, and the response is witness in truth to the validity of that life" (p. 71). Hence—contrary to Franklin's statement on page 17 that "it is the risen Jesus, not the one who walked in Palestine who saves"—"it is the whole event of Jesus which saves", and this includes the incarnate life as well as the resurrection (p. 100).

Franklin has a number of words with impressive emotional associations which do him steady service. He mentions (without demur) the judgement of a colleague that the story of the empty tomb is "a profoundly significant myth" (p. 145). But it is as a characterization of what he calls the fourth gospel's "ontological approach to the person of Jesus" (p. 92) that the word 'profound' is most useful. It is "a profound interpretation of Jesus" (p. 45), "the profoundest of all writings" (quoted on p. 40 from William Temple), "a profound testimony to the whole event of Jesus" (p. 46). Its discourses constitute "a profound meditation" and it "unfolds the real significance of Jesus in a singularly profound and telling way" (p. 47). 'Inspired' serves also to characterize it. It is "an inspired meditation" (p. 46) and preachers should present it as "an inspired response to the Lord's risen and exalted presence in our midst" (p. 50). One can envisage a suitably solemn-faced response from congregations. Franklin allows that we do, however, need to ask "whether John has got his response quite right" (p. 52) and that in fact "there can be little doubt" that, in stressing Jesus's divinity, he "failed to take seriously the real humanity of Jesus which is so obvious in the synoptic presentation of him" (p. 53).

Franklin knows quite well that not only John but other evangelists too did not restrict themselves to writing up and reworking existing traditions, but were sometimes "perhaps even creators of material" (p. 28) and "created narratives which embodied belief in a historical and factual form" (p. 146). But the adjective 'creative' has positive associations which Franklin puts to good effect. Hence he does not say that stories were made up so as to give the appearance of fulfilling OT 'prophecies', but rather: "The Old Testament exerted a truly creative influence upon the evangelists" (pp. 65, 67). For him, this puts no question mark over what they say, but is evidence of its truth: that they linked Jesus "so firmly to the Old Testament is of the greatest significance in enabling us to accept their basic truth" (p. 70). Nevertheless, since each of them was not simply recording facts, but must be seen as "a much more creative exponent of the total significance of Christianity"

(p. 35), we have some difficulty in extracting what is truly factual from their narratives. The "creative situation" in the early church "both adds to and so inevitably clouds the words of Jesus in his actual time on earth" (p. 16). Yet this "creative situation" was due to the influence of the Spirit: the evangelists were persons who had experienced "encounters" with God who had "grasped", "seized", and "taken hold" of them in the "whole event" of Jesus (pp. 18, 19, 46),

Such an 'encounter' underlies the way in which one evangelist corrects another. Franklin's illustration of this is Matthew's emendation of Mark's account of the request of the sons of Zebedee for a position of authority in Jesus's kingdom (Mk. 10 and Mt. 20). In Mark the request is made by the disciples themselves, in Matthew by their mother, and in a form "less harsh, less presumptuous". Mark's version of the incident is the less pleasing to the Christian reader and for that reason "almost certainly nearer to the original factors". But Matthew could correct it on the basis of supernatural knowledge:

> Matthew knew his risen Lord, he experienced his risen presence and he therefore knew how his disciples, now reverenced by Matthew's church, would have acted. For him . . . it 'must' have been the mother. Nothing else was appropriate to the present belief and to Matthew's sense of oneness with the past.

In sum, all four evangelists (even Mark) had, alongside their written sources and oral traditions about Jesus, another source of "legitimate information", namely "the living Jesus in their midst. . . . His experienced presence could shape, refine, clarify and correct what other sources contained" (p. 64). As these other sources—certainly Mark as a source for Matthew and Luke—were authored by persons who enjoyed the same 'experienced presence', it is strange that they needed to be corrected—unless this 'presence', far from being a positive factor, had led them to introduce all manner of fantasies.

But for Franklin, the aberrations of the evangelists are due not to the Spirit, but to the "outlook, presuppositions and background" of their times. These factors "inevitably put constraints upon them"—as, according to Franklin, they did even on Jesus himself—and "stopped the full significance of Jesus from being seen" (p. 93). How do we know that he was more significant than even they realized? Because since their time, "the continuing work of God's spirit" has been "guiding the church towards all truth" (p. 87). This is surely a very charitable estimate of what Franklin calls the near "two thousand years of Christian witness" (p. 177).

To appeal to 'the spirit' is felt to be an adequate response to all damaging objections, beginning with those raised against the foundation documents. If it be objected that the gospels are not stenographic reports of words and actions of Jesus, but the work of various believing communities of later date, the reply is made that these documents are nonetheless reliable because the relevant communities were inspired by the spirit of the risen Lord.

Franklin's conclusion is that the preacher can say, on the authority of the scholar, that all is well with Christian belief, and that, while the gospels "do not give us an easy way into Jesus's thinking, his development or his inner beliefs", if we take them "as a whole" and view their "overall sweep, direction and atmosphere", we can nevertheless "arrive at a picture which gives an adequate statement of him" (pp. 106f). On this basis we find that "we cannot explain either the life of Jesus or the response to him in any less a way than that they are in fact the actions of God himself" (p. 166). There can be no better illustration than Franklin's book of Räisänen's complaint (which we met in chapter 2 above) that the scholar is wont to turn into the pious preacher. Franklin's plea that Christian faith should be "less strident and more humble than it was before" (p. 165) represents a mere residual awareness of problems and difficulties over this faith.

Preachers do not tackle issues like these. Even if a clergyman were trained at a college which did not shield him from the problems, his flock is usually not eager to listen to any explanation of them, and has no desire to hear how the faith has been put in question. Sermons and religious broadcasts are nearly always worded as though New Testament scholarship did not exist. Most believers are never informed of just how flimsy is the historical evidence for the stories about Jesus they take for gospel.

Notes

For the key to books and articles cited in an abbreviated form, see pp. xvff above.

Introduction

1. M. Wiles, *The Remaking of Christian Doctrine.* London: SCM, 1974, p. 49.
2. A. Hastings, *The Theology of a Protestant Catholic.* London: SCM; Philadelphia: Trinity, 1990, pp. 1–2.
3. Philo, quoted by R.M. Grant, 'The Christ at the Creation', in *Jesus in History and in Myth*, edited by R.J. Hoffmann and G.A. Larue (Buffalo: Prometheus, 1986), p. 159. Cf. Dodd (as cited in note 5 below) pp. 66, 276: "Philo's Logos is in many places almost a doublet of Wisdom." Cf. R.G. Hamerton-Kelly's statement: "The Logos is a Hellenistic-Jewish term for pre-existent Wisdom" (*Pre-Existence, Wisdom and the Son of Man* (Cambridge: University Press, 1973), p. 241.
4. E. Schweizer, 'Zur Herkunft der Präexistenzvorstellung bei Paulus', *Evangelische Theologie*, 19 (1959), p. 69.
5. C.H. Dodd, *The Interpretation of the Fourth Gospel.* Cambridge: Cambridge University Press, 1968, pp. 274–77.
6. Commentators have pleaded, defensively, that, although Paul posits Jesus's pre-existence, the doctrine is not elaborated or stressed in his letters (see, for instance M. de Jonge, *Christology in Context: The Earliest Christian Response to Jesus*, Philadelphia: Westminster, 1988, pp. 43, 48). James Dunn has even disputed—by taking Paul to mean other than what he says—that the doctrine is present at all in Paul's thinking (*Christology in the Making: A New Testament Inquiry into the Origins of the Incarnation*, 2nd edition, London: SCM, 1989). Dunn's arguments have been extensively and severely criti-

cized, and in a long 'Foreword' to this second edition of his
book, where he responds to criticisms, he allows that some
regard his suggestions as "insubstantial and wholly implausible, if not absurd, if not perverse" (p. xviii). John Macquarrie,
however, has treated them sympathetically in his *Jesus Christ
In Modern Thought* (London: SCM; Philadelphia: Trinity,
1990). Like Dunn, he wants Paul's language on Jesus's pre-
existence to be understood as "metaphorical and not literal"
(p. 57). This approach to Paul naturally appeals to him, for if
Paul had really regarded the earthly Jesus as the incarnation
of a supernatural figure, "that would have been a denial of
his true humanity and a lapse into mythology" (p. 390).

7. G.W.E. Nickelsburg Jr. has traced the history of the genre
   known as the 'wisdom tale'. See his *Resurrection, Immortality and Eternal Life in Intertestamental Judaism* (Cambridge, Mass: Harvard University Press; London: Oxford
   University Press, 1962).

8. Eleazar appeals to God to accept his death, with that of
   the other martyrs, as an expiation for the sins of the people: "Take my soul to ransom their souls" (4 Maccabees
   6:28–29). At the end of the book it is said that this is what
   in the event happened: the courageous deaths of the martyrs "have as it were become a ransom for our nation's
   sin." Through their "blood" and "the propitiation of their
   death", the nation's guilt has been expiated (17:21–22).

9. See Sam K. Williams, *Jesus's Death as a Saving Event:
   Background and Origin of a Concept* (Missoula: Scholars,
   1975), pp. 230ff. He gives evidence that 4 Maccabees must
   have been written "at least a decade" earlier than the
   period of Paul's literary activity" (p. 202).

10. Josephus, *Antiquities of the Jews*, Book 12, chapter 5 and
    Book 13, chapter 14.

11. J. Barr, *Fundamentalism*. 2nd edition, London: SCM, 1981,
    pp. 162–63.

1. The Commentator's Task

1. Friedrich Meinecke, *Die Entstehung des Historismus*. Munich
   and Berlin: Oldenbourg, 1936, pp. 115–16, 122, 124, 211, 254.

2. I owe this formulation to J. Beversluis's book, *C.S. Lewis and the Search for a Rational Religion,* Grand Rapids: Eerdmans, 1985, p. 52—a trenchant criticism of a still highly regarded apologist.

3. N.T. Wright, *Who was Jesus?,* London: SPCK, 1992, p. ix.

4. B. Croce, *History as the Story of Liberty,* English translation by Sylvia Sprigge, London: Allen and Unwin, 1941, pp. 19, 78–79, 85–86. Some of these passages show that Croce's bias was pro-metaphysical, as well as pro-Christian. For him, Ranke was too much concerned to recover the events of the past and too little able or willing to philosophize about them; his "philosophically indifferent" mind was not even capable of falling into the errors perpetrated by the "weighty" and "sovereign" minds of Vico and Hegel—errors which they of course "possessed in themselves the power of correcting."

5. R.G. Collingwood, *The Idea of History.* Oxford: Clarendon, 1946, p. 147.

6. M.J.S. Rudwick, in M.R. House *et al.* (eds.), *The Devonian System,* London: Palaeontological Association, 1979, p. 20.

7. D. Hume, *Enquiry Concerning the Principles of Morals,* 1751, section 9, end of appendix 1.

8. The late F.F. Bruce, a well-known conservative theologian of Manchester University, declared (*Documents,* p. 14n.) that the Tübingen school "restated the origins of Christianity in terms of Hegelian metaphysics", and so exemplified the principle that, if the facts are otherwise, "so much the worse for the facts". This perennial criticism of Baur and his followers is adequately refuted in P.C. Hodgson's monograph on him (*The Formation of Historical Theology,* New York: Harper and Row, 1966). Even Karl Barth, no friend of critical theology, allowed that "a man who was to be found at his desk all his life, summer and winter, from four in the morning, does not at any rate look like one who is in a position to improvise history because he is in possession of Hegel's third act" (*Protestant Theology in the Nineteenth Century,* English translation, London: SCM, 1972, p. 505). The charge against Baur has often been broadened in Britain into an accusation that "German the-

ologians" are in general blinkered by philosophy. The
Anglican theologian A.C. Headlam complained in 1914
that they "almost invariably carry into the region of history some particular philosophical theory by which they
are prejudiced." This is quoted by R. Morgan in an informative article on Anglican reactions to German gospel
criticism ('Non Angli sed Angeli', in *New Studies in Theology*, I, edited by S. Sykes and D. Holmes, London: Duckworth, 1980, p. 9). Recently, the vogue of existentialism
among certain German theologians has led J.W. Montgomery to suppose that, if only they will cast aside their
philosophy, they will see themselves faced with scriptures
that are inerrant (See above, p. 67).

9. H. Räisänen, *Beyond New Testament Theology*. London:
   SCM, 1990, p. 97.

10. H. Wansbrough, *Jesus, The Real Evidence*. London:
    Catholic Truth Society pamphlet, 1984, p. 3.

11. "Constantine in the fourth century and Theodosius in the
    fifth decided that the only way to overcome Porphyry's
    objections was to put his books to the torch." In A.D. 448
    the imperial church condemned all copies of his *Against
    the Christians* to be burned, and was thus able to eradicate
    "all traces" of it (R.J. Hoffmann, *Porphyry's 'Against the
    Christians'*, Amherst, NY: Prometheus, 1994, pp. 17, 155,
    164). Hoffmann has reconstructed part of Porphyry's
    books from quotations in a Christian opponent.

12. Koester's article 'History and the Development of Mark's
    Gospel: From Mark to *Secret Mark* and "Canonical" Mark'
    (in *Colloquy on NT Studies: A Time for Reappraisal and
    Fresh Approaches*, edited by B. Corley, Macon: Mercer Uni-
    versity Press, 1983, pp. 35–57) tackles the well-known
    objection that if, as is generally supposed, Matthew and
    Luke both independently made use of Mark, it is surpris-
    ing that they sometimes agree with each other against him
    in certain phrases in material they share with him and
    have, by hypothesis, taken from him. Koester finds the
    solution to lie in the existence of different forms of Mark.
    He argues that the Mark used by Matthew and Luke was a

shorter proto-Mark, that this was later expanded at Alexandria to include gnostic views—Morton Smith's claim to have discovered a fragment of a secret Alexandrian gospel of Mark is relevant here—and that our canonical Mark is an abbreviation of this expansion. Koester is particularly concerned with the well-known discrepancy between Mk. 4:11 (where Jesus tells the disciples: "Unto you is given the mystery of the kingdom") and the parallel passages in Matthew and Luke (both of which have "is given *to know* the mysteries . . . "). He argues that the original proto-Mark used the plural 'mysteries', referring to a plurality of parables that need to be decoded; that in the 'secret' Alexandrian gnostic gospel this was changed to the singular (as a designation of the entire preaching of Jesus) which survived when this gospel was purified of gnostic views to form our canonical Mark. I discuss the whole pericope Mk. 4:10–12 above, p 123.

13. C. Thiede, *Jesus: Life or Legend?*, Oxford: Lion, 1990, pp. 83–84. What I asserted in the books Thiede had in mind was not that Jesus never existed at all, but that the Jesus of the gospels, a teacher and miracle-worker crucified under Pontius Pilate, never existed.

14. Writing of the situation in England, Adrian Hastings observes that, although "there had long been a notable gap between academic theology and what one may call the theology of the pew", a significant link between them had nevertheless remained until the 1970s; whereas this is now no longer so: "The theology of Gore, Temple, Ramsey, or Farrer was, most certainly, one the Church could live and thrive with. The same cannot be said for that of Nineham, Hick, or Cupitt." "One cannot", he adds, "reject the scholarly conclusions of able theological thinkers simply because they are too destructive of the core of the tradition of Christian faith and theology. If the destruction is to be avoided the conclusions must be demonstrated to be unconvincing", and "that may not be easy" (*A History of English Christianity 1920–1985*, London: Collins, 1986, pp. 662–63).

2. 'Catholic Truth' on the Historicity
of Jesus

1. A.G. Hunter, *Christianity and Other Faiths in Britain*, London: SCM, 1985, p. 40. I have discussed the two gospel birth and infancy narratives very fully in chapter 3 of *WWJ*.

2. By 'early Christian epistles', I mean, first, those of the letters ascribed in the canon to Paul which were in fact written by him, namely Romans, 1 and 2 Corinthians, Galatians, Philippians, 1 Thessalonians, and Philemon; second, Colossians (which whether by him or by one of his pupils is almost as early), 2 Thessalonians, and Ephesians. (That these three, although ascribed to Paul, were written only after his death is, says Furnish (*Jesus*, p. 93), the view of many scholars, and he himself endorses it.) Finally, I include Hebrews, 1 Peter, and James in this early epistolic literature.

3. Nineham, *Explorations*, p. 193 n.6; cf. Philippians 3:17 and 4:9 ("Be ye imitators together of me", do what you "learned and received and saw in me"); 1 Corinthians 4:16 ("Be ye imitators of me"); the added words "even as I am of Christ" (11:1) refer only to willingness to accept pain and suffering, as Christ did (cf. *HEJ*, p. 35).

4. 2 Peter, widely regarded as the very latest of all the books in the NT (compare above, p. 89), obviously has (at 1:16–18) some relationship to the story of Jesus's Transfiguration, as related in Mk. 9:2–7. The Pastoral epistles (1 and 2 Timothy and Titus) are ascribed to Paul in the canon, but most scholars agree that they were written early in the second century (compare above, pp. 80f). In one of them (1 Timothy 6:13) Jesus is said to have "made the good confession in his testimony before Pontius Pilate."

5. G. Stanton, review of my *DJE* in *TLS*, 29 August 1975, p. 977, repeated in his *The Gospels and Jesus*, Oxford University Press, 1989, p. 140.

6. Romans 15:18–19; 1 Corinthians 12:10 and 28; 2 Corinthians 12:12.

7. Furnish (*Jesus*, p. 65) says it is "especially important" to note that Paul "nowhere employs a traditional saying of Jesus to help present or support his own most basic affirmations about the gospel. Those are presented and supported primarily with reference to Jesus's death and resurrection." He adds (p. 70) that Paul "shows little interest in the historical circumstances of Jesus's death", and mentions neither the time or the place, nor anything about the trial, "nor who was with him or any final words he may have spoken. And while Paul knows of an entombment . . . , he does not indicate where it was or who was responsible for it."

8. Paul is here saying that there are Christians sufficiently strong in faith to eat food of all kinds, and others weaker in faith who are vegetarians; and the former should show consideration towards the latter, just as Christ did not "consider himself", but gave himself up to death for all alike (Romans 14:15; 15:3).

9. H. Räisänen, *Jesus, Paul, and Torah: Collected Essays*, English translation. Sheffield: Academic Press, 1992, pp. 141–42, 144–45. These passages are from an essay originally published in 1982. In the Preface to the second, revised edition of his *Paul and the Law* (Tübingen: Mohr, 1987, p. xviii), Räisänen thinks he may have overemphasized the 'spontaneity' of the rise of the law-free gentile mission: "It may, after all, not have been *just* a case of 'action preceding theology'." Those who initiated it "may have had a theological rationale for their action as well", namely "a spiritualized view of the Torah, pre-formed in the Diaspora. They would have preferred, for theological reasons, a 'circumcision of the heart' to a circumcision in the 'flesh' (Romans 2:29; cf. Philippians 3:3)"; and they would have regarded their giving up of certain commandments "not as a destructive critique of the law, but rather as a reinterpretation of its true meaning".

10. Goulder, who interprets the evidence very differently from me, nevertheless notes (*Midrash*, pp. 148f) that Paul's "failure to appeal to texts which would have been highly effec-

tive had he known them becomes critical on occasion. In 1 Corinthians 6 he is arguing against the practice of Christians going to law, and gives eight verses to shaming the Corinthians by logic: why does he not ram the point home" by quoting Jesus's dictum "if any man would go to law with thee, and take away thy coat, let him have thy cloke also" (Mt. 5:40)? Again, chapters 8 and 9 of 2 Corinthians are devoted to appealing for support for a financial collection. One cannot, says Goulder, but admire the variety and quality of the arguments Paul here uses which include citations of Proverbs and Psalms. But he does not "cap it all" with "give and it shall be given unto you" (Lk. 6:38), nor any of "a dozen other Matthean or Lucan texts". All that Paul can do here by way of reference to Jesus is to point to his "generosity" in condescending to come to earth in human form at all (2 Corinthians 8:9). Again and again it is to the incarnation and crucifixion (both in unspecified circumstances) to which Paul appeals, not to anything in Jesus's life. I have argued (above, pp. 28f) that the 'words of the Lord' he knew were spoken by the risen, not the earthly Jesus.

11. S.G. Wilson, 'From Jesus to Paul: The Contours and Consequences of a Debate', in *From Jesus to Paul* (Studies in Honour of F.W. Beare), edited by P. Richardson and J.C. Hurd, Waterloo (Ontario): Laurier University Press, 1984, p. 3.

12. The passages in Proverbs, in the Wisdom of Solomon, and in Ecclesiasticus to which I have referred above (pp. xxvf), together with other similar passages in the Wisdom literature, show that "the hypostatized Wisdom of late Jewish literature . . . is an anonymous heavenly redeemer figure" (W. Schmithals, *The Office of Apostle in the Early Church*, English translation London: SPCK, 1971, p. 126). These passages invite the inference that "the early Christian myth of a descending-ascending redeemer was taken over from Hellenistic Judaism" (C.H. Talbert, *What is a Gospel? The Genre of the Canonical Gospels*, London: SPCK, 1978, p. 77). The personification of Wisdom may have been orig-

inally merely poetic, but later Hellenistic writings take it literally and make Wisdom a personage who descends from heaven with saving intent.

13. Cf. 1 Corinthians 1:24, quoted above, p. xxvi; Talbert, as cited in the previous note, p. 73; and *HEJ*, pp. 38–39.

14. Mt. 4:24, RSV. Matthew has added this verse to his Marcan source in order to supply Jesus with an audience for the Sermon on the Mount (also absent from Mark) which follows immediately: "There followed him great multitudes" (4:25), and "seeing the multitudes he went up into the mountain" (5:1). Nevertheless, Mark too stresses the extent of Jesus's following, which included "a great multitude" from Galilee, Judea, Jerusalem, Idumea, and also from "beyond Jordan and about Tyre and Sidon" (Mk. 3:7 8). And Mark twice represents him as miraculously feeding thousands at a time.

15. Ian Wilson, *Are These the Words of Jesus?* Oxford: Lennard, 1990, p. 14. I responded to earlier misrepresentation from Mr. Wilson in the 2nd edition of *DJE*, pp. 206–07.

16. A. Fridrichsen, *The Problem of Miracle in Primitive Christianity*, English translation (from the French of 1925), Minneapolis: Augsburg, 1972, pp. 33, 35. In his view (p. 43), 2 Corinthians 5.16 adequately explains why Paul rarely cites from Jesus's life. But in fact, as I show (above p. 24), this passage is not to the point.

17. W. Wrede, *Paul*, English translation (from the German of 1904), London: Green, 1907, p. 91: for Paul, "the earthly life of Christ is the opposite of his divine glory; it is this humiliation alone which chains the interest of the apostle." Wrede accepts that the gospels portray a Jesus who was a historical personage; but he insists that this Jesus, as portrayed in them, "did *not* determine the Pauline theology" (pp. 165–66. Author's italics). He supposes that Paul believed in a celestial Christ before he was converted to belief in this historical personage, to whom he then transferred all the conceptions which he already had of Christ, "for instance, that he had existed before the world

and had taken part in its creation" (p. 151). This theory in fact fails to harmonize Paul's view of Jesus's life on earth with that of the gospels: humiliation and obscurity are not compatible with fame, power, and influence.

18. A.E. Harvey, *Jesus and the Constraints of History*, London: Duckworth, 1982, pp. 98–99.

19. Furnish (*Jesus*, p. 112) says that we cannot be certain when the three Pastoral epistles (which include 1 Timothy) were written, "although a date sometime in the first two decades of the second century seems likely." The epistles of Ignatius of Antioch are assigned to the early second century even by conservative scholars (cf. J.A.T. Robinson, *Redating the NT.* London: SCM, 1976, pp. 4, 162n.).

20. J.L. Houlden characterizes the author of 1 Timothy (and of the other two Pastoral epistles) as "a man of the Hellenistic world, perhaps Asia Minor, able to draw upon the varied intellectual resources of the time" (*The Pastoral Epistles.* Harmondsworth: Penguin, 1976, p. 44). Ignatius was Bishop of Antioch, Syria, and addressed his letters to five churches in western Asia Minor.

21. Ignatius declares (epistle to the Magnesians, chapter 10) that "to profess Jesus Christ while continuing to follow Jewish customs is an absurdity." In his epistle to the Philadelphians he warns against persons who campaigned among the Christian community for the maintenance of such practices, or for a return to them. He calls them "plausible wolves" and "poisonous weeds" (chapters 2 and 3) and says they make use of the OT prophets to propound Judaism to Christians, and will believe only what they find in the "ancient records", i.e. the OT (chapters 6 and 8). At least some of them (according to chapter 6) were uncircumcised, and so may have been people of mixed descent or gentiles. He regards them as a threat to the unity of the church which included both gentiles and Jews who had abandoned Jewish practices. Cf. Joan E. Taylor, 'The Phenomenon of Early Jewish-Christianity: Reality or Scholarly Invention?', *Vigilae Christianae*, 44 (1990), pp. 318–19. She gives the following summary of the development of Chris-

tianity away from orthodox Judaism: "There was the early Jewish Church, Jewish ethnically and religiously with Gentile converts which, after Paul's mission and fierce debate, accepted the Gentiles into the Church without the requirement of accepting the praxis of Judaism. Thereafter, ethnic Jews in the Church gradually began to fall away from Jewish praxis. By the beginning of the second century, the religion of the Church was perceived as something other than Judaism. Some members of the Church disagreed with this development and undertook missions to Judaise (and re-Judaise) certain communities. By the middle of the second century few Jews within the Church continued to maintain the praxis of Judaism" (p. 326).

22. Mk. 7:3–4 states that "the Pharisees and all the Jews" follow certain practices; but it is not true that 'all the Jews' followed the practices here specified, and the whole passage has been dropped by Matthew and Luke, possibly because they were aware of Mark's error. E. Schweizer thinks that the "detailed itemization" of Mk. 7:4 "indicates the scorn of the non-Jew for such absurd practices" (*The Good News According to Mark*. London: SPCK, 1971, p. 148). Other recent commentators also think it likely that Mark was a gentile. H. Anderson regards the report of the Baptist's death (Mk. 6:17ff) as insensitive to inaccuracies regarding the members of Herod's family and Palestinian practices (*The Gospel of Mark*, New Century Bible, London: Oliphants, 1976, p. 31).

23. Redford gives only a page reference to Kümmel's *Introduction*, but is obviously relying on the English translation of the 14th edition of the German original (London: SCM, 1965, pp. 68–70). My references are to the English translation of the 17th fully revised edition (SCM, 1975), p. 97. For further details of Mark's geographical errors, see *WWJ*, p. 169 n.9.

24. S.R. Sutherland, *God, Jesus and Belief.* Oxford: Blackwell, 1984, pp. 137, 174.

25. M.E. Boring, *Sayings of the Risen Jesus: Christian Prophecy in the Synoptic Tradition.* Cambridge: Cambridge University Press, 1982, pp. 111f. Cf. Boring's *The Continuing*

Voice of Jesus: Christian Prophecy and the Gospel Tradition,
Louisville, Kentucky: Westminster, 1991. He here notes
(pp. 24, 46) that, by creating a narrative framework for
Jesus's life, Mark bound 'words of the Lord' to the pre-
Easter Jesus, and made it more difficult for prophetic oracles to be accepted into the developing canonical tradition
of Jesus's words. Mark even mentions prophets as posing a
certain danger to the life of the church, and this may well
indicate that he "opposed or was suspicious of the
prophetic phenomenon" (p. 68). Boring complains (p. 28)
that scholars still tend to see the sayings material "too
much through post-Markan eyes".

26. 1 Corinthians 9:14 states that "the Lord ordained that they
which proclaim the gospel should live of the gospel." This
claim that preachers are entitled to financial support from
their Christian community is similar to Jesus's statement
"the labourer is worthy of his hire" (Lk. 10:7; Matthew has
"of his food", 10:10). Because of this similarity 1 Corinthians 9:14 has sometimes been adduced as evidence of Paul's
knowledge of the synoptic tradition. But this ruling on
finance and the one on divorce (compare above, p. 30) were
community regulations which were secured by anchoring
them to the authority of Jesus. Priests at all times have
claimed such support and represented the claim as the will
of God. It can only invite cynical inferences if it is suggested
that Paul knew the synoptic tradition, yet drew on practically none of it except when a salary matter was at issue.
'The workman is worthy of his hire' is a proverb, and that a
proverb well known in the Graeco-Roman world could be
put into the mouth of Jesus is evidenced at Acts 20:35,
where Paul is made to allege that "Jesus himself said, It is
more blessed to give than to receive." No such logion is
recorded in the gospels, even though one of them (Luke)
was written by the author of Acts.

27. W. Schmithals, *Die Gnosis in Korinth*, 3rd edition. Göttingen: Vandenhoeck and Ruprecht, 1969, pp. 117–122. He
points out that the possibility of a ritual cursing of Jesus
in Christian worship at Corinth is not as farfetched as it

might seem, for Origen knew of gnostics (Ophites) who "do not admit anyone into their meeting unless he has first pronounced curses against Jesus" (*Contra Celsum*, vi, 28). Such gnostics, says Schmithals, could have found support in the curse pronounced on crucified persons in Deuteronomy 21:23—a passage to which Paul himself alludes in Galatians 3:13. There is no need to suppose any linkage between Ophites and Corinthians, for, he adds, it is characteristic of all gnostic Christology to distinguish sharply between Jesus the man and Christ the supernatural heavenly personage. David E. Aune rejects Schmithals's interpretation of the passage in 1 Corinthians and thinks that 'Jesus be cursed' is merely "a hypothetical Pauline construct" (*Prophecy in Early Christianity*, Grand Rapids: Eerdmans, 1983, p. 257). Aune's book gives a valuable account of prophecy in the whole Graeco-Roman world, although his interpretation of the Christian evidence is very conservative.

28. H. Maccoby, *Paul and Hellenism*. London: SCM, 1991, pp. 91–93.

29. J.C. VanderKam says of the Qumran meal that, however one interprets it, "its messianic character, the prominence of bread and wine, the fact that it was repeated regularly and its explicit eschatological associations do recall elements found in the New Testament treatments of the Lord's Supper" (*The Dead Sea Scrolls Today*. Grand Rapids: Eerdmans; London: SPCK, 1994, p. 175). He instances other overlaps of organizational and ritual practices, and of some major doctrinal tenets which suggest that the Qumranites and the early Christians were "children of a common parent tradition in Judaism" (p. 162). Maccoby stresses the pagan parallels and concludes that the "principal affinities" of the Christian eucharist are with "the ritual meal of the mystery religions" (*op. cit.* in previous note, p. 90).

30. R.P.C. Hanson, in *Theology and Change* (Essays in memory of Alan Richardson), edited by R.H. Preston. London: SCM, 1975, p. 113.

31. Kümmel, *Introduction*, pp. 423–24. Since Kümmel wrote this, J.A.T. Robinson's *Redating the New Testament* (as cited in note 19 above) has made what J.H. Elliott has called "a valiant attempt" to salvage the authenticity of 1 Peter. But Elliott, with many others, remains unconvinced. See his *A Home for the Homeless: A Sociological Exegesis of 1 Peter*, London: SCM, 1982, p. 271. On Robinson's general conservativeness see p. 105 above.

32. H. Räisänen, *Beyond New Testament Theology*, as cited in note 9 to chapter 1 above pp. xii–xiii.

33. I have attempted a detailed account of "criteria of historicity" in *JEC*, chapter 8.

3. Pagan and Jewish Attitudes to Jesus

1. T.D. Barnes, 'Pagan Perceptions of Christianity', in his *From Eusebius to Augustine*. Aldershot (Hampshire): Variorum, 1994, p. 232.

2. The style of this passage is genuinely Tacitean, especially the cynical aside about Rome; and a Christian interpolator would not have needlessly referred to the Christians' betrayal of their fellows. It has been objected that Tacitus mentions Pilate on only this occasion, yet fails to tell us what province he governed, and that this suggests a Christian interpolater writing for Christians who did not need to be told who he was. But in fact Tacitus implies that Pilate functioned in Judea; for he says not only that the originator of Christianity died under him, but also that the movement originated in Judea. It was also objected that the passage contains the phrase 'Tiberio imperitante' ('when Tiberius was emperor') and that emperors were not then so designated, as the pretence was kept up that they still ruled under republican forms as 'princeps senatus', so that one would expect 'Tiberio principe' or something similar. But Tacitus uses the phrase 'Tiberio imperitante' elsewhere in the *Annals* (iii, 24 and iv, 62) and refers to Claudius in the same way (xiii, 32 and 42). H. Furneaux notes in

his edition of the *Annals* (volume 2, Oxford: Clarendon, 1907, p. 374) that the verb is one of the frequentative forms which Tacitus so often prefers. Writing early in this century, Furneaux still found it necessary to defend the authenticity of the passage against sceptics (pp. 416–17). Today that is no longer necessary.

3. Cf. W.H.C. Frend, *Martyrdom and Persecution in the Early Church*. Oxford: Blackwell, 1965, p. 111.

4. J.J. Walsh, 'On Christian Atheism', *Vigiliae Christianae*, 45 (1991), pp. 264–65.

5. Hans Conzelmann, art. 'Jesus Christus', in *Religion in Geschichte und Gegenwart*, 3rd edition, edited by K. Galling. Tübingen: Mohr, 1959, vol. 3, p. 622.

6. F.F. Bruce, *Jesus and Christian Origins Outside the New Testament*. London: Hodder and Stoughton, 1974, p.30n.

7. *Josephus's Jewish Antiquities*, Books 18–19, in *Josephus*, vol. 9, Loeb Classical Library, London: Heinemann, 1965, pp. 106–08 and n.

8. F. Jacoby, *Fragmente der griechischen Historiker*, vol. 2 B (Leiden: Brill, 1962), p. 1156, and the companion volume of commentary (with the same date and place of publication) pp. 835–36.

9. R.T. France, *The Evidence for Jesus*, London: Hodder and Stoughton, 1986, p. 24.

10. R.M. Grant, *Eusebius as Church Historian*, Oxford: Clarendon, 1980, pp. 99–100 and references in note 19. The quotation is from Eusebius's *Chronicle of Jerome*.

11. Jacoby, commentary volume cited in note 8 above, p. 843.

12. Rabbi (Hebrew 'my master') became added shortly after NT times as a title of respect to the names of Jewish religious teachers (e.g. Rabbi Johanan). F.C. Grant and H.H. Rowley note in their revised edition of Hastings's *Dictionary of the Bible* (Edinburgh: Clark, 1963, art. 'Rabbi') that although Jesus is addressed in this way by his disciples in the gospels, this "may be anachronistic", as "the title did not exist in the time of Jesus."

13. S. Sandmel, *Judaism and Christian Beginnings*, New York: Oxford University Press, 1978, p. 397.

14. J.N. Birdsall, 'The Continuing Enigma of Josephus's Testimony About Jesus', *Bulletin of the John Rylands Library*, 67 (1985), p. 618.

15. The Sadducees comprised a Jewish politico-religious sect which, in contrast to the Pharisees, accepted only the written laws of the Pentateuch (the first five books of the OT) and not the oral traditions which had developed from them, nor doctrines explicit only in the later books of the OT. Hence, as we learn in the NT, they did not believe in bodily resurrection (Mt. 22:23), nor in angels or spirits (Acts 23:8). Modern scholars, says Sandmel, believe them to have represented "a social segment, the Jerusalem upper classes, whose lives were intertwined with the priests and the nobility". He adds that "it is also reasonable to suppose that, living in proximity to the Temple, the Sadducees were fully satisfied in their needs by the Temple rituals, so that they felt no compulsion toward that progressive adulation of Scripture which marked the Pharisees and the commoners in the synagogue" (*op. cit.* in note 13 above, p. 157). As a group, the Sadducees did not survive the destruction of the temple in A.D. 70.

16. On Vespasian, see Josephus's *Jewish War*, vi, 5, 4; on Theudas and the Egyptian his *Antiquities of the Jews*, xx, 5, 1 and 8,6.

17. Mark and Matthew nowhere say that carrying out capital sentences was beyond the competence of the Sanhedrin. They would surely have been glad to record it, had they known of it, so as to explain why Jesus, already in their accounts tried and "condemned" by the Sanhedrin "to be worthy of death" (Mk. 14:64), nevertheless has to be extradited to Pilate. Even in the fourth gospel Pilate seems to know nothing of this restriction of the Sanhedrin's authority; for, having himself found no case against Jesus, he tells the Jews to crucify Jesus themselves if they are so minded (19:6. Commentators reconcile this with 18:31 [where he has already been told that "it is not lawful for us to put any man to death"] by calling it sarcasm). In any case, this whole pericope is no eyewitness report, and the

Jews' statement that they cannot themselves kill their victim may simply be the evangelist's way of bringing home to us—for the first time within his passion narrative—that they are bent on having him killed; and Pilate's telling them to kill him themselves may serve to introduce their response: "We have a law and by that law he ought to die, because he made himself the Son of God" (19:7).

18. Jean Juster, *Les Juifs dans l'empire romain*, Paris: Geuthner, 1914, vol. 2, pp. 140–41.

19. E. Schürer, *Geschichte des jüdischen Volkes im Zeitalter Jesu Christi*, vol. 1, Leipzig, 1901, p. 581. Schürer's view is accepted by the author of the article on Josephus in *Paulys Real-Encyclopädie der Altertumswissenschaft*, revised by G. Wissowa, vol. 9, Stuttgart: Metzler, 1916, column 1993 It is, however, possible, as P. Winter notes in the new English version of Schürer's book (*The History of the Jewish People in the Age of Jesus Christ*, edited by G. Vermes and F. Miller, volume 1, Edinburgh: Clark, 1973, p. 430n.), that Origen, and Eusebius following him, confused Hegesippus with Josephus. On this view, Origen may have read in Hegesippus how the Jews had paid for their murder of James, but later thought he had read it in Josephus. If he did in fact make such a mistake, the basis for it may have been that his text of Josephus did make *some* mention of James as the brother of Jesus; and if so, the passage as we have it in Book 20 of the *Antiquities* will have existed (whether as genuine or as an interpolation) by the time of Origen. Ian Wilson alleges that "the information from Origen is incontrovertible evidence that Josephus referred to Jesus before any Christian copyist would have had a chance to make alterations" (*Jesus, the Evidence*, London: Weidenfeld and Nicolson, 1984, p. 61). This is absurd. Origen wrote in the third century; Josephus's book had been available since the end of the first.

20. The scribes were the 'writers', and as this occupation made them very familiar with the scriptures, they were the interpreters of the sacred writings. Their successors in the second century A.D. were the rabbis.

21. The testimony of Hegesippus and Clement of Alexandria concerning James is recorded by Eusebius, *Ecclesiastical History*, ii, 1 and 23.

22. Pinchas Lapide, *The Resurrection of Jesus:* English Translation (from the German) by W.C. Linss, London: SPCK, 1984, pp. 32f, 34.

23. M. Grant, *Jesus*, London: Weidenfeld and Nicolson, 1977, p. 42.

24. On Jesus in the Koran, see my *Belief and Make-Believe*, pp. 107f, and (much more fully) H. Räisänen, *Das Koranische Jesusbild*, Helsinki: Finnische Gesellschaft für Missiologie, 1971.

25. G. Vermes, review of Lapide's book in *TLS*, 1 February 1985.

4. Hard-Line Protestantism: The Case of J.W. Montgomery

1. J.W. Montgomery, 'Did Jesus Exist?', *New Oxford Review* (Berkeley, Ca), vol. 60, 1993, reprinted in the Lutheran *Christian News*, 17 May, 1993. I replied to Prof. Montgomery in *Christian News*, 13 September, 1993, where his rejoinder to my reply was also published. He continued the discussion in the *New Oxford Review* of May, 1994. My quotations from him are from the above material, except for those from two books of his which I call *Crisis* and *The Law* (details of them are given on p. xviii above). I give page references when quoting from these two books, but not when quoting from the articles.

2. I have attempted a full discussion of 'Miracles and the Nature of Truth' in chapter 8 of my *Religious Postures*.

3. On this difference between John and the synoptics, the article 'John, Son of Zebedee' in the second volume of the old *Encyclopaedia Biblica* (first published in London by Black in 1901) is (like P.W. Schmiedel's other articles in this four-volume work) still instructive. He wrote (*art.cit.*, § 20): "None of the sick mentioned by the synoptics as

having been healed by Jesus is recorded to have lain under his infirmity for thirty-eight years (Jn. 5:5). The blind man who is healed has been blind from birth (9:1). Jesus walks across the whole lake, not over a portion of it only (6:21). Lazarus is not raised on the day of his death, like the daughter of Jairus or the son of the widow of Nain [neither of whom is mentioned in John] but after four days have elapsed", that is, Schmiedel added, at a time when, according to Jewish belief, the soul has irrevocably departed from the body.

4. *WWJ* includes detailed discussion of the recent attempt by Gary Habermas and others to defend the historicity of the resurrection; and I note there (p. 79) that in my *JEC* of 1971 I found it necessary to come to terms with the conservative case on the virgin birth because at that time the doctrine was still stoutly defended. John Robinson's attempt to assign early dates to various NT books is discussed in my *HEJ*.

5. What I wrote was: now that statements rejecting traditional Christian interpretations of the NT "are coming from Christians *who have taken the trouble to make a thorough study of the evidence,* is it not time to look elsewhere than in the Scriptures for guidance in our living?" In quoting this, Montgomery omitted the clause that I have here italicized.

6. "Biblical inerrancy is under severe attack in our time not because of empirical data militating against the view, but because of the climate of philosophical opinion presently conditioning Protestant theology" (Montgomery, *Crisis*, p. 33). He has existentialism particularly in mind.

7. Montgomery refers in this context to Annie Jaubert's harmonization of synoptic and Johannine chronology (cf. above, pp. 112f) and declares that "archaeological work daily confirms biblical history" (*Crisis*, p. 20). Cf. his quite unjustified claim concerning the recently discovered inscription naming Pontius Pilate (above, p. 70).

8. Maurice Wiles gives this as a summary of Irenaeus's position in his 'Orthodoxy and Heresy', in *Early Christianity:*

Origins and Evolution to A.D. 600, Festschrift for W.H.C.
Frend, edited by I. Hazlett, London: SPCK, 1991, p. 202;
reprinted in Wiles's *A Shared Search: Doing Theology in
Conversation With One's Friends,* London: SCM, 1994,
pp. 67–68.

Irenaeus's method of countervailing what he regarded
as false teaching was to exaggerate the continuity (and
hence, he supposed, the reliability) of orthodox tradition
by alleging that the bishops of the Christian communities
of his time had predecessors who could be traced back to
apostolic founders. Thus, although Paul's epistle to the
Romans shows that there was a Christian community at
Rome prior to him, Irenaeus holds that the church there
was founded by Paul and Peter, jointly; and he lists their
supposed successors. His list includes 'Sixtus', and as this
means 'sixth', he posits five non-apostolic precedessors,
the first of whom he names 'Linus' and identifies with the
Linus mentioned at 2 Timothy 4:21. He seems to have chosen this name simply because Linus is the last male person
named as Paul's companion in this epistle, taken as written by Paul, and at Rome, immediately before his martyrdom. In the epistle that immediately follows this one in
the canon, it is said that "the bishop must be irreproach-
able" (Greek *anenklētus,* Titus 1:7). This seems to have
given Irenaeus his next name, Anakletus, followed by
Clement, supposed author of the extant anonymous letter
addressed by the church of Rome to that of Corinth, and
traditionally dated at the end of the first century. Where
the fourth and fifth names on the list came from we cannot tell (see the whole passage quoted in *A New Eusebius:
Documents Illustrative of the History of the Church to* A.D.
337, edited by J. Stevenson, London: SPCK, 1957, pp.
118–19). Such arguments, says S.G. Hall, "have nothing to
do with historical information" (*Doctrine and Practice in
the Early Church,* London: SPCK, 1991, p. 61).

Irenaeus sometimes contradicts himself in making the
past fit his Christianity. On the one hand he gives Jesus the
age of thirty before a three-year ministry, and has him cru-

cified under Pilate in the reign of Tiberius (*Against Heresies*, I, 27, 2 and II, 22, 3–4). But in order to accommodate what he read at Jn. 8:57, he supposes that Jesus nearly reached the age of fifty (*Ibid.*. II, 22,5), and so has to make Pilate the Procurator of Claudius (*Epideixsis*, i.e. *Demonstration of the Apostolic Preaching*, 74).

9. On Sherwin-White and Finley, see my *Belief and Make-Believe*, p. 265 n.4.

10. Jean Imbert, *Le procès de Jésus*, 2nd edition, Paris: Presses Universitaires, 1984, pp. 26, 123; Weddig Fricke, *Standrechtlich Gekreuzigt. Person und Prozess des Jesus aus Galiläa*, Hamburg: Rowohlt, 1988 or later reprint.

11. See Anderson's contribution to *Is Christianity Credible?*, essays by various hands, introduced by David Stacey, London: Epworth, 1981.

12. W.F. Albright, who died in 1971, was an American Near Eastern scholar and archaeologist who aimed to restore confidence in the Bible—I illustrated how in *JEC*, p. 127n.—and who influenced many evangelical theologians. He believed that modern archaeological and other discoveries make it "clear that God has been preparing the way for a revival of basic Christianity through enlightened faith in His Word" (*History, Archaeology, and Christian Humanism*, London: Black, 1965, p. 297). In his view, "all the authors of the NT were certainly or probably Jews" (p. 296), and the NT "cannot be later than the spread of Gnosticism after the middle decades of the first century A.D." (p. 44). We would need to know how long after precisely which decades this puts gnosticism before we could make any inference about the date of the NT material. In his commentary on Matthew (written jointly with C.S. Mann and published by Doubleday in the Anchor Bible Series) Albright is more precise and says that the four gospels "must have been composed in substantially their extant written form no earlier than the late 60s and no later than the 70s or early 80s" (1971 reprint, p. clxviii). In his *New Horizons in Biblical Research* (London, etc.: Oxford University Press, 1966, p. 46) he dates the fourth gospel at "the

late 70s or early 80s".

13. D. Parker, 'Scripture is Tradition', *Theology*, 94 (1991), p. 12. Cf. P.M. Head's article 'Christology and Textual Transmission: Reverential Alterations in the Synoptic Gospels' (*Novum Testamentum*, 35 (1993), p. 111), where he notes that "Gospel manuscripts from the second century are very scarce, with only two fragments of John's Gospel definitely written before A.D. 200 (i.e. P^{52} and P^{90})." He adds that, although fragmentary manuscripts of the synoptic gospels are extant from around 200, "of all the synoptic manuscripts which can be dated to the fourth century or earlier, only two (P^{45} and P^{75}, both of the third century) contain more than a chapter."

14. Many, says Elliott, have "fondly argued that, of the myriad textual variants in our fund of extant mss., few affect key doctrinal matters". He adds that if they read Ehrman, they will find that "the text was regularly adjusted in such areas as the birth of Jesus, the agony in the garden, the institution of the Eucharist, Jesus's death, his cry of dereliction, resurrection and ascension. . . . And these adjustments were made not by those who were labelled as heretics, but by the 'proto-orthodox', to use Ehrman's term." Again, "Ehrman vividly shows how scribes have preserved or created within the mss. they were copying reflections of early Christological debates that helped to shape mainstream Christianity" (*Nov Test* 36 [1994], pp. 405–06).

15. Few scholars support Montgomery's confident dating of P^{52} at A.D. 100. Lindars (*John*, 1972, p. 43) does not query Aland's assessment of "130 at the latest"; Barrett (*John*, p. 110) says 130 or 140 at the latest. Even J.A.T. Robinson commits himself to nothing more than "not much later than the first quarter of the second century" (*The Priority of John*, London: SCM, 1985, p. 37).

16. *World Christian Encyclopaedia: A Comparative Study of the Churches and Religions in the Modern World*, edited by D.B. Barrett, Oxford University Press, 1982, p. v.

17. J.A. Kleist: his edition of the extant quotations from and references to Papias's books is included in volume 6 of

Ancient Christian Writers, Cork: Mercier, 1948, pp. 114–124.

18. Details in Haenchen, *JE,* pp. 19–20 and in his *Die Apostelgeschichte,* 6th edition, Göttingen: Vandenhoeck and Ruprecht, 1968, note on pp. 8–10. Cf. also Kümmel, *Introduction,* p. 488. Even Wenham (*Redating,* pp. 139–140) allows that all three Anti-Marcionite prologues—to Mark, Luke, and John (there was presumably also one to Matthew, but it is not extant)—are "of uncertain date" and should not be given "undue weight".

19. This cannot be true if the early fifth-century historian Philip Sidetes (cited in Kleist, note 17 above) is right to say that Papias states in his book that those whom Christ raised from the dead lived until Hadrian's reign (A.D. 117–138). Accordingly, Gundry sets Sidetes aside as unreliable. It is noteworthy that even so conservative a scholar as M. Hengel declines to do this, and finds himself unable to date Papias's work earlier than Hadrian (*Studies in the Gospel of Mark,* English translation London: SCM, 1985, p. 149).

20. R.H. Gundry, *Mark: A Commentary on his Apology for the Cross,* Grand Rapids: Eerdmans, 1993, p. 1034. Papias's passage about the two Johns, quoted by Eusebius (*Ecclesiastical History,* iii, 39) is as follows:

> If ever anyone came who had followed the presbyters, I inquired into the words of the presbyters, what Andrew or Peter or Philip or Thomas or James or John or Matthew, or any other of the Lord's disciples, had said, and what Aristion and the presbyter John, the Lord's disciples, were saying.

Eusebius comments on this:

> It is here worth noting that he twice counts the name of John, and reckons the first John with Peter and James and Matthew and the other Apostles, clearly meaning the evangelist, but by changing his statement places the second with the others outside the number of the Apostles, putting Aristion before him and clearly calling him a presbyter.

21. Someone named Mark is mentioned in verse 24 of Paul's letter to Philemon, in Colossians 4:10, 2 Timothy 4:11 and

1 Peter 5:13. There is also a "John named Mark" in Acts. This difference in name suggests someone different from the Mark (or several Marks) of the epistles.

22. Goulder observes that the name Peter occurs nineteen times in Mark; Simon (the same person—see the next note) occurs eight times, James and John ten times each: "In contrast none of the other eight faithful apostles is ever mentioned independently" (*Midrash*, p. 141). Mark also represents Peter (with his brother) as the first disciple to be called (1:16) and places him first on the list of the twelve (3:16).

23. 'Cephas' is not a proper name but an Aramaic word meaning 'rock', while 'Peter' is a translation of this word into Greek. In the synoptics there is no mention of Cephas, but the most prominent disciple is called Simon, and—in different circumstances in each gospel—Jesus gives him the title 'Peter'.

24. "The existence in the first half of the second century of i. the *Gospel of the Nazaraeans* (in Aramaic or Syriac, and attested by Hegesippus, Eusebius, Epiphanius and Jerome) which showed a close relationship with the canonical Matthew, and ii. *The Gospel of the Ebionites* (quoted by Epiphanius . . . and called by him the 'Hebrew Gospel') which is more closely related to Matthew than to any other of the canonical Gospels, may explain why Papias spoke of translations (or interpretations) of the *logia* which he incorrectly considered to be the Gospel [of Matthew]. Both these Semitic Gospels are virtually targumistic renderings of the canonical Matthew" (D. Hill, *The Gospel of Matthew* (New Century Bible), London: Oliphants, 1972, p. 26. 'Targums' are Aramaic translations or paraphrases).

25. J. Kürzinger, *Papias von Hierapolis und die Evangelien des NT*, Regensburg: Pustet, 1983, pp. 22–23, 33–34, 49–60. This book also gives all the ancient quotations from and references to Papias, in the original languages and in German translation, and an annotated bibliography of modern studies of Papias.

26. P.W. Schmiedel, art. 'Gospels', §147, in *Encyclopaedia Bib-*

lica, as cited in note 3 above).

27. These patristic statements about the origin of Mark are assembled and discussed by V. Taylor, *Mark*, pp. 1–8.

28. Cf. *Dictionary of the Bible*, as cited in note 12 to chapter 3 above (p. 223), art. 'Gospel'. Also H. Koester, 'From the Kerygma-Gospel to Written Gospels', *NTS*, 35 (1989), pp. 376, 380–81. The word 'gospel' occurs more than fifty times in the Pauline epistles, but rarely elsewhere in the NT. C.F. Evans thinks it may have been "a word of Pauline coinage" or "taken by Paul from the terminology of the Christian mission field to denote the message of salvation" (*The Beginning of the Gospel*, London: SPCK, 1968, p. 16). Koester (*Ancient Christian Gospels*, London: SCM, 1990, p. 36) concludes that the word continued to be used in the sense of the proclamation of the saving message about Christ or the coming of the kingdom until, ca. A.D. 150, Marcion made it a technical designation for a written document; and that his motive for introducing this novel usage was to protest against "the still undefined and mostly oral traditions to which the churches of his day referred as their dominical and apostolic authority".

29. G.M. Hahneman, *The Muratorian Fragment and the Development of the Canon*, Oxford: Clarendon, 1992, p. 110.

30. Montgomery ascribes this computer work wrongly to Morton and Macgregor, and says, wrongly, that they found no letters to be genuinely Pauline except Romans and Galatians (*Crisis*, p. 86).

31. A. Kenny, *A Stylometric Study of the New Testament*, Oxford: Clarendon, 1986, pp. 107, 114, 118.

32. D. Lamont, *God's Word and Man's Response*, London: Inter-Varsity Fellowship, 1946, p. 7; quoted by Steve Bruce, *Firm in the Faith*, Aldershot (Hants) and Brookfield (Vermont): Gower, 1984, p. 4. Bruce's book is a valuable study of conservative Protestantism.

33. J. Wellhausen, *Einleitung in die drei ersten Evangelien*, Berlin: Reimer, 1905, pp. 47, 52. Wellhausen's observations on the synoptics are called "gems" by R. Morgan and J. Barton (see their *Biblical Interpretation*, Oxford Univer-

sity Press, 1988, p. 334). N. Perrin says they are "amazingly prophetic of what was to come", namely the 'form-criticism' of K.L. Schmidt and others (See Perrin's *What is Redaction Criticism?*, London: SPCK, 1970, p. 14); for Wellhausen regarded Mark's account of the Galilean ministry as composed of small units which had existed earlier, independent of each other, in oral tradition, and from which the evangelist could construct only an arbitrary sequence which gives no true chronology and pays scant regard to place as well as to time—the setting being often quite vague ('the wilderness', 'the mountain', 'the house'). And the Christian community made a substantial contribution to the teaching ascribed to Jesus in, for instance, Matthew's Sermon on the Mount (Wellhausen, *op. cit*, pp. 43, 53, 56, 86, 115, and also his *Das Evangelium Marci*, Berlin: Reimer, 1904, pp. 9, 16).

34. R. Bultmann, *Die Geschichte der synoptischen Tradition*, Göttingen: Vandenhoeck and Ruprecht, 1970, p. 27; compare *DJE*, p. 93 n.2. S. Barton has recently noted that Mark's stories of the call of the disciples (1:16–20 and 2:13–14) have been shaped according to the pattern of the biblical call story, exemplified in the call of Elisha by Elijah (1 Kings 19:19–21). This pattern comprises a summons to follow and a response involving the renunciation of household and/or occupational ties: "The appearance of the divinely appointed messenger, the authoritative summons to share his mission and the consequent subordination of otherwise legitimate commitments are elements which the Marcan stories share in common with the scriptural prophetic tradition." These stories thus have "a strong conventional quality" (*Discipleship and Family Ties in Mark and Matthew*, Cambridge University Press, 1994, p. 61).

35. R.H. Gundry, *The Use of the Old Testament in St. Matthew's Gospel*, Leiden: Brill, 1967, pp. 182–83.

36. C. Thiede, as cited in note 12 to chapter 1 above, p. 36.

37. K.J. Schulte, 'Der Tod Jesu in der Sicht der modernen Medizin', *Berliner Medizin*, 14(1963), pp. 210–220.

38. Cf. 1 Jn. 5:6: He "came not with the water only, but with

the water and with the blood." The idea there, as at Jn. 19:34 (where water and blood issue from Jesus's side) is that not only the eucharist but also baptism owes its efficacy to the Lord's death: it is in virtue of his death that sins are forgiven at baptism, the opening of a fountain of grace. Ignatius of Antioch expressed the idea when he wrote, early in the second century: "He submitted to baptism so that by his Passion he might sanctify water" (Letter to the Ephesians, section 18).

39. Lindars, *John*, 1990, p. 22. He adds that the beloved disciple "is one of the Twelve who at crucial moments gives expression to the evangelist's own views. He represents true discipleship, understanding the necessity of the death of Jesus when all others fail. He is thus a foil to Peter, who in spite of being the acknowledged leader failed by denying Jesus three times."

40. In a letter quoted by Eusebius (*Ecclesiastical History*, v, 20) Irenaeus named the author of the fourth gospel as John and claimed that as a boy he had heard his own teacher, the aged Polycarp, tell of having heard of Jesus's wonders directly from this John and from "the others who had seen the Lord." If Polycarp had been wont to speak of the John who had taught him as 'a disciple of the Lord', the boy Irenaeus could easily have taken this as meaning not merely a Christian, but a personal acquaintance of Jesus. Polycarp himself, in his extant letter to the Philippians, gives no indication of having known any of the apostles. He shows some knowledge of the gospels of Matthew and Luke, but none of the fourth gospel—a fact which "has never yet been satisfactorily accounted for by those who maintain with Irenaeus (a) that this gospel was written by John the son of Zebedee and (b) that Polycarp was a disciple of this same John" (P.N. Harrison, *Polycarp's Two Epistles*, Cambridge: University Press, 1936, p. 257). Barrett (*John*, p. 105) notes that a life of Polycarp, somewhat later than Irenaeus, is extant (written under the name of Pionius) and "says nothing of any contact between Polycarp and John. Like most hagiographs it magnifies its subject

as far as possible; but it describes Polycarp as the third
bishop of his see (the first having been appointed not by
John but by Paul)." The author "would have recounted
Polycarp's association with John if he could have found a
shred of evidence to suggest it." That Irenaeus exaggerated
the continuity of Christian tradition is evident from his
calling Papias "a hearer of John". Eusebius shows that this
cannot be true, for he quotes (*op. cit*, iii, 39) the relevant
passage from Papias and accuses Irenaeus of having confused the apostle John with a presbyter named John. We
saw (above, p. 72) that in this passage Papias does not
even claim direct acquaintance with the presbyters, but
only with their pupils. And as Barrett says (*loc. cit*), a
notable error in Irenaeus's account of the one Father
(Papias) does not inspire confidence in his report of the
other (Polycarp).

41. Clement of Alexandria, quoted by Eusebius, *op. cit*, vi, 14.

42. Cf. Montgomery's *Crisis*, p. 41, where he adduces 1 Jn.
1:1–4 as evidence of the author's "objective empirical contact with the incarnate Christ."

43. J.L. Houlden (*A Commentary on the Johannine Epistles*,
revised edition, London: Black, 1994) observes that the
whole passage "borders on incoherence" (p. 45), that it is
possible that the writer is "writing as if he were an eyewitness, deliberately setting out to deceive in order to further
his case", but more probable that he is consciously taking
the mantle of orthodoxy in that he "speaks for and is at
one with all those who have thought rightly about Jesus
'from the beginning'—and of course that includes those
who first saw, heard and felt" (p. 53). Houlden adds that
the author's use of the expression 'to see with the eyes' is
"a positive aid" to him: its ambiguity—"to see with the
eyes is to have faith"—"helps to bind him to those who
stand behind him, those who literally saw Jesus and witnessed the original events."

44. R.J. Bauckham, '2 Peter: An Account of Research', in *Aufstieg und Niedergang der römischen Welt*, edited by W.
Haase et al, Berlin and New York: de Gruyter. Abteilung II

(Principat), volume 25 (5), 1988, pp. 3719, 3741—42. Meier calls J.A.T. Robinson's attempt to place all the writings of the NT before A.D. 70 "a dazzling tour de force that fails to convince" and says that Robinson "does not even attempt a serious argument for the hopeless case of 2 Peter" (*Marginal*, p. 50 n.5)—even though he does discuss 2 Peter at some length.

45. D. Guthrie, *Hebrews to Revelation: New Testament Introduction*, London: Tyndale, 1962, pp. 168, 174.

46. J.N.D. Kelly, *The Epistles of Peter and of Jude*, London: Black, 1969, pp. 235–36.

47. E. Grässer, *Das Problem der Parusieverzögerung*, 3rd edition, Berlin and New York: de Gruyter, 1977, p. 136.

48. S.G. Wilson, *The Gentiles and the Gentile Mission in Luke-Acts*, Cambridge: Cambridge University Press, 1973, pp. 73, 78, 80, 82–85.

49. C.H. Dodd, *The Interpretation of the Fourth Gospel*, Cambridge: Cambridge University Press, 1970, p. 147.

50. Cf. Haenchen, *JE*, p. 280. Cf. p. 35 above, concerning what Haenchen regards as interference from the final editor in chapter 6 of John.

51. A.T. and R.P.C. Hanson, *Reasonable Belief*, Oxford University Press, 1980, p. 196.

52. M.D. Goulder, review of J.M. Rist's *On the Independence of Matthew and Mark*, Cambridge University Press, 1978, in *JTS*, 30 (1979), pp. 266–67. Rist's book is one of the few recent attempts to deny any literary dependence of the one gospel on the other, and is here severely criticized.

53. S.E. Johnson, *The Griesbach Hypothesis and Redaction Criticism*, Atlanta: Scholars, 1991.

54. See, for instance, the symposium *The Two-Source Hypothesis: A Critical Appraisal*, edited by A.J. Bellinzoni Jr., Mercer University Press, 1985. J.B. Tyson observes at the end of this volume that, after reading the evidence collected in it for and against the hypothesis, "it is difficult to avoid the conclusion that nothing convincing has emerged from this long and tortuous debate" (p. 438).

55. Romans 4:25 (Jesus our Lord "was delivered up for our

trespasses and raised for our justification"); 1 Corinthians
15:3 (Christ "died for our sins"); 1 Peter 2:24 (He "bare our
sins in his body upon the tree" and "by his stripes ye were
healed").

56. *Peter in the New Testament*, edited by R.E. Brown et al.,
London: G. Chapman, 1974, p. 107. Details are given on
the same page: "He who is called a 'man of little faith'
(14:31) is soon afterwards praised for having expressed a
faith so perceptive that it can be explained only as a gift of
God (16:17–18). And yet the Peter who is blessed for this
(16:17) is within a few lines cursed as 'Satan' and a 'stum-
bling block' for Jesus precisely because he thinks the
thoughts of men and *not* the thoughts of God" (16:23).

57. *The New Bible Commentary Revised*, edited by D. Guthrie
et al., London: Inter-Varsity Press, 1970, p. 925 (This section is written by I.H. Marshall).

58. James Barr, *Fundamentalism*, 2nd edition, London: SCM,
1981, pp. 57, 61. This whole section of Barr's book—on
'harmonization'—merits careful study.

59. M.C. Parsons, *The Departure of Jesus in Luke-Acts*,
Sheffield: Academic Press, 1987, p. 195.

60. A brief summary of the differences and the common
ground between John and the synoptics is given by S. Barton, 'The Believer, the Historian, and the Fourth Gospel',
Theology, 96 (1993), pp. 289–302.

61. An obvious example is the story of the anointing of Jesus
(cf. note 73 below). Another is Peter's 'confession' that
Jesus is "the Christ". John has no direct parallel to the
incident in the other three gospels which provokes this
confession, but in another context he does make Peter,
speaking for the twelve, give Jesus a christological title
("We have believed and know that thou art the Holy One
of God", Jn. 6:69). In Mark and Matthew, Peter follows his
'confession' with unwillingness to believe plain speaking
from Jesus about his forthcoming death and resurrection,
and this earns him the severe rebuke "get thee behind me,
Satan." John has nothing, here or elsewhere, corresponding to this, but—less appropriately—makes Jesus respond

directly to Peter's confession that he is "the Holy One" with a rebuke—not, however, of Peter, but of Judas ("Did I not choose you the twelve, and one of you is a devil?"). Cf. *HEJ*, pp. 130ff on John's reworking of traditional material.

62. An example of Zahn's technique is what he makes of Jesus's relation to John the Baptist. The fourth evangelist makes the two men missionize at the same time (3:22–24). This enables him to show that Jesus was by far the more successful and more important of the two, and that this was acknowledged even by the Baptist himself (3:30 and 4:1. Why the Baptist continued with his admittedly inferior water baptism once it had achieved what he himself says was its purpose—namely to make Jesus "manifest to Israel" (1:31–34)—remains unexplained). The synoptics, however, represent the Baptist as having been confined to prison before Jesus begins his own preaching (Mk. 1:14). For Zahn, there is no contradiction: Jesus first acted with the Baptist, as in the fourth gospel; then the Baptist was imprisoned, and only then did Jesus begin the ministry specified in the synoptics. As according to Zahn the fourth evangelist presupposed readers familiar with the synoptics, his statement (at Jn. 3:24) that the Baptist "was not yet cast into prison" is to be understood as a clear pointer to such readers that the contact between Jesus and the Baptist that has just been described occurred prior to the preaching of Jesus familiar to them from the synoptics (Theodor Zahn, *Introduction to the New Testament*, English translation, volume 3, Edinburgh: Clark, 1909, p. 258).

63. J.A.T. Robinson, *The Priority of John*, London: SCM, 1983, p. 128.

64. I discuss *Honest to God* in Part 3 of my *Belief and Make-Believe*, and *Redating the New Testament* throughout *HEJ*.

65. J.V.M. Sturdy, in *JTS*, 30 (1979), p. 256.

66. Lindars, *John*, 1972, p. 443. Brown (*Death*, pp. 76–77) gives a brief resumé of swings of opinion concerning how John is related to the synoptics. Some commentators hold that John did at least know Mark. Brown replies that John's account of Jesus's public ministry is really close to

Mark's only in chapter 6 (the multiplication of the loaves and the walking on the water), and that while their passion narratives share "a general outline", their dissimilarities of items and wording far outnumber the similarities (*Death*, pp. 77, 80–81). The overlap with Mark in John's chapter 6 has frequently been attributed to use by both evangelists of an earlier collection of miracle stories.

67. *The New Bible Commentary Revised* (as cited in note 57 above) says: "By far the most satisfactory solution is that Jesus cleansed the Temple twice" (p. 875, written by C.E. Graham Swift).

68. H.F.D. Sparks, *A Synopsis of the Gospels*, Part II, *The Gospel According to St. John with the Synoptic Parallels*, London: Black, 1974.

69. Matthew (21:18–19) avoids making Jesus look silly by deleting Mark's "it was not the season of figs", but still makes him petulantly curse and kill the tree for not satisfying his hunger. Luke was surely wiser to delete the whole incident.

70. Although the RV uses the word 'temple', the Greek here, both in John, and in Mark and Matthew, has ναός, 'sanctuary', i.e. the most sacred inner' part of the temple, and not the usual word for 'temple' (ἱερόν, used, for instance at Mk. 13:1–2, where Jesus prophesies that no one stone shall be left upon another of the great temple buildings). Those who mock Jesus at his crucifixion likewise say that he threatened to destroy the "sanctuary" (Mk. 15:29); and at his death it is the veil of the "sanctuary" that is torn from top to bottom (15:38)—a symbolic destruction of it.

71. See 4Q Florilegium, quoted by A. Dupont-Sommer, *The Essene Writings from Qumran*, English translation Oxford: Blackwell, 1961, pp. 311–12.

72. "Some passages in Mark (1:45; 3:20; 6:5; 7:24; 9:22–23) seem to put limitations on what Jesus was able to do; Matthew modifies or eliminates all those passages, and so the Matthean reader would have the impression that Jesus's power was limitless" (Brown, *Death*, p. 435).

73. If it is unlikely that Jesus cleansed the temple twice, it is

even less likely that he was anointed three times: on the feet, in Galilee early in his ministry while dining in a Pharisee's house, by an immoral woman (Lk. 7:37–50); on the feet, in Bethany (within two miles of Jerusalem) by Mary the sister of Martha and Lazarus, at dinner in their house, before his triumphal entry into Jerusalem (Jn. 12:1–8); and on the head, in Bethany by an unnamed woman in the house of Simon the leper, after the triumphal entry (Mk. 14:3–9 and Mt. 26:6–13). These are radically different forms of a single underlying story (cf. *WWJ*, pp. 118–123).

74. Annie Jaubert, *La date de la Cène*, Paris: Gabolda, 1957; English translation *The Date of the Last Supper*, Staten Island: Alba House, 1965.

75. The Catholic theologian H. Küng finds that, in spite of intense critical scrutiny of the gospels, it is not possible to reconstruct what happened at Jesus's trial, of which neither eyewitness statements nor original documents are available. He summarizes the objections that have so often been made to the gospel accounts (*Christ sein*, Zürich: Ex Libris, 1976, pp. 320–21). Imbert (p. 124) finds these remarks astounding. J.C. Vanderkam (Professor of Old Testament studies at the University of Notre Dame) says "there is no evidence that the writers of the Gospels followed different calendar systems", and declares that John obviously had "a larger purpose" (a theological one) "in arranging the events in the passion week as he does" ('The Dead Sea Scrolls and Christianity', in Shanks, *Scrolls*, pp. 195–96.

76. J.A. Fitzmyer, *The Dead Sea Scrolls: Major Publications and Tools for Study*, revised edition, Atlanta: Scholars, 1990, p. 186.

77. Brown, *Death*, pp. 1311–12, where he points out that in Mark, Luke, and John, the only obstacle mentioned as preventing the women from entering the tomb is the stone. These three evangelists would certainly have had to explain how the women expected to enter if there were a guard placed there precisely to prevent entry. In these gospels "the stone is already removed or rolled back when the women

get there. How can we reconcile that with Matthew's account where, while the women are at the sepulcher, an angel comes down out of heaven and rolls back the stone?" It is also not plausible that "the Jewish authorities knew the words of Jesus about his resurrection and understood them, when his own disciples did not"; and "that the guards could lie successfully about the astounding heavenly intervention". But these implausibilities "touch only on the minor details" of Matthew's story, whereas the very existence of a guard "touches on its heart".

78. Mark has derived this from the final verse of Isaiah (66:24), where Yahweh prophesies that the pious will watch deceased sinners being eternally tormented: "And they shall go forth, and look upon the carcases of the men that have transgressed against me; for their worm shall not die, neither shall their fire be quenched." D. Kidner, commenting on this in the *New Bible Commentary Revised* (as cited in note 57 above) observes (p. 625) that in the synagogue the verse previous to this final one ("all flesh shall come to worship before me") is read again after the latter "to soften the ending of the prophecy". Kidner himself, however, finds this final verse "a true ending": What else can result to men who prefer their idols and their pork "to so evident a God of grace"?

79. J. Boswell, *Life of Johnson*, edited by G.B. Hill in six volumes, volume 2, Oxford: Clarendon, 1934, p. 443 (20 March 1776).

5. The Gospel of Mark—History or Dogma?

1. I have given an assessment of Strauss's work on the NT in *Religious Postures*, chapter 2.

2. "No critical theologian believes Mark's report on the baptism of Jesus, the raising of Jairus's daughter, the miraculous feedings, the walking of Jesus on the water, the transfiguration, or the conversation of the angel with the women at the tomb, in the sense in which he records

them. If the theologian sees facts *behind* such information he is nevertheless compelled to grant that they have undergone a very substantial transformation and distortion" (Wrede, *Secret*, pp. 9–10).

3. E.P. Sanders, *Jesus and Judaism*, London: SCM, 1985, p. 330.

4. The implication of the passage is that the disciples suppose Jesus to be telling them to bake or buy bread, but in either case to beware of Pharisaic or Herodian attempts to poison it. Even today some commentators can note that this is so, with barely a hint that it is ridiculous of Mark to impute such thinking to the disciples. See, for instance, C.F.D. Moule *ad. loc.* in *The Gospel According to Mark*, Cambridge University Press, 1965, p. 62: "The disciples solemnly take Jesus's proverbial words literally, thinking, since they have forgotten to bring sandwiches, that they are being warned against accepting poisoned food from others."

5. On Sanday's "intemperate language" about Wrede, see C. Tuckett's introduction to the collection of essays edited by himself under the title *The Messianic Secret*, London: SPCK; Philadelphia: Fortress, 1983, p. 9.

6. J.C. Meagher, *Clumsy Construction in Mark's Gospel: A Critique of Form- and Redaktionsgeschichte*, New York: Mellen, 1979 (Toronto Studies in Theology, volume 3), p. 117.

7. Eta Linnemann, *Gleichnisse Jesu*, 6th edition, Göttingen. Vandenhoeck and Ruprecht, 1975, p. 180. She offers the following reconstruction:

Verses of Mk. 4 *(material added at each stage is underlined)*	1. In the pre-Marcan oral tradition, the parable of the sower (4:3–9) was followed immediately by two further parables—the seed which grows secretly and the mustard seed (verses 26–32). Both represent the kingdom of God as something great coming unexpectedly from inconspicuous beginnings.
3–9	
26–32	

2
3–9
26–32
33

2. A framework for this was then provided with verses 2 (he taught the multitude "many things in parables") and 33 ("with many such parables spake he the word unto them").

2
3–9
10
(original)
13–20

26–32

33

3. Into this the original form of verse 10 was inserted ('the disciples asked him about the parable', singular, namely the parable of the sower he has just spoken in verses 3–9); and this was followed by Jesus' surprise that they had not understood it ("know ye not this parable?", verse 13) and by his interpretation of it (verses 14–20), which tells them to hold fast to the faith even if it brings tribulation and persecution. If these verses (10 and 13–20) are deleted as a secondary addition, the change of audience specified in verse 10— from the multitude to the disciples—is eliminated, and we are left with Jesus consistently addressing the multitude from verses 2 to 33.

2
3–9
10
(Marcan)
11–12
13–20
21–25
26–32
33

4. Mark then interpolated verses 11 and 12, and at the same time changed 'parable' of verse 10 into 'parables' and added logia exhorting the faithful to profess their faith openly (verses 21–25). These were added because they reiterate the point already made in the interpretation of the sower parable in verses 14–20.

5. Finally, verses 1 and 34 give a setting to the whole.

8. I discuss the conflict between predestinarian and other ideas in the NT in chapter 5 of *Belief and Make-Believe*.

9. K.L. Schmidt, *Der Rahmen der Geschichte Jesu*, Berlin, 1919: photographic reprint 1964 by the Wissenschaftliche Buchgesellschaft, Darmstadt. There is no English translation, but brief quotations are given, in English, in W.G. Kümmel's *The New Testament: The History of the Investigation of its Problems*, London: SCM, 1970, pp. 328–330.

10. C.H. Dodd, 'The Framework of the Gospel Narrative', *Expository Times*, 43 (1931/32), pp. 396, 400.

11. R.H. Lightfoot, *History and Interpretation in the Gospels*, London: Hodder and Stoughton, 1935, pp. 16–17.

12. R.H. Lightfoot, *The Gospel Message of St. Mark*, Oxford: Clarendon, 1952 (corrected from the first edition of 1950), p. 11.

13. D.E. Nineham, 'The Order of Events in St. Mark's Gospel—An Examination of Dr. Dodd's Hypothesis', in Nineham's *Explorations*, p. 14: This article is a criticism of the article by Dodd mentioned in note 10 above.

14. E.P. Sanders and Margaret Davies, *Studying the Synoptic Gospels*, London: SCM and Philadelphia: Trinity, 1989, p. 134. I have discussed this valuable book in *Belief and Make-Believe*, pp. 132–143.

15. K.L. Schmidt, 'Die Stellung der Evangelien in der allgemeinen Literaturgeschichte', in *Eucharisterion*, Festschrift for H. Gunkel, edited by H. Schmidt, volume 2, Göttingen: Vandenheock and Ruprecht, 1923, pp. 76, 89.

16. M. Reiser, *Syntax und Stil des Markusevangeliums*, Tübingen: Mohr, 1984, p. 35.

17. C. Bryan, *A Preface to Mark. Notes on the Gospel in its Literary and Cultural Settings*, New York: Oxford University Press, 1993, pp. 17, 53–54.

18. C.P. Anderson, 'The Trial of Jesus as Jewish-Christian Polarization: Blasphemy and Polemic in Mark's Gospel', in *Anti-Judaism I*, p. 115.

19. Wellhausen saw that when Mark makes Jesus call people to 'believe the gospel' or sacrifice everything for 'the gospel', he is larding Jesus's words with later "Christian trimmings"; for the meaning is quite clearly and anachro-

nistically that they should accept Christianity. In such passages as Mk. 14:9 ("wheresoever the gospel shall be preached throughout the whole world") the reference is not to the teaching of Jesus or to the promises he extended; 'the gospel' has come to mean the later Christian proclamation *about* him (*Einleitung in die ersten drei Evangelien*, Berlin: Reimer, 1905, pp. 110, 111, 113).

20. Cf. E. Haenchen's valuable commentary on Mark and canonical passages parallel to it: *Der Weg Jesu*, 2nd edition, Berlin: de Gruyter, 1968, p. 442.

21. W.H.C. Frend, *Martyrdom and Persecution in the Early Church*, Oxford: Blackwell, 1965, p. 220.

22. "The persecution of A.D. 95 and 96 was the creation of Eusebius", writing a full two centuries later, "not of Domitian" (T.C. Wilson, 'The Problem of the Domitiatic Date of Revelation', *NTS*, 39 (1993), p. 605; cf. L.L. Thompson, *The Book of Revelation: Apocalypse and Empire*, New York: Oxford University Press, 1990, p. 104ff).

23. A.N. Sherwin-White, 'The Early Persecutions and Roman Law', appendix 5 to his *The Letters of Pliny: A Historical and Social Commentary*, Oxford: Clarendon, 1966, pp. 774, 784.

24. N. Perrin, *What is Redaction Criticism?* London: SPCK, 1970, p. 52.

25. E.M. Blaiklock, *Jesus Christ, Man or Myth*, Hornebush, New South Wales: Anzea, 1983, p. 37.

26. R.H. Gundry, *Mark*, as cited in note 20 to chapter 4 above, pp. 6, 196.

27. K. Aland, 'Über die Möglichkeit der Identifikation kleiner Fragmente neutestamentlicher Handschriften mit Hilfe des Computers', in *Studies in New Testament Language and Text*, Festschrift for G.D. Kilpatrick, edited by J.K. Elliott, Leiden: Brill, 1976, pp. 15–17.

28. C.H. Roberts, 'On Some Presumed Papyrus Fragments of the New Testament from Qumran', *JTS*, 23 (1972), pp. 446–47.

29. The other relevant articles by Aland are his 'Neutestamentliche Papyri, III', *NTS*, 20 (1973/74), pp. 357–381, and

'Die Papyri aus Höhle 7 von Qumran', in *Supplementa zu den neutestamentlichen und den kirchlichen Entwürfen*, edited by Beate Köster et al., Berlin and New York: de Gruyter, 1990. Cf. also VanderKam, *The Dead Sea Scrolls Today*, as cited in note 29 to chapter 2 above, pp. 159, 166.

30. See Elliott's reviews of Wenham's *Redating* in *Nov Test*, 34 (1992), pp. 200–01 and of Thiede's *The Earliest Gospel Manuscript?* Exeter: Paternoster, 1992 in *Nov Test* 36 (1994), pp. 98–100. Elliott notes that B.M. Metzger refuses, in the third edition of his *Text of the New Testament*, to accept O'Callaghan's claims, which have found much more favour with popular writers than with scholars.

31. E. Haenchen, *Die Apostelgeschichte*, as cited in note 18 to chapter 4 above, p. 647.

32. R.M. Grant, *Miracle and Natural Law in Graeco-Roman and Early Christian Thought*, Amsterdam: North Holland Company, 1952, p. 173. Cf. C.F. Evans's comment that the ideas and vocabulary of the gospel miracle stories lead us into "that strange twilight zone in the ancient world between medicine and magic which is appropriately described by the word 'thaumaturgy' with its double connotation of marvel and effective action" (*The Beginning of the Gospel*, London: SPCK, 1968, p. 30).

33. W. Schadewaldt, 'The Reliability of the Synoptic Tradition', in M. Hengel, *Studies in the Gospel of Mark*, English translation London: SCM, 1985, p. 100.

34. Hengel, as cited in previous note, p. 11.

35. Cf. E. Haenchen, as cited in note 20 above, for the importance of some of these factors in originating traditions that Jesus worked miracles.

6. The 'Sayings Gospel' Q

1. W.H. Kelber, *The Oral and the Written Gospel*, Philadelphia: Fortress, 1983, p. 197. Psalm 22 is particularly important as what B. Lindars has called a "quarry for pictorial detail in writing the story of the Passion" (*New Testament Apolo-*

getic, London: SCM, 1961, p. 90). The purpose of the quarrying was, of course, to show that the Passion occurred because God willed it. Cf. Acts 2:23: "He was delivered up by the determinate counsel and foreknowledge of God." Mack summarizes scholarly comments on the passion narratives of all four gospels as "a series of efforts to be critical about the composition of the text while refusing to give up its claim to historical report" (*Myth*, p. 251).

2. On the existence of Q, see Kümmel's clear account in *Introduction*, pp. 63ff. Much more detailed but less readable is D. Catchpole, *The Quest for Q*, Edinburgh: Clark, 1993. C.M. Tuckett gives a helpful survey in his 'The Existence of Q', in *The Gospel Behind the Gospels: Current Studies on Q*, edited by R.A. Piper, Leiden: Brill, 1995, pp. 19–47.

3. Cf. H.C. Kee, *What Can We Know About Jesus?* (in the series 'Understanding Jesus Today'), Cambridge: Cambridge University Press, 1990, p. 42.

4. The standard text for Q studies in America, where most of the present work is being done, is J. Kloppenborg's *Q Parallels: Synopsis, Critical Notes and Concordance*, Sonoma, CA: Polebridge, 1988. The International Q Project and the Q Project of the Society of Biblical Literature at Claremont are still working to achieve a definitive text. Their decisions are published periodically in *JBL*.

5. For instance, the accusation that Jesus works miracles by "Beelzebub, the prince of the devils" is met by him with three responses (Q 11:17–18, 19, 20), followed by a saying about binding the strong man and then by the logion "he that is not with me is against me." Matthew has all these items in the same order.

6. The request for a sign appears at Mk. 8:11–12 and is placed by Matthew (at 16:1–4) in the Marcan sequence. But the request also appears in Q 11:29–30, paralleled of course in Matthew (at 12:38–40).

7. J.S. Kloppenborg, *The Formation of Q: Trajectories in Ancient Wisdom Collections*, Philadelphia: Fortress, 1987, pp. 42–50.

8. See H.O. Guenther's 'The Sayings Gospel Q and the Quest for Aramaic Sources', in *Early Christianity, Q and Jesus*, edited by J.S. Kloppenborg with L.E. Vaage (*Semeia* 55, 1991), Atlanta: Scholars, 1992, pp. 41–76. This is a lucid account of the history of the futile quest for Aramaic originals behind the NT writings. Reiser (as cited in note 16 to chapter 5 above, p. 165) finds the style and syntax of Mark characteristic of simple current everyday Greek.

9. Jacobson gives the following account of the fundamental difference between Q and Mark concerning the Baptist. Q 3:16–17 speaks of two baptisms, John's baptism of water in preparation for the coming judgement, and the baptism of wind (pneuma) and fire by Yahweh, which constitutes the judgement itself. In Mark there is still a two-baptism scheme, but there the contrast is between the inferior water baptism of John and the superior Spirit baptism of Jesus (1:8). Again, both Q and Mark cite Malachi 3:1 with reference to John; but in Q the meaning is that John was the forerunner of Yahweh's judgement, whereas Mark's use of the passage (1:1ff) makes John Jesus's forerunner. Q 7:31–35 places both of them in a common front against "this generation" which has rejected them both (A.D. Jacobson, 'The Literary Unity of Q', in *The Shape of Q*, edited by J.S. Kloppenborg, Minneapolis: Fortress, 1994, p. 107).

10. C.M. Tuckett, 'On the Stratification of Q: A Response', in *Semeia* 55, as cited in note 8 above, p. 217.

11. This is the argument of A.D. Jacobson, *The First Gospel. An Introduction to Q*, Sonoma: Polebridge, 1992, p. 74.

12. Cf. Kloppenborg, '"Easter Faith" and the Sayings Gospel Q', in *The Apocryphal Jesus and Christian Origins*, edited by R. Cameron (*Semeia*, 49, 1990), Atlanta: Scholars, 1990, p. 81.

13. The Gospel of Thomas is part of an ancient Coptic library discovered by a peasant from the village of Nag Hammadi in Upper Egypt. Meier explains that Coptic is the latest form of the ancient Egyptian language. It came into use as an almost exclusively Christian language in the second

century A.D., began to be written in the Greek alphabet augmented by seven characters from the popular form of Egyptian known as demotic, and supplemented with numerous Greek loanwords (*Marginal*, pp. 152f). He allows that there are "weighty" arguments for dating the underlying Greek original of the Gospel of Thomas as early as the second half of the first century; but he gives his reasons for inclining "with all due hesitation" to the view that it is later and dependent on the synoptic tradition (pp. 129f). Unscientific motives have often influenced the dating and evaluation of this gospel and other apocryphal material. Meier justly notes (p. 140) that both scholars and popularizers have been glad to take it as reliable supplementation of the tantalizingly sparse canonical information about the historical Jesus. On the other hand it is equally true that conservative Christian scholars have been anxious to disallow anything not included in the canon.

14. On this, cf., apart from Mack and the authors to whom he refers, F.G. Downing, *Cynics and Christian Origins*, Edinburgh: Clark, 1992.

15. C.M. Tuckett, 'A Cynic Q?', *Biblica*, 70 (1989), p. 374. But see L.E. Vaage's reply to Tuckett, defending the Cynic analogy: 'Q and Cynicism: On Comparison and Social Identity', in *The Gospel Behind the Gospels*, as cited in note 2 above, pp. 199–229.

16. Jacobson, as cited in note 11 above, pp. 149–150.

17. H.W. Attridge, 'Reflections on Research into Q', in *Semeia* 55, as cited in note 8 above, p. 224.

18. "Easter, appearance and spirit" are "coded signs, usually capitalized", which "mark the point beyond which the scholar chooses not to proceed with investigation, indeed the point beyond which reasoned argument must cease." They are allowed to establish "a point of origin that is fundamentally inaccessible to further probing or clarification". On this basis, "everything else can be examined rigorously without threatening the notion of originary uniqueness" (Mack, *Myth*, p. 7 and note on pp. 7–8).

19. Mack, *Myth*, p. 88. Cf. Guenther, as cited in note 8 above, p. 44: "Haenchen's conclusion that Luke's portrait of Christianity's advance from Jerusalem to Rome is not a historical one but flowed 'entirely from the pen of Luke' is . . . blatantly ignored by scholars who employ Acts for their reconstruction of Christian origins." The reference is to Haenchen's commentary on Acts (cf. n. 18 to chapter 4 above). It is available in English translation (Oxford: Blackwell, 1971).

7. Are the Gospels Anti-Semitic?

1. L.T. Johnson, 'The NT's Anti-Jewish Slander and the Conventions of Ancient Polemic', *JBL*, 108 (1989), p. 410.

2. F.W. Beare, *The Epistle to the Philippians* (Black's New Testament Commentaries), 3rd edition, London: Black, 1973, pp. 107f.

3. Cf. A. du Toit, 'Vilification as a Pragmatic Device in Early Christian Epistolography', *Biblica*, 75 (1994), pp. 403–412. He mentions, as characteristic of "the hyperbolical and often stereotyped character of [ancient] vilificatory utterances", Josephus's fulminations that Apion has "the mind of an ass and the impudence of a dog" (*Contra Apionem*, 2, 7).

4. Moshe Weinfeld gives evidence that rabbinic sources accuse Pharisees of not practising what they preach, of ostentatiously wearing cloaks, of showing off phylacteries and fringes, of demanding the first place at dinner, and of tithing trivial things ('The Charge of Hypocrisy in Matthew 23 and in Jewish Sources', in *The New Testament and Christian-Jewish Dialogue*, Studies in Honour of David Flusser, edited by M. Lowe, *Immanuel* 24/25: Ecumenical Research Fraternity in Israel, 1990, p. 58. The sectarians of the Dead Sea Scrolls villified the Pharisees—as hypocrites according to K. Schubert—because Pharisees were realists "sceptical about ultra-eschatological speculations and expectations". He adds that the NT designation of them as hypocrites "must be understood against this back-

ground" ('Jewish Religious Parties and Sects', in *The Crucible of Christianity*, edited by A. Toynbee, London: Thames and Hudson, 1969, p. 90).

5. Marxists classify people as peasants, proletariat, land owners, industrialists, and so forth, and the classification depends on external conditions: men chance to be born into one class or the other, or come to it from the accidents of education. Only to a small extent does social class depend on congenital qualities, on virtues, vices, and intellectual capacity. What is common to a class is merely those tendencies which the conditions of life in it tend to encourage or develop. There may be some point in saying that a certain set of individuals are scoundrels, traitors, brutal, or anything else, but if the classification depends on external conditions, to ascribe such characters to a whole class is absurd, and is like saying that people who travel on buses are always impatient. International hatred has the same irrational basis. The German (or Englishman) is hated not because of any defects of character, but because he was born in Germany (or England) of German (or English) parents.

6. A.J. Saldarini concludes his careful study *Pharisees, Scribes and Sadducees*, Edinburgh: Clark, 1988, with the comment: "Data on the Pharisees is so sparse and difficult to evaluate that any historical reconstruction must remain incomplete and uncomfortably hypothetical" (p. 277). He stresses the slimness of second temple evidence, and the unreliability of the rabbinic sources, which "date from later centuries and do not purport to be historical" (p. 8). He adds: "It is very likely that the pre–70 Pharisees contributed to the emergence of the post–70 rabbis, but evidence is not abundant."

7. Mk. 7:6 Well did Isaiah prophesy of you hypocrites (genitive plural)

Mt. 15:7 Ye hypocrites, well did Isaiah prophesy of you . . .

Mk. 12:15 But he, knowing their hypocrisy, said unto them, why tempt ye me?

Mt. 22:18 Why tempt ye me, ye hypocrites?

8. D.E. Garland (*The Intention of Matthew 23*, Leiden: Brill, 1979, p. 70) points out that the 'woes' in the Q passage Mt. 11:21–23 (= Lk. 10:13–15) and in Mt. 23 are formulated with οὐαι plus the second person pronoun, followed by the name of those specifically addressed, and then a clause introduced by ὅτι ('for', 'because'), identifying the sin which evoked the woe. He shows that these features are not present in passages where οὐαι may be taken as expressing lamentation (18:7, 24:19, 26:24). An exception in Mt. 23 is the fifth woe (verses 25–26), which (for the first time) allows a chance of remedying the misbehaviour specified, and so is not announcing irrevocable damnation: those who can improve their conduct are not yet the 'sons of hell' of verse 15, who will inevitably be sent there (verse 33).

9. Isaiah 5:8 and 11; Habakkuk 2:9. Zechariah 11:17 is another example: "Woe to my worthless shepherd who deserts his flock! May the sword smite his arm and his right eye! Let his arm be wholly withered, and his right eye utterly blinded!" (RSV). The formula is meant as an effective curse, a form of words that will bring about its own fulfilment, in accordance with ideas universally underlying verbal magic. I have discussed the origin and nature of magic in my *What's in a Name?*, Chapter 3.

10. Even membership of the Christian community does not automatically guarantee admission to the kingdom of heaven, as is clear from the parables of the wheat and the tares and of the fish net (Mt. 13:24–30; 47–50; cf. 13:41f). Peter holds the keys (16:19) and so can presumably withhold entry.

11. Mt. 23 begins by accepting without reservation the authority of the scribes and Pharisees as teachers. They "sit on Moses's seat", and so the Christian disciples should "do and observe all things whatsoever they bid you", but not imitate their "works", because they do not carry out their own rigorous prescriptions. These verses 2–3 have no synoptic parallel, are out of line with Jesus's clear rejection of Pharisaic teaching concerning the sabbath in an earlier

passage (12:1–8), with his equally clear rejection of the "tradition" of the scribes and Pharisees at 15:2–6, and with his warning against the "leaven" of the Pharisees and Sadducees, understood (in a verse present only in Matthew) as referring to their "teaching" (16:12). The endorsement of this teaching at the beginning of chapter 23 is also out of line with what follows there. Verses 8–10 affirm that the Christian disciples are "brothers" of equal status and so need no teacher or master other than God or Christ. It would follow that the attention to scribal or Pharisaic pronouncements recommended in verses 2–3 is unnecessary. And verse 5 (again without synoptic parallel) goes against these verses in a different way, complaining not (as in verse 3) that scribes and Pharisees fail to do appropriate 'works', but that their works are performed from impure motives, for ostentation. Mt. 23 surely represents not a single continuous discourse, but an amalgam of various units of tradition of different provenance.

12. E. Haenchen, 'Matthäus 23', in *Gott und Mensch: Gesammelte Aufsätze*, Tübingen: Mohr, 1965, p. 39n. My whole account of Mt. 23 is deeply indebted to this article.

13. See Luise Schottroff, 'Die Erzählung vom Pharisäer und Zöllner als Beispiel für die theologische Kunst des Überredens', in *Neues Testament und Christliche Existenz*, Festschrift für H. Braun, edited by herself and H.D. Betz, Tübingen: Mohr, 1973, pp. 439–461. To extract information about Pharisaic piety from Lk. 18:10ff would be, she says, like trying to find truths about women from jokes about 'women at the wheel' (p. 452). In the prayer often adduced as a rabbinic parallel, the speaker thanks God who, by his grace, has spared him the fate of the impious; whereas in Luke's parable, the Pharisee thanks God that he is not as the rest of men, implying that *all* others are steeped in vice.

14. Cf. Nehemiah 9:26–27. The Jews "were disobedient and rebelled against thee and cast thy law behind their back and slew thy prophets which testified against them to turn them again unto thee, and they wrought great provoca-

tions. Therefore thou deliveredst them into the hand of their adversaries." In actual fact the OT names only two prophets (and they not among the three major and twelve minor ones) who died violently: Uriah son of Shemaiah (Jeremiah 26:20–23) and Zechariah son of Jehoiada (2 Chronicles 24:20–22).

15. See D.R.A. Hare, *The Theme of Jewish Persecution of Christians in the Gospel According to St. Matthew*, Cambridge University Press, 1967, pp. 104f. For instance, there is no αὐτων at Mk. 3:1, 6:2 and 13:9, but the equivalent passages in Matthew (12:9, 13:54 and 10:17) have added it. Mark does have the αὐτων at 1:23 and 39, but does not attempt the consistency that is so striking in Matthew.

16. B. Przybylski, 'The Setting of Matthean Anti-Judaism', in *Anti-Judaism I*, p. 195. The man obviously had great faith in Jesus, and is said in Mark (5:22) and in Luke (8:41) to be "a ruler of the synagogue", whereas in Matthew he figures simply as "a ruler" (9:18).

17. E. Buck, 'Anti-Judaic Sentiments in the Passion Narrative According to Matthew', in *Anti-Judaism I*, pp. 168–170, 177.

18. Brown (*Death*, pp. 59–63) has helpful remarks on the extent and nature of the material in Matthew's passion narrative not found in Mark. He notes its "strongly anti-Jewish character" and regards it as "popular" stuff, "reflecting the anti-Jewish attitude and vocabulary of many ordinary Christians in Matthew's time" (p. 1431).

19. Because of Israel's guilt, the kingdom is to be taken from it and given to another nation (21:43, no synoptic parallel). The Jews ("the sons of the kingdom") shall be "cast forth into the outer darkness" (8:12) and the gospel is to be preached to gentiles (24:14; 28:19). OT prophets can speak harshly of their own people, but they persist in the hope that, after Israel has been properly punished for its faithlessness, it will be restored to privilege (Cf. Mary C. Callaway, 'A Hammer that Breaks Rocks in Pieces: Prophetic Critique in the Hebrew Bible', in *Anti-Semitism and Early Christianity*, edited by C.A. Evans and D.A. Hagner, Min-

neapolis: Fortress, 1993, p. 37). There is no such qualification in Matthew: the invitation to the Messianic banquet has been persistently refused (22:8ff) and there is no suggestion that it will be offered again.

20. S.G. Wilson, *Luke and the Law*, Cambridge University Press, 1983, pp. 64, 112.

21. The fourth gospel does not mention scribes, makes the Pharisees an authoritative body, part of the governing class with considerable power in Jerusalem side by side with the priests, and combines all Jesus's opponents into these two categories. Matthew and John are the only canonical evangelists to represent a combination of "the chief priests and the Pharisees" as aligned against Jesus. (Jn. 7:32; 18:3; cf Mt. 21:45, absent from Mark's version of the same narrative and represented in Luke by a mention of "the scribes and chief priests"). Martyn and Hummel have argued that thereby Matthew and John set the hostile Jewish authorities of their own time side by side with those persons who had power in the temple before it was destroyed (J.L. Martyn, *History and Theology in the Fourth Gospel*, New York: Harper and Row, 1968, p. 72; R. Hummel, *Die Auseinandersetzung zwischen Kirche und Judentum im Matthäusevangelium*, 2nd edition, Munich: Kaiser, 1963, p. 16).

22. See E.W. Gritsch and M.H. Tanenbaum, *Luther and the Jews*, published in 1983 by the Lutheran Council in the U.S.A.

8. Ethics and Religious Belief

1. H.D. Betz, *Essays on the Sermon on the Mount*, Philadelphia: Fortress, 1985, p. 22.

2. This significant difference between Mark and Matthew is pointed out by W.D. Davies, *The Setting of the Sermon on the Mount*, Cambridge University Press, 1966, pp. 100, 107.

3. J. Neusner, *Judaism and the Beginning of Christianity*, London: SPCK, 1984, pp. 64, 85–87.

4. G. Strecker, *The Sermon on the Mount: An Exegetical Commentary*, English translation, Edinburgh: Clark, 1988, p. 108.

5. In this connection it is of interest that Matthew's expres-

sion "poor in spirit" in his version of the beatitudes (5:3) is found in one of the Qumran scrolls, but in no other ancient text. See J.C. VanderKam, 'The Dead Sea Scrolls and Christianity', in Shanks, *Scrolls*, p. 188.

6. This inculcation of hatred is Q material. The parallel passage of Mt. 10:37 has mitigated its hardness: "He that loveth father or mother, son or daughter more than me is not worthy of me."

7. Canon Harvey notes: "In face of the hard saying in Mark 'How hard it is (for the rich) to enter the kingdom of God' (10:24), some manuscripts offer a convenient qualification by adding the words, 'for those who *place their trust* in riches'." Such "pragmatic adjustments" are evidence of a "tendency to make Jesus's strenuous commands seem 'sensible'" (*Commands*, p. 144). Jesus's instruction to the rich man at Mk. 10:21 ("go, sell whatsoever thou hast and give to the poor, and thou shalt have treasure in heaven") is retained by Matthew and Luke, but Matthew makes it more palatable by adding the qualification "if thou wouldest be perfect" (19:21).

8. D. Parker, 'The Early Traditions of Jesus's Sayings on Divorce', *Theology*, 96 (1993), pp. 372, 379. He adds: "The differences in emphasis, not only between Mt. 5, Mk. 10, Mt. 19 and Lk. 16, but between different versions of these Gospels, show the oral period and the first centuries of the written period to have been a continuum of re-interpretation. Even after the development of 'standard', 'ecclesiastical' texts . . . variant forms survived."

9. A.E. Harvey, 'Marriage, Sex and the Bible (I)', *Theology*, vol. cit. in previous note, p. 367.

10. The fullest study of Paul's inconsistent attitude to the Jewish law is Räisänen's *Paul and the Law*, 2nd edition revised and enlarged, Tübingen: Mohr, 1987. He shows that, for Paul, "the law . . . is a thing of the past. Christians are no longer under it. . . . Yet Paul can exhort his readers to Christian love by emphasizing that love is the fulfilment of that very law. He can also motivate various moral or otherwise practical instructions by appealing to words of the

law. Now as before the law is justified in putting a claim on man, even on the Christian. The special thing with the Christians is that they alone fulfil that just requirement. Paul underlines that, far from annulling the law, he actually establishes it. He is thus quite reluctant to admit how far he has actually gone in his rejection of the law." He "wants to have his cake and eat it" and does the one or the other "depending on the situation" (p. 82). He is "first and foremost a missionary, a man of practical religion who develops a line of thought to make a practical point, to influence the conduct of his readers", and who is quite capable the next moment of putting forward a contradictory line of thought to make a different point, or when struggling with a different problem (p. 267).

11. J. Kent, *The Unacceptable Face: The Modern Church in the Eyes of the Historian*, London: SCM, 1987, pp. 66, 68.

12. J. Barr, *Biblical Faith and Natural Theology*, Oxford: Clarendon, 1993, p. 220.

13. On Falwell, see Steve Bruce, 'The Moral Majority: the Politics of Fundamentalism in Secular Society', in *Studies in Religious Fundamentalism*, edited by Lionel Caplan, London: Macmillan, 1987, pp. 177–194.

14. On this as on other matters, Paul does not argue consistently. See S.G. Wilson, 'Paul and Religion', in *Paul and Paulinism*, Essays in honour of C.K. Barrett, edited by Morna Hooker and by Wilson, London: SPCK, 1982. He there notes (pp. 342–43, 348) that, since Paul's central conviction was that Christ alone mediates redemption, he had to show that earlier religions, Jewish and gentile, had failed. Hence he expatiates on the moral perversity of gentiles (Romans, chapter 1), finds that Jews and Greeks are "all under sin" so that "there is none righteous, no not one" (3:9–10), and yet cannot resist strengthening his denunciation of Jews in chapter 2 by shaming them with the example set by pious gentiles (2:14–16). The admission that such persons exist compromises the argument of 7:14–25 that only belief in Christ can lead to moral behaviour.

EPILOGUE

1. The ideas expressed in this story of the healing of the woman with an issue of blood "are of the essence of Graeco-Roman magical notions" (D.E. Aune, 'Magic in Early Christianity', *Aufstieg und Niedergang der Römischen Welt*, II, 23.2, edited by W. Haase, Berlin: de Gruyter, 1980, p. 1536). Jesus's healing power is represented as quite independent of his will, for even the woman's surreptitious touching of his garments suffices to cure her immediately. He himself notices the diminution of power in his own body: the woman's touch has made it overflow like electricity. That the power is in his clothes as much as in his body is what Hugh Anderson calls "a crude feature, very common in ancient healing stories, that for us today savours of magic or superstition" (Commentary on Mark in 'New Century Bible' series, London: Oliphants, 1976, p. 152). He notes that this same feature is present in Acts 19:11–12, where Paul's "handkerchiefs or aprons" are applied to sick persons who are thereby healed. The papyrologist Friedrich Preisigke has given many similar examples from pre-Christian and Christian times, including a sixth century account of how a silken cloak, laid for the night over the coffin of St. Martin, acquired so much of the saint's power that it successfully healed the king of Spain (*Die Gotteskraft der frühchristlichen Zeit*, Leipzig and Berlin: de Gruyter, 1922, pp. 15–17. J.M. Hull has drawn attention to this neglected little book in his *Hellenistic Magic and the Synoptic Tradition*, London: SCM, 1974, pp. 109–114). Resistance to such crude ideas is documented already in Matthew's rewriting (9:20–22) of the Marcan pericope. In Matthew the woman expects magic, but does not get it. There is no 'power' issuing from Jesus or from his clothes; he simply addresses her with the words "thy faith hath made thee whole", and it is then (not when, two verses earlier, she touched the fringe of his garment) that she is instantly cured.

Index of
New Testament
References

(References to Q are included under Luke)

Matthew

Mark

Luke and Q

John

Acts

Romans

1 Corinthians

2 Corinthians

Galatians

Ephesians

Philippians

Colossians

1 Thessalonians

1 Timothy

2 Timothy

Titus

Jude

Revelation

General Index

Page numbers in parentheses indicate pages where an author is quoted (or his views alluded to) but not named. Thus Beare 324 (228) means that this author is alluded to on p. 228, where a superscript will direct the reader to a note on p. 324, where Beare is named and details of his work are given.